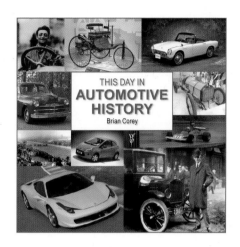

THIS DAY IN
AUTOMOTIVE
HISTORY
Brian Corey

Also from Veloce

Biographies

- A Chequered Life – Graham Warner and the Chequered Flag (Hesletine)
- A Life Awheel – The 'auto' biography of W de Forte (Skelton)
- Amédée Gordini ... a true racing legend (Smith)
- André Lefebvre, and the cars he created at Voisin and Citroën (Beck)
- Chris Carter at Large – Stories from a lifetime in motorcycle racing (Carter & Skelton)
- Cliff Allison, The Official Biography of – From the Fells to Ferrari (Gauld)
- Edward Turner – The Man Behind the Motorcycles (Clew)
- Driven by Desire – The Desiré Wilson Story
- First Principles – The Official Biography of Keith Duckworth (Burr)
- Inspired to Design – F1 cars, Indycars & racing tyres: the autobiography of Nigel Bennett (Bennett)
- Jack Sears, The Official Biography of – Gentleman Jack (Gauld)
- Jim Redman – 6 Times World Motorcycle Champion: The Autobiography (Redman)
- John Chatham – 'Mr Big Healey' – The Official Biography (Burr)
- The Lee Noble Story (Wilkins)
- Mason's Motoring Mayhem – Tony Mason's hectic life in motorsport and television (Mason)
- Raymond Mays' Magnificent Obsession (Apps)
- Pat Moss Carlsson Story, The – Harnessing Horsepower (Turner)
- 'Sox' – Gary Hocking – the forgotten World Motorcycle Champion (Hughes)
- Tony Robinson – The biography of a race mechanic (Wagstaff)
- Virgil Exner – Visioneer: The Official Biography of Virgil M Exner Designer Extraordinaire (Grist)

Toys & models

- Britains Farm Model Balers & Combines 1967-2007, Pocket Guide to (Pullen)
- Britains Farm Model & Toy Tractors 1998-2008, Pocket Guide to (Pullen)
- Britains Toy Models Catalogues 1970-1979 (Pullen)
- British Toy Boats 1920 onwards – A pictorial tribute (Gillham)
- Diecast Toy Cars of the 1950s & 1960s (Ralston)
- Ford In Miniature (Olson)
- GM In Miniature (Olson)
- Plastic Toy Cars of the 1950s & 1960s (Ralston)
- Tinplate Toy Cars of the 1950s & 1960s (Ralston)

General

- 1½-litre GP Racing 1961-1965 (Whitelock)
- AC Two-litre Saloons & Buckland Sportscars (Archibald)
- Alfa Romeo 155/156/147 Competition Touring Cars (Collins)
- Alfa Romeo Giulia Coupé GT & GTA (Tipler)
- Alfa Romeo Montreal – The dream car that came true (Taylor)
- Alfa Romeo Montreal – The Essential Companion (Classic Reprint of 500 copies) (Taylor)
- Alfa Tipo 33 (McDonough & Collins)
- Alpine & Renault – The Development of the Revolutionary Turbo F1 Car 1968 to 1979 (Smith)
- Alpine & Renault – The Sports Prototypes 1963 to 1969 (Smith)
- Alpine & Renault – The Sports Prototypes 1973 to 1978 (Smith)
- An Incredible Journey (Falls & Reisch)
- Anatomy of the Classic Mini (Huthert & Ely)
- Anatomy of the Works Minis (Moylan)
- Armstrong-Siddeley (Smith)
- Art Deco and British Car Design (Down)
- Autodrome (Collins & Ireland)
- Automotive A-Z, Lane's Dictionary of Automotive Terms (Lane)
- Automotive Mascots (Kay & Springate)
- Bahamas Speed Weeks, The (O'Neil)
- Bentley Continental, Corniche and Azure (Bennett)
- Bentley MkVI, Rolls-Royce Silver Wraith, Dawn & Cloud/Bentley R & S-Series (Nutland)
- Bluebird CN7 (Stevens)
- BMC Competitions Department Secrets (Turner, Chambers & Browning)
- BMW 5-Series (Cranswick)
- BMW Z-Cars (Taylor)
- BMW Boxer Twins 1970-1995 Bible, The (Falloon)
- BMW Cafe Racers (Cloesen)
- BMW Classic 5 Series 1972 to 2003 (Cranswick)
- BMW Custom Motorcycles – Choppers, Cruisers, Bobbers, Trikes & Quads (Cloesen)
- BMW – The Power of M (Vivian)
- Bonjour – Is this Italy? (Turner)
- British 250cc Racing Motorcycles (Pereira)
- British at Indianapolis, The (Wagstaff)
- British Café Racers (Cloesen)
- British Cars, The Complete Catalogue of, 1895-1975 (Culshaw & Horrobin)
- British Custom Motorcycles – The Brit Chop – choppers, cruisers, bobbers & trikes (Cloesen)
- BRM – A Mechanic's Tale (Salmon)
- BRM V16 (Ludvigsen)
- BSA Bantam Bible, The (Henshaw)
- BSA Motorcycles – the final evolution (Jones)
- Bugatti – The 8-cylinder Touring Cars 1920-34 (Price & Arbey)
- Bugatti Type 40 (Price)
- Bugatti 46/50 Updated Edition (Price & Arbey)
- Bugatti T44 & T49 (Price & Arbey)
- Bugatti 57 2nd Edition (Price)
- Bugatti Type 57 Grand Prix – A Celebration (Tomlinson)
- Caravan, Improve & Modify Your (Porter)
- Caravans, The Illustrated History 1919-1959 (Jenkinson)
- Caravans, The Illustrated History From 1960 (Jenkinson)
- Carrera Panamericana, La (Tipler)
- Car-tastrophes – 80 automotive atrocities from the past 20 years (Honest John, Fowler)
- Chrysler 300 – America's Most Powerful Car 2nd Edition (Ackerson)
- Chrysler PT Cruiser (Ackerson)
- Citroën DS (Bobbitt)
- Classic British Car Electrical Systems (Astley)
- Cobra – The Real Thing! (Legate)
- Competition Car Aerodynamics 3rd Edition (McBeath)
- Competition Car Composites A Practical Handbook (Revised 2nd Edition) (McBeath)
- Concept Cars, How to illustrate and design – New 2nd Edition (Dewey)
- Cortina – Ford's Bestseller (Robson)
- Cosworth – The Search for Power (6th edition) (Robson)
- Coventry Climax Racing Engines (Hammill)
- Daily Mirror 1970 World Cup Rally 40, The (Robson)
- Daimler SP250 New Edition (Long)
- Datsun Fairlady Roadster to 280ZX – The Z-Car Story (Long)
- Dino – The V6 Ferrari (Long)
- Dodge Challenger & Plymouth Barracuda (Grist)
- Dodge Charger – Enduring Thunder (Ackerson)
- Dodge Dynamite! (Grist)
- Dorset from the Sea – The Jurassic Coast from Lyme Regis to Old Harry Rocks photographed from its best viewpoint (also Souvenir Edition) (Belasco)
- Draw & Paint Cars – How to (Gardiner)
- Drive on the Wild Side, A – 20 Extreme Driving Adventures From Around the World (Weaver)
- Ducati 750 Bible, The (Falloon)
- Ducati 750 SS 'round-case' 1974, The Book of the (Falloon)
- Ducati 860, 900 and Mille Bible, The (Falloon)
- Ducati Monster Bible (New Updated & Revised Edition), The (Falloon)
- Ducati Story, The - 6th Edition (Falloon)
- Ducati 916 (updated edition) (Falloon)
- Dune Buggy, Building A – The Essential Manual (Shakespeare)
- Dune Buggy Files (Hale)
- Dune Buggy Handbook (Hale)
- East German Motor Vehicles in Pictures (Suhr/Weinreich)
- Fast Ladies – Female Racing Drivers 1888 to 1970 (Bouzanquet)
- Fate of the Sleeping Beauties, The (op de Weegh/Hottendorff/op de Weegh)
- Ferrari 288 GTO, The Book of the (Sackey)
- Ferrari 333 SP (O'Neil)
- Fiat & Abarth 124 Spider & Coupé (Tipler)
- Fiat & Abarth 500 & 600 – 2nd Edition (Bobbitt)
- Fiats, Great Small (Ward)
- Fine Art of the Motorcycle Engine, The (Peirce)
- Ford Cleveland 335-Series V8 engine 1970 to 1982 – The Essential Source Book (Hammill)
- Ford F100/F150 Pick-up 1948-1996 (Ackerson)
- Ford F150 Pick-up 1997-2005 (Ackerson)
- Ford Focus WRC (Robson)
- Ford GT – Then, and Now (Streather)
- Ford GT40 (Legate)
- Ford Midsize Muscle – Fairlane, Torino & Ranchero (Cranswick)
- Ford Model Y (Roberts)
- Ford Small Block V8 Racing Engines 1962-1970 – The Essential Source Book (Hammill)
- Ford Thunderbird From 1954, The Book of the (Long)
- Formula One - The Real Score? (Harvey)
- Formula 5000 Motor Racing, Back then ... and back now (Lawson)
- Forza Minardi! (Vigar)
- France: the essential guide for car enthusiasts – 200 things for the car enthusiast to see and do (Parish)
- From Crystal Palace to Red Square – A Hapless Biker's Road to Russia (Turner)
- Funky Mopeds (Skelton)
- Grand Prix Ferrari – The Years of Enzo Ferrari's Power, 1948-1980 (Pritchard)
- Grand Prix Ford – DFV-powered Formula 1 Cars (Robson)
- GT – The World's Best GT Cars 1953-73 (Dawson)
- Hillclimbing & Sprinting – The Essential Manual (Short & Wilkinson)
- Honda NSX (Long)
- How to Restore & Improve Classic Car Suspension, Steering & Wheels (Parish, translator)
- Immortal Austin Seven (Morgan)
- Inside the Rolls-Royce & Bentley Styling Department – 1971 to 2001 (Hull)
- Intermeccanica – The Story of the Prancing Bull (McCredie & Reisner)
- Italian Cafe Racers (Cloesen)
- Italian Custom Motorcycles (Cloesen)
- Jaguar, The Rise of (Price)
- Jaguar XJ 220 – The Inside Story (Moreton)
- Jaguar XJ-S, The Book of the (Long)
- Japanese Custom Motorcycles – The Nippon Chop – Chopper, Cruiser, Bobber, Trikes and Quads (Cloesen)
- Jeep CJ (Ackerson)
- Jeep Wrangler (Ackerson)
- The Jowett Jupiter – The car that leaped to fame (Nankivell)
- Karmann-Ghia Coupé & Convertible (Bobbitt)
- Kawasaki Triples Bible, The (Walker)
- Kawasaki Z1 Story, The (Sheehan)
- Kris Meeke – Intercontinental Rally Challenge Champion (McBride)
- Lamborghini Miura Bible, The (Sackey)
- Lamborghini Urraco, The Book of the (Landsem)
- Lambretta Bible, The (Davies)
- Lancia 037 (Collins)
- Lancia Delta HF Integrale (Blaettel & Wagner)
- Lancia Delta Integrale (Collins)
- Land Rover Series III Reborn (Porter)
- Land Rover, The Half-ton Military (Cook)
- Laverda Twins & Triples Bible 1968-1986 (Falloon)
- Lea-Francis Story, The (Price)
- Le Mans Panoramic (Ireland)
- Lexus Story, The (Long)
- Little book of microcars, the (Quellin)
- Little book of smart, the – New Edition (Jackson)
- Little book of trikes, the (Quellin)
- Lola – The Illustrated History (1957-1977) (Starkey)
- Lola – All the Sports Racing & Single-seater Racing Cars 1978-1997 (Starkey)
- Lola T70 – The Racing History & Individual Chassis Record – 4th Edition (Starkey)
- Lotus 18 Colin Chapman's U-turn (Whitelock)
- Lotus 49 (Oliver)
- Marketingmobiles, The Wonderful Wacky World of (Hale)
- Maserati 250F In Focus (Pritchard)
- Mazda MX-5/Miata 1.6 Enthusiast's Workshop Manual (Grainger & Shoemark)
- Mazda MX-5/Miata 1.8 Enthusiast's Workshop Manual (Grainger & Shoemark)
- Mazda MX-5 Miata, The book of the – The 'Mk1' NA-series 1988 to 1997 (Long)
- Mazda MX-5 Miata Roadster (Long)
- Mazda Rotary-engined Cars (Cranswick)
- Maximum Mini (Booij)
- Meet the English (Bowie)
- Mercedes-Benz SL – R230 series 2001 to 2011 (Long)
- Mercedes-Benz SL – W113-series 1963-1971 (Long)
- Mercedes-Benz SL & SLC – 107-series 1971-1989 (Long)
- Mercedes-Benz SLK – R170 series 1996-2004 (Long)
- Mercedes-Benz SLK – R171 series 2004-2011 (Long)
- Mercedes-Benz W123-series – All models 1976 to 1986 (Long)
- Mercedes G-Wagen (Long)
- MGA (Price Williams)
- MGB & MGB GT– Expert Guide (Auto-doc Series) (Williams)
- MGB Electrical Systems Updated & Revised Edition (Astley)
- Micro Caravans (Jenkinson)
- Micro Trucks (Mort)
- Microcars at Large! (Quellin)
- Mini Cooper – The Real Thing! (Tipler)
- Mini Minor to Asia Minor (West)
- Mitsubishi Lancer Evo, The Road Car & WRC Story (Long)
- Montlhéry, The Story of the Paris Autodrome (Boddy)
- Morgan Maverick (Lawrence)
- Morgan 3 Wheeler – back to the future!, The (Dron)
- Morris Minor, 60 Years on the Road (Newell)
- Moto Guzzi Sport & Le Mans Bible, The (Falloon)
- The Moto Guzzi Story - 3rd Edition (Falloon)
- Motor Movies – The Posters! (Veysey)
- Motor Racing – Reflections of a Lost Era (Carter)
- Motor Racing – The Pursuit of Victory 1930-1962 (Carter)
- Motor Racing – The Pursuit of Victory 1963-1972 (Wyatt/Sears)
- Motor Racing Heroes – The Stories of 100 Greats (Newman)
- Motorcycle Apprentice (Cakebread)
- Motorcycle GP Racing in the 1960s (Pereira)
- Motorcycle Road & Racing Chassis Designs (Noakes)
- Motorcycling in the '50s (Clew)
- Motorhomes, The Illustrated History (Jenkinson)
- Motorsport In colour, 1950s (Wainwright)
- MV Agusta Fours, The book of the classic (Falloon)
- N.A.R.T. – A concise history of the North American Racing Team 1957 to 1983 (O'Neil)
- Nissan 300ZX & 350Z – The Z-Car Story (Long)
- Nissan GT-R Supercar: Born to race (Gorodji)
- Northeast American Sports Car Races 1950-1959 (O'Neil)
- Norton Commando Bible – All models 1968 to 1978 (Henshaw)
- Nothing Runs – Misadventures in the Classic, Collectable & Exotic Car Biz (Slutsky)
- Off-Road Giants! (Volume 1) – Heroes of 1960s Motorcycle Sport (Westlake)
- Off-Road Giants! (Volume 2) – Heroes of 1960s Motorcycle Sport (Westlake)
- Off-Road Giants! (volume 3) – Heroes of 1960s Motorcycle Sport (Westlake)
- Pass the Theory and Practical Driving Tests (Gibson & Hoole)
- Peking to Paris 2007 (Young)
- Pontiac Firebird – New 3rd Edition (Cranswick)
- Porsche 356 (2nd Edition) (Long)
- Porsche 908 (Födisch, Neßhöver, Roßbach, Schwarz & Roßbach)
- Porsche 911 Carrera – The Last of the Evolution (Corlett)
- Porsche 911R, RS & RSR, 4th Edition (Starkey)
- Porsche 911, The Book of the (Long)
- Porsche 911 – The Definitive History 2004-2012 (Long)
- Porsche – The Racing 914s (Smith)
- Porsche 911SC 'Super Carrera' – The Essential Companion (Streather)
- Porsche 914 & 914-6: The Definitive History of the Road & Competition Cars (Long)
- Porsche 924 (Long)
- The Porsche 924 Carreras – evolution to excellence (Smith)
- Porsche 928 (Long)
- Porsche 944 (Long)
- Porsche 964, 993 & 996 Data Plate Code Breaker (Streather)
- Porsche 993 'King Of Porsche' – The Essential Companion (Streather)
- Porsche 996 'Supreme Porsche' – The Essential Companion (Streather)
- Porsche 997 2004-2012 – Porsche Excellence (Streather)
- Porsche Boxster – The 986 series 1996-2004 (Long)
- Porsche Boxster & Cayman – The 987 series (2004-2013) (Long)
- Porsche Racing Cars – 1953 to 1975 (Long)
- Porsche Racing Cars – 1976 to 2005 (Long)
- Porsche – The Rally Story (Meredith)
- Porsche: Three Generations of Genius (Meredith)
- Powered by Porsche (Smith)
- Preston Tucker & Others (Linde)
- RAC Rally Action! (Gardiner)
- Racing Colours – Motor Racing Compositions 1908-2009 (Newman)
- Racing Line – British motorcycle racing in the golden age of the big single (Guntrip)
- Rallye Sport Fords: The Inside Story (Moreton)
- Renewable Energy Home Handbook, The (Porter)
- Roads with a View – England's greatest views and how to find them by road (Corfield)
- Rolls-Royce Silver Shadow/Bentley T Series Corniche & Camargue – Revised & Enlarged Edition (Bobbitt)
- Rolls-Royce Silver Spirit, Silver Spur & Bentley Mulsanne 2nd Edition (Bobbitt)
- Rootes Cars of the 50s, 60s & 70s – Hillman, Humber, Singer, Sunbeam & Talbot (Rowe)
- Rover P4 (Bobbitt)
- Runways & Racers (O'Neil)
- Russian Motor Vehicles – Soviet Limousines 1930-2003 (Kelly)
- Russian Motor Vehicles – The Czarist Period 1784 to 1917 (Kelly)
- RX-7 – Mazda's Rotary Engine Sportscar (Updated & Revised New Edition) (Long)
- Scooters & Microcars, The A-Z of Popular (Dan)
- Scooter Lifestyle (Grainger)
- Scooter Mania! – Recollections of the Isle of Man International Scooter Rally (Jackson)
- Singer Story: Cars, Commercial Vehicles, Bicycles & Motorcycle (Atkinson)
- Sleeping Beauties USA – abandoned classic cars & trucks (Marek)
- SM – Citroën's Maserati-engined Supercar (Long & Claverol)
- Speedway – Auto racing's ghost tracks (Collins & Ireland)
- Sprite Caravans, The Story of (Jenkinson)
- Standard Motor Company, The Book of the (Robson)
- Steve Hole's Kit Car Cornucopia – Cars, Companies, Stories, Facts & Figures: the UK's kit car scene since 1949 (Hole)
- Subaru Impreza: The Road Car And WRC Story (Long)
- Supercar, How to Build your own (Thompson)
- Tales from the Toolbox (Oliver)
- Tatra – The Legacy of Hans Ledwinka, Updated & Enlarged Collector's Edition of 1500 copies (Margolius & Henry)
- Taxi! The Story of the 'London' Taxicab (Bobbitt)
- This Day in Automotive History (Corey)
- To Boldly Go – twenty six vehicle designs that dared to be different (Hull)
- Toleman Story, The (Hilton)
- Toyota Celica & Supra, The Book of Toyota's Sports Coupés (Long)
- Toyota MR2 Coupés & Spyders (Long)
- Triumph & Standard Cars 1945 to 1984 (Warrington)
- Triumph Bonneville Bible (59-83) (Henshaw)
- Triumph Bonneville!, Save the – The inside story of the Meriden Workers' Co-op (Rosamond)
- Triumph Motorcycles & the Meriden Factory (Hancox)
- Triumph Speed Twin & Thunderbird Bible (Woolridge)
- Triumph Tiger Cub Bible (Estall)
- Triumph Trophy Bible (Woolridge)
- Triumph TR6 (Kimberley)
- TT Talking – The TT's most exciting era – As seen by Manx Radio TT's lead commentator 2004-2012 (Lambert)
- Two Summers – The Mercedes-Benz W196R Racing Car (Ackerson)
- TWR Story, The – Group A (Hughes & Scott)
- Unraced (Collins)
- Velocette Motorcycles – MSS to Thruxton – New Third Edition (Burris)
- Vespa – The Story of a Cult Classic in Pictures (Uhlig)
- Vincent Motorcycles: The Untold Story since 1946 (Guyony & Parker)
- Volkswagen Bus Book, The (Bobbitt)
- Volkswagen Bus or Van to Camper, How to Convert (Porter)
- Volkswagens of the World (Glen)
- VW Beetle Cabriolet – The full story of the convertible Beetle (Bobbitt)
- VW Beetle – The Car of the 20th Century (Copping)
- VW Bus – 40 Years of Splitties, Bays & Wedges (Copping)
- VW Bus Book, The (Bobbitt)
- VW Golf: Five Generations of Fun (Copping & Cservenka)
- VW – The Air-cooled Era (Copping)
- VW T5 Camper Conversion Manual (Porter)
- VW Campers (Copping)
- Volkswagen Type 3, The book of the – Concept, Design, International Production Models & Development (Glen)
- Volvo Estate, The (Hollebone)
- You & Your Jaguar XK8/XKR – Buying, Enjoying, Maintaining, Modifying – New Edition (Thorley)
- Which Oil? – Choosing the right oils & greases for your antique, vintage, veteran, classic or collector car (Michell)
- Wolseley Cars 1948 to 1975 (Rowe)
- Works Minis, The Last (Purves & Brenchley)
- Works Rally Mechanic (Moylan)

Also available ...
eBook
Download now from
www.digital.veloce.co.uk

Also available ...
Apps
Download now from
www.digital.veloce.co.uk

Hubble & Hattie

Belvedere

www.veloce.co.uk

First published in October 2017 by Veloce Publishing Limited, Veloce House, Parkway Farm Business Park, Middle Farm Way, Poundbury, Dorchester DT1 3AR, England. Fax 01305 250479 / e-mail info@veloce.co.uk / web www.veloce.co.uk or www.velocebooks.com. ISBN: 978-1-787110-68-7; UPC: 6-36847-01068-3.

© 2017 Brian Corey and Veloce Publishing. All rights reserved. With the exception of quoting brief passages for the purpose of review, no part of this publication may be recorded, reproduced or transmitted by any means, including photocopying, without the written permission of Veloce Publishing Ltd. Throughout this book logos, model names and designations, etc, have been used for the purposes of identification, illustration and decoration. Such names are the property of the trademark holder as this is not an official publication. Readers with ideas for automotive books, or books on other transport or related hobby subjects, are invited to write to the editorial director of Veloce Publishing at the above address.

British Library Cataloguing in Publication Data – A catalogue record for this book is available from the British Library. Typesetting, design and page make-up all by Veloce Publishing Ltd on Apple Mac. Printed in India by Parksons Graphics.

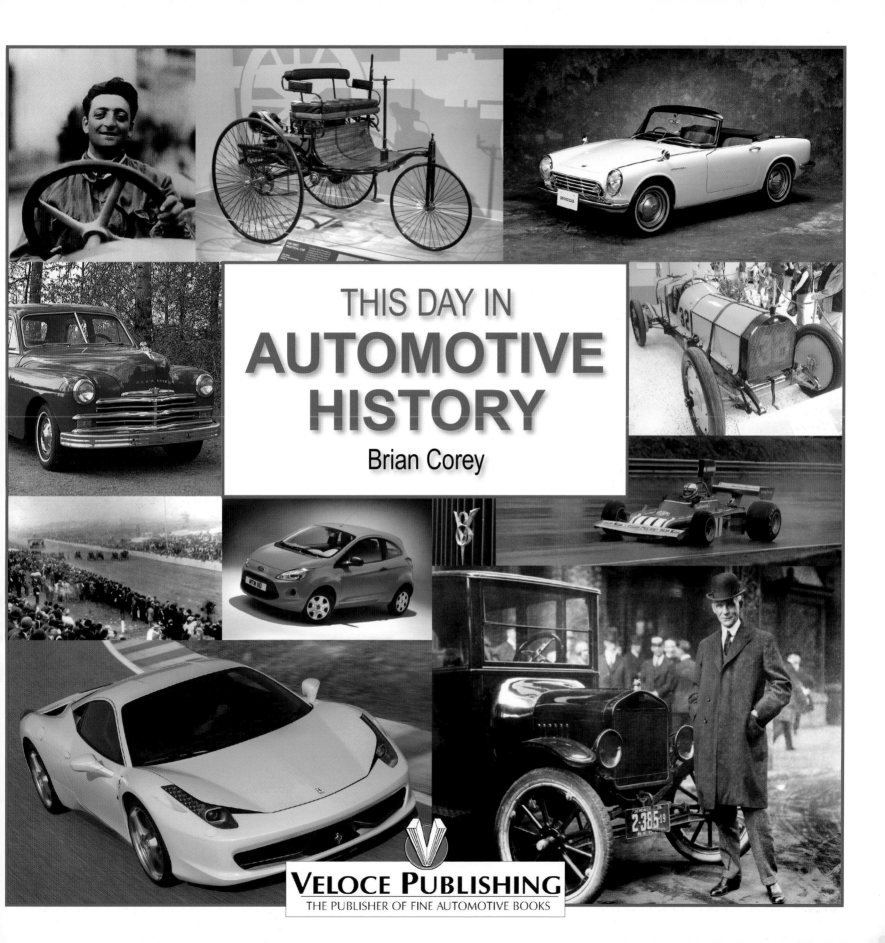

THIS DAY IN
AUTOMOTIVE
HISTORY

Brian Corey

VELOCE PUBLISHING
THE PUBLISHER OF FINE AUTOMOTIVE BOOKS

Contents

Introduction and acknowledgements 5

January 6

February 23

March 38

April 54

May 69

June 85

July 100

August 116

September 131

October 146

November 162

December 177

Appendix: Picture sources 192

Index 195

Introduction

Have you ever climbed into your car and thought about the story both it and its ancestors might tell? It is no secret that the automobile has changed our world. Throughout the last four centuries, a series of interconnected events have led to the existence of the auto industry and the vehicles of today. This book tells many of those fascinating tales that have shaped the automotive world. From the first self-powered vehicles to modern advances in technology, many topics surrounding the history of the automobile are discussed within these pages. The births and deaths of automotive innovators, the rise and fall of car companies lost to history, incredible days at the racetrack, heated rivalries between industry giants, important inventions, the introduction of some of the greatest cars ever built, and many more true events from around the world are described in their day in automotive history. The next time you buckle in, be sure to think about where your car came from. Not just the factory it left, but the blood, sweat and tears that went into it. Think about the investments, the testing, the design and the napkin it was first sketched on.

My earliest, and certainly some of my favorite memories, include a car (or two, for that matter). Just about everyone who has a love affair with the automobile can relate. From their first time behind the wheel to falling in love at lookout point, one's relationship with personal transportation is shaped by their day-to-day lives. For me, the passion first developed as a youngster riding in my parents' Volkswagen Bus, and also pretending I was a race car driver while sitting in my uncle's RX-7 with my cousin. I came to love the experience of being in a car, and well before I could drive I found myself appreciating cars and trucks for their aesthetic value. I grew curious about automotive design and engineering, and the people who created these beautiful machines. I spent many summer days of my youth frequenting auto shows, learning about different makes and models, and when I was 13 my parents helped me purchase my first car – a 1949 Plymouth Special Deluxe coupé, which I still own to this day. After joining the Port Gardner Vintage Auto Club, I began taking auto tech classes in high school, furthering my interest and knowledge of all things cars. While studying journalism in college I figured out what stories I wanted to tell, combining my love of writing and cars seemed obvious. And so the research began …

Acknowledgements

This book is for anyone with the slightest interest in the history of the automobile, but it never would have come to be if it weren't for a few people. Thank you to everyone who allowed their wonderful photos and artwork to be used in this book by contributing their works under Creative Commons licensing*. This book really wouldn't be what it is without you. To my friends who continuously support me, my teachers who have inspired me, and to my family for unconditional love. Extra thanks to my parents, Jack and Diane, for never saying no to any rusty jewels being parked in their driveway.

Brian Corey

Publisher's note: for those pictures reproduced under Creative Commons licenses, captions are numbered, with full details given in the Appendix, in accordance with the terms of the license.

January 1, 1942
Hold the line

On this day in 1942, amidst the US entry into WWII, an order was issued from the United States Office of Production Management to put a freeze on the production and delivery of civilian automobiles throughout the United States as part of the national war effort. Civilian production would end completely on February 22nd of that year, leaving a stockpile of 520,000 cars that would be available for purchase only by citizens who the government deemed as 'essential drivers.' Brightwork materials, such as chrome, were limited on any personal vehicles produced in January and February, due to their necessity for war production. This resulted in automobiles that were referred to as blackout cars, where moldings were painted rather than finished with bright metal.

A 1942 Chevrolet blackout sedan. Chromium was needed for the war effort so automakers had to curtail the use of brightwork, resulting in painted finishes on what would normally be chrome trim. (Brian Corey)

Also on this day: 1904 – Earl Russell received the first vehicle registration plate in Great Britain, number A1, for his Napier. **1919** – Edsel Ford succeeded his father Henry as President of Ford Motor Company. **1952** – Michael Allen and Colin Chapman founded the Lotus Engineering Company.

A 1942 Ford, featuring painted finishes instead of chrome. (Public domain)

January 2, 1994
Chrysler introduces the Neon

Chrysler introduced the Neon on this day in 1994, selling the car under the Chrysler, Dodge and Plymouth nameplates over the vehicle's lifetime. The Neon was a successful model for Chrysler, as it continuously met its sales goals until being discontinued in 2005. This compact two- or four-door car served as Chrysler Corp's entry into the small car market. The Neon tended to have a hard time keeping up with other small cars when it came to comfort, but it made up for it in power. While other manufacturers added accessories, Chrysler added speed. When the Neon R/T debuted in 1998 it could hit 60mph (100km/h) in 7.6 seconds, making the cars competitive in SCCA Solo autocross and showroom-stock road racing.

Also on this day: 1915 – Armand Peugeot, founder of Peugeot, died at age 65. **1974** – E L Cord, founder of Cord Corporation, died at age 79. **1988** – Lexus debuted at the Los Angeles Auto Show.

A second generation (2003-2005) Dodge Neon. (Public domain)

Dodge Neon (racing edition) taking laps at Infineon Raceway Park.
(Photo by Ernesto Andrade [1])

January 3, 1969
F1 champion Michael Schumacher is born

Michael Schumacher at the 2012 Chinese Grand Prix.
(Photo by emperornie [2])

Seven-time Formula One World Champion Michael Schumacher was born on this day in 1969 in Hürth, West Germany. Schumacher began his F1 career at the 1991 Belgian Grand Prix. The race started amongst much hype, after he had qualified for the seventh position. Come race day, however, Schumacher couldn't make it past the first lap due to clutch problems. This was no omen for the rest of his career. He won his first championship in 1994, and followed it up the next year with another. He barely missed titles in 1997 and 1998, and then broke his leg in 1999, putting an end to yet another title run. He returned in 2000 hungry for gold. He would win that year's championship, as well as those of 2001, 2002, 2003 and 2004. Before retiring in 2012, Schumacher set records for the most World Championships (7), Grand Prix wins (91), fastest laps (77) and wins in a single season (13).

Schumacher drove the Benetton B194 below to his first Drivers' World Championship in 1994.
(Photo by Flominator [3])

Also on this day: **1926** – Pontiac was introduced by General Motors. **1992** – The Citroën Xantia went on sale. **2008** – Ford named Tata Motors as the highest bidder for Jaguar and Land Rover.

January 4, 2011
The last Mercury is built

Reproduction of a 1939 Mercury magazine advertisement.

Introduced by Edsel Ford in 1938 for the 1939 model year, Mercury cars were promoted to suit the middle-ground buyer, between an introductory Ford and its luxury line, Lincoln. Despite the original, unique design of the Mercury Eight, for decades following, to save on development costs, Mercurys were essentially rebadged Ford or Lincoln models. Regardless of its attempts to create new and interesting options for buyers, such as the Liquimatic Transmission (the first semi-automatic transmission developed by Ford), by June of 2010 Mercury owned just 1 per cent of the market in the United States, and Ford was forced to announce that the brand would be discontinued. It was on this day in 2011 that the final Mercury, a Grand Marquis, rolled off the line.

Also on this day: **1930** – Cadillac introduced its first V16-powered car. **1975** – Fire ripped through the TVR engineering facility in Blackpool, England, causing much damage.

A fourth generation Mercury Grand Marquis, similar to the last Mercury to roll off the assembly line. (Public domain)

January 5, 1933

The Golden Gate Bridge breaks ground

Having been declared one of the 'Wonders of the Modern World' by the American Society of Civil Engineers, the Golden Gate Bridge is now one of the most recognizable landmarks in San Francisco, California, and throughout all of the United States. Construction on the bridge began on this day in 1933. Because San Francisco was poorly connected to surrounding communities due to its position in the bay, many residents and laborers wanted a bridge across the bay to ease the commute for the growing city, which at this time was connected mainly by a ferryboat that operated across San Francisco Bay. Engineer Joseph Strauss designed the bridge at a final budget of $38 million. Finishing ahead of schedule and under budget, the bridge hosted a grand opening ceremony on May 27, 1937 that saw more than 200,000 people walk or skate across it.

Also on this day: 1955 – An AC Ace was first imported to the US. **1962** – Buick announced its plans to resume the importing of Opels.

The Golden Gate Bridge by night, with part of downtown San Francisco visible in the background. (Photo by Carol M Highsmith, Library of Congress Catalog, public domain)

Looking across the Golden Gate Bridge. (Public domain)

United States Vice President Charles Curtis, Clessie Cummins & Indiana Governor Harry Leslie in Indianapolis with a Cummins-powered Packard.
(Photo courtesy of Cummins Inc, all rights reserved)

January 6, 1930

The first long-distance diesel automobile trip

Founded in 1919, the Cummins Engine Company went out to prove that diesel engines were a viable option for passenger car travel. To show the feasibility of diesel technology, founder Clessie Cummins installed one of his engines in a used Packard, and drove it from Indianapolis to New York City and back, completing his round trip journey on this day in 1930. He used only 30 gallons of fuel at a cost of less than $3. This was the first of several publicity drives Cummins would complete, including one in 1935 from New York to Los Angeles, using just $7.63 in fuel.

Also on this day: 1920 – Walter Chrysler joined Willys-Overland as Executive VP and General Manager. **1954** – The Kaiser Darrin roadster went on sale. **1980** – US President Jimmy Carter introduced a $1.2 billion bailout bill to prevent Chrysler from failing.

At the 1931 Indianapolis 500 the #8 Cummins Special became the first Indy 500 race car to run the entire race nonstop. It finished in 13th place and used $1.40 worth of furnace oil. (Photo by Brian Corey)

January 7, 1985
A different kind of car company

What started as a codename for a new small car from General Motors in the mid 1980s, ended up becoming a car brand all its own. In June of 1982, discussions of a new compact were heating up in GM, and first publicized by Chairman Roger B Smith in November 1983. Just more than a year later, on this day in 1985, Saturn Corporation was officially founded. A concept car soon followed, but GM was still planning on releasing the vehicle under one of its other brands, likely Chevrolet, Oldsmobile or Pontiac. Plans changed, and the Saturn SC and Saturn SL went into production in 1990 for the 1991 model year at the Spring Hill, Tennessee assembly plant. Saturn was marketed as "a different kind of car company," featuring unique models, and operating a separate retailer network than other GM brands.

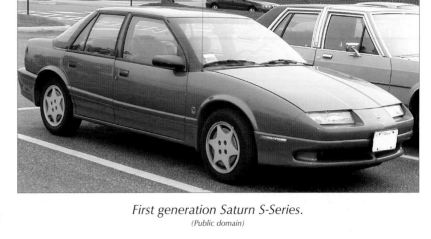

First generation Saturn S-Series.
(Public domain)

Also on this day:
1924 – The first General Motors vehicle manufactured outside of North America came off a Copenhagen assembly line: a Chevrolet truck.
1989 – The Dodge Viper concept debuted.

The Saturn Sky, introduced for the 2007 model year, shared the same platform as the Pontiac Solstice and the Opel GT in Europe.
(Photo by Greg Gjerdingen [4])

William Vanderbilt in 1903.
(Photo by Theodore C Marceau, public domain)

January 8, 1944
Auto racer William Vanderbilt dies

The Vanderbilt family is easily associated with wealth, but early auto racing? William Kissam Vanderbilt II was born in 1878, and discovered a love for automobiles after riding a steam-powered tricycle in France. By age 20 he was acquiring motor vehicles of all sorts, his first being a French De Dion-Bouton tricycle. In 1904 he set a land speed record of 92.30mph (148.54km/h) in a Mercedes at Daytona Beach. The same year he founded America's first automobile trophy race, the Vanderbilt Cup. It was held in Long Island, New York, and offered a large cash prize. Vanderbilt hoped to drive interest in racing to get automakers to build better, faster cars. Contestants from around the world entered the inaugural race held on October 8, 1904. Vanderbilt continued racing and collecting cars throughout his life until he passed away on this day in 1944.

Also on this day: 1927 – The Marmon 8 debuted in New York City.
2002 – Bentley unveiled the Arnage T in Detroit, Michigan.

Start of the 1908 Vanderbilt Cup. (Public domain)

January 9, 1958

Japan invades the US

On January 9, 1958, the Imported Car Show was held in Los Angeles, officially bringing Nissan, under the Datsun name, and Toyota to the United States for the first time. While some Datsuns and Toyotas came home with servicemen in the early 1950s, this was the first time that the two companies presented their cars to the American public outside of testing. The vehicles that were shown included a Datsun 1000 and a Toyota Toyopet Crown. Although Toyota had opened a Hollywood dealership in October of the previous year, sales didn't begin until after the show. Toyota quickly discovered its underpowered sedans were not popular. Datsun, on the other hand, understood that more powerful engines were desired in America. Ray Lemke opened the first US Datsun dealership on October 8, 1958 in San Diego.

Also on this day: **1909** – The Badger Four Wheel Drive Auto Company was formed. **2009** – Cuba lifted a decade long ban on new taxi driver licenses.

January 10, 1942

Jeep contract awarded to Ford

Prior to the US entering WWII, the US Army contacted 135 companies and asked for prototypes of a four-wheel drive reconnaissance car. American Bantam delivered a working model for testing on September 21, 1941, and the Army found it met all of its criteria, except for engine torque. The Army sent the blueprints to Willys-Overland and Ford, along with a list of hopeful improvements. Following testing of the Bantam, along with the new Willys and Ford models, the Willys MB design was awarded a production contract. As the United States entered WWII the Army knew it would need more vehicles than Willys could manufacture. To boost production of what would become known as the Jeep, Ford was granted a contract to build copycat versions of the Willys design on this day in 1942.

Also on this day: **1959** – Stirling Moss won the New Zealand Grand Prix. **1979** – The last Volkswagen Type 1 "Beetle" convertible was produced.

This modified yellow 1960 Datsun 1200 wasn't much different from the Datsun 1000 that debuted in 1958. It originally featured a 48hp engine and a four speed column shifter.
(Photo by Vetatur Fumare [5])

A right hand drive 1959 Toyopet Crown, similar to the model that debuted in LA in 1958. (Photo by Iwao [6])

Willys Jeep with a trailer that could have been produced by American Bantam.
(Photo by Joe Ross [7])

A Ford GPW jeep named 'AL' that belonged to Company A of the 50th Armored Infantry Battalion of the 6th Armored Division US (Super Sixth). Taken after disembarking Normandy Beach in June, 1944.
(Public domain)

January 11, 1937
GM goes on strike

The United Automobile Workers was founded in May 1935 to focus on improving working conditions in automaker facilities. Membership grew quickly and it had success in organizing a sit-down strike that started on December 30, 1936 at the GM Fisher Body Plant No 2 in Flint, Michigan. On this day in 1937 violence erupted at the strike site as police tried to prevent the strikers from receiving a food delivery from local supporters. Dubbed the "Battle of the Running Bulls" by the autoworkers – bulls a reference to the police force – both the strikers and police reported injuries. As many as 14 autoworkers were hurt by gunfire, but no fatalities were recorded. The riot resulted in the National Guard being called in, but it never advanced on the buildings. The strike lasted for more than a month and ended with GM agreeing to give the UAW bargaining rights.

Also on this day: **1917** – Ford introduced the Model TT truck. **1919** – The Essex automobile made its public debut.

National Guard with machine gun overlooking Chevrolet factories number nine and number four. Flint, Michigan.

Left: A striker with his fiancée (sit-down strike romance) in the Women's Auxiliary room in Pengally Hall, Flint, Michigan. Right: Young striker off sentry duty, sleeping on assembly line of auto seats. (Photos by Sheldon Dick for the Farm Security Administration Office of War Information, public domain)

January 12, 1904
Henry Ford sets new speed record

Before the Ford Motor Company was founded, Henry Ford collaborated with bicycle racer Tom Cooper to build two racing cars in 1902. The vehicles were relatively interchangeable, both featuring a 1156 cu in (18.9-liter) inline-4 engine that produced between 70 and 100hp. Two weeks before their first scheduled race the cars would not start, so Ford sold his stake in them for $800 to Cooper and early auto racer Barney Oldfield, but retained rights to publicity and promotions. Painted red and yellow, and named 999 and Arrow, respectively, the bare-bones cars would prove ferocious on the track once up and running. It was on this day in 1904 Henry Ford drove the 999 himself, with mechanic Ed Huff at the throttle, to a new automobile land speed record of 91.37mph (140.05km/h) on an ice track over a frozen lake.

Also on this day: **1921** – William Durant founded Durant Motors Inc after being fired from General Motors. **1973** – Clifton R Wharton Jr became the first black man elected to the Ford Motor Company Board of Directors.

Left: Henry Ford (standing) and Barney Oldfield in 1902, with the '999' racing automobile. (Public domain)

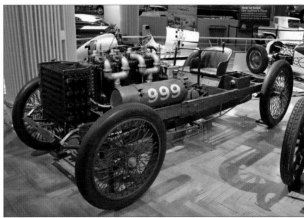

The 999 at The Henry Ford Museum. (Photo by Joe Ross [8])

January 13, 1906

The first AMCMA auto show

Founded just weeks prior, the American Motor Car Manufacturers Association held its first auto show on this day in 1906 to build public interest in the new type of transportation. As the doors opened at the 69th Regiment Armory in New York City, the crowd enjoyed a peek at many vehicles being produced in America. The association, made up mostly of motorcar builders and executives, aimed to become the leading advocator for the advancement of the automotive industry. By 1910, the AMCMA show moved to the Grand Central Palace in New York, and featured 79 manufacturers from the US and abroad, as well as hundreds more exhibitors of parts and accessories.

Also on this day: **1920** – Charles Kettering was named VP of General Motors. **2004** – Rolls-Royce employees celebrated the 500th Phantom built at Goodwood.

TRELLIS DECORATIVE SCHEME OF THE GRAND CENTRAL PALACE SHOW

These images, taken from The Motor World, Volume 21, printed in 1909, illustrate the anticipated Grand Central Palace Show that took place from December 31, 1909 to January 7, 1910. The image above shows the interior of the Grand Palace; on the right can be seen the layout of one area of the show.

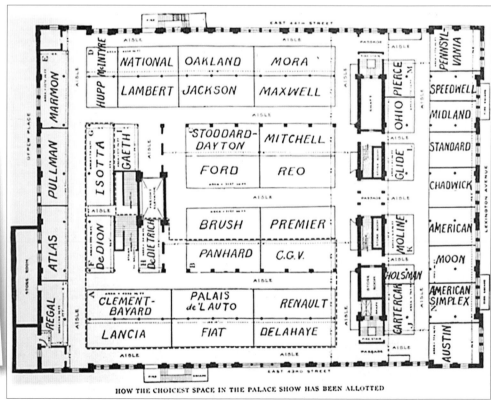

HOW THE CHOICEST SPACE IN THE PALACE SHOW HAS BEEN ALLOTTED

January 14, 1954
The Hudson and Nash merger

In what was the largest corporate merger in US history at the time, Nash-Kelvinator Corporation joined with Hudson Motor Car Company to form American Motors Corporation (AMC) on this day in 1954. The merger was led by Nash-Kelvinator CEO George Mason, in hopes of building a company strong enough to compete with the Big Three of General Motors, Ford and Chrysler. Within a year Mason died of pneumonia, and his assistant George Romney was named the new president. Under Romney, the company focused on a small car line for AMC and the Hudson and Nash names were phased out. By 1960, AMC was named the third most popular brand of automobile in

The AMC Rambler helped push AMC into the top three by 1960. This 1960 Rambler American Wagon offered space and great fuel economy.
(Photo by Greg Gjerdingen [9])

The Metropolitan, first built by Nash in 1953, remained a key part of the AMC lineup through 1961, as they continued to push smaller cars.
(Photo by Brian Corey)

the US, in part thanks to the new Rambler American. For the next two decades AMC would experience relative success, producing some of America's most iconic cars of the 1960s and 1970s, including the AMX, Gremlin and Pacer.

Also on this day: **1896** – Daimler Motor Co was incorporated by Harry Lawson. **1982** – The third generation Chevrolet Camaros and Pontiac Firebirds made their public debut.

1971 AMC Javelin AMX.
(Photo by Greg Gjerdingen [10])

January 15, 1909
The son of Ettore

Gianroberto Bugatti was born in Germany on this day in 1909, the same year his father Ettore founded Automobiles E Bugatti. Following the end of WWI, Gianroberto, known as Jean, became an integral part of his father's company. At the age of 23, Jean led the design of the Bugatti Type 41 Royale, and later developed four separate bodies for the Type 57, often regarded as one of Bugatti's finest touring models. It was, unfortunately, his love of the automobile that would cause his death. On August 11, 1939, at the age of 30, Jean was killed while testing the Type 57 tank-bodied car that had recently won a Le Mans race. He lost control of the vehicle after hitting a cyclist who had snuck on to the test track, resulting in a devastating impact with a tree.

Also on this day: **1936** – Henry Ford organizes the Ford Foundation. **1979** –The Formula One Ferrari 312T4 debuts, which Enzo Ferrari calls the ugliest car to ever leave his factory.

1931 Bugatti Type 41 'Royale' Cabriolet Weinberger.
(Photo by Yahya S [11])

1936 Bugatti 57G Tank that was driven by Jean-Pierre Wimille and Robert Benoist to victory at the 1937 24 Hours of Le Mans. (Photo by ilikewaffles11 [12])

Left: 1936 Bugatti Type 57SC Atlantic.
(Photo by Brian Corey)

January 16, 1853
André Michelin is born

Portrait of André Michelin.
(Public domain)

André Michelin was born in Paris, France, on this day in 1853. While running the farm and agricultural equipment business started by his grandfather, André Michelin encountered a cyclist seeking help repairing his inflatable bicycle tire. The pneumatic bike tire was invented the year prior by John Dunlop, but, after being presented with the tire trouble, André, along with his brother Édouard, developed improvements to the design that would reduce the chances of it going flat, while also easing repairs. In 1891, two years after founding the Michelin Tire Company, the brothers received a patent for the detachable tire. Michelin would go on to create the radial tire, first fitted on a Citroën, and patented in 1946.

An 1898 poster by O'Galop, creator of the Michelin Man.

Also on this day: **1905** – The Sunbeam Motor Company was founded in Wolverhampton, England. **1948** – The Ford F-Series trucks were introduced. **1958** – The first Scarab sports car was road tested.

January 17, 1953
Introducing, Corvette!

America's sports car, the Chevrolet Corvette, made its public debut at the Waldorf-Astoria Hotel in New York City during General Motors' Motorama, on this day in 1953. Designed by Harley Earl, the Corvette was the first all-fiberglass-bodied sports car built in the United States. The excitement that surrounded the Corvette's debut led GM to rush the car into production. A temporary assembly line was soon put together in an old customer pick-up station at a GM plant in Flint, Michigan. The first production Corvettes, each hand built, left the factory on June 30. All 300 Corvettes produced for 1953 were polo white convertibles with red interiors and black tops. Due in part to poor marketing, a number of them were left unsold at the end of the year. Others blame the Blue Flame six-cylinder and two-speed automatic transmission for the troubled sales.

1953 Chevrolet Corvette. (Photo by Jeff Wilcox [13])

Also on this day:
1922 – George Selden, former US patent holder for the automobile, died, aged 78. **1964** – The first Porsche 904 Carrera GTS was sold. **1999** – Renault acquired a 20 per cent interest in Nissan.

Porsche 904/8 during training for the 1000km race at the Nürburgring in 1964. (Photo by Lothar Spurzem [14])

1924 Bentley 3 Litre. (Public domain)

January 18, 1919
Bentley is founded

While touring the DFP automobile factory Walter Owens Bentley noticed an aluminum paperweight, leading to the idea of using the lightweight metal to produce engine cylinders. W O, as he was known, took the idea home to North London and began producing aluminum cylinders for aero engines during the Great War for the Sopwith Camel airplane. His successes led to the founding of Bentley Motors Limited on this day in 1919. The first vehicle carrying his name would be delivered two years later, featuring an innovative 4-valve per cylinder engine designed by Clive Gallop. Bentley quickly earned a roaring reputation, but it was a first place finish at the 24 Hours of Le Mans in 1924 that helped secure business-saving financial backing from Captain Woolf Barnato.

Also on this day: **1907** – Hispåno-Suiza debuted in England. **1937** – Horse-drawn buggies were banned from traffic in the West End of London. **1953** – The inaugural Argentine Grand Prix took place.

Red label Speed four-seater tourer, 1927. (Photo by Tim Green [15])

January 19, 1954

GM announces $1 billion expansion

On this day in 1954, General Motors (GM) announced a $1 billion investment into the expansion of its automotive ventures. GM was founded in 1908 as a holding company, and quickly acquired brands such as Oldsmobile, Buick and Oakland. The initial growth helped GM become the largest automotive business in the early part of the century, a position it held for decades. Its 1954 investment was geared toward overall expansion of its numerous brands, which by then included Cadillac and Chevrolet. This monstrous investment led to models that have been cherished through the ages, including the Tri-Five Chevrolets and V8 laden Corvettes.

Also on this day: 1896 – Japan witnessed its first motor vehicle, a Hildebrand & Wolfmuller motorcycle from Germany. **1971** – Ford of Britain introduced the GT70. Only six were produced.

A custom 1955 Chevrolet Bel-Air. GM's billion dollar expansion assisted in the development of the Tri-Five Chevys. (Photo by James [16])

January 20, 1946

Meet Frazer and Kaiser

Following WWII, many entrepreneurs foresaw the need for new commodities for returning soldiers, including houses and automobiles. Successful shipbuilder Henry J Kaiser was one of those people, and he pursued multiple ventures, including cars. To build automobiles Kaiser partnered with Graham-Paige Motors, leading to the Kaiser-Frazer Corporation being founded in August 1945, named after Kaiser and Graham-Paige CEO Joseph Frazer. It was on this day in 1946 that non-running prototypes of the new Frazer and the Kaiser K85 front wheel-drive car debuted at the Waldorf Astoria Hotel in New York City. Several setbacks led to the front-wheel drive idea being scrapped, and

1948 Frazer Standard. (Photo by Greg Gjerdingen [18])

1949 Kaiser Virginian 2. (Photo by Jack Snell [17])

instead the same body and drivetrain were used for both of the first Frazer and Kaiser vehicles.

Also on this day: 1924 – Legion Ascot Speedway opened in Los Angeles. **1949** – The Buick Riviera debuted.

January 21, 1862

Opel opens for business

Before manufacturing automobiles Opel first produced sewing machines in a cowshed in Russelsheim, Hessen, Germany. Founded on this day in 1862 by Adam Opel, the business moved from the cowshed in 1888 after beginning bicycle production. Opel's sons took over the business following their father's death in 1895, and shortly thereafter developed a partnership with a locksmith named Friedrich Lutzmann, who had been working on automobile designs. The first Opel autos were built in 1899. Limited success of the venture resulted in the partnership dissolving. Two years later the brothers signed a licensing agreement with Automobiles Darracq France, to produce cars with an Opel body on a Darracq chassis that was powered by a two-cylinder engine. Opel debuted its first vehicle of its own complete design at the 1902 Hamburg Motor Show. These cars would go into production four years later, and the Opel Darracq partnership ended the following year.

Opel Patent Motor Wagen circa 1899. (Public domain)

Also on this day:
1901 – The first Paris Motor Show was held. **1918** – Emil Jellinek, founder of Mercedes, died. **1954** – General Motors debuted the Firebird XP-21 turbine concept car.

The Firebird XP-21, later known as the Firebird I.
(Photo by Karrmann [19])

January 22,

1950
Preston Tucker walks free

Tucker Torpedo.
(Photo by Brian Corey)

Preston Tucker.
(Photo courtesy of the Tucker Automobile Club of America, Inc [20])

After decades in the auto industry Preston Tucker dreamed up a revolutionary new car, giving way to the Tucker Torpedo. The innovative vehicle featured a padded steering wheel, safety glass, a roll bar and center Cyclops headlight, all powered by a 334 cu in (5.47-liter) aircraft engine. There was much public interest in his vehicle, but even after securing $17 million in funding and purchasing a factory, he was still short on cash for final development and mass production. To raise the money Tucker sold dealerships and accessories, including seat covers and luggage, before the car even started down the assembly line. A fraud case followed, brought on by the Securities and Exchange Commission, alleging that he illegally acquired the funds from investors. It was on this day in 1950 a not guilty verdict was delivered, but the trial and negative press destroyed the company, and only 51 complete Tuckers ever left the assembly line.

Also on this day: 1944 – Henry Ford II was elected as Vice President of Ford. **1976** – The first SEAT 124D was manufactured in Portugal.

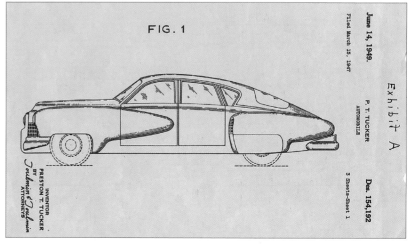

Tucker Torpedo patent. (Public domain)

January 23, 1980
Death of a designer

Giovanni Michelotti made many incredible contributions to the European sports car market before passing away on this day in 1980. Having designed bodies for Ferrari, Maserati, Standard Triumph and others while working at coachbuilders Stabilimenti Farina, Vignale and Carrozzeria Allemano, Michelotti was able to open his own studio in 1959. Throughout his career he would bring an astounding portfolio of cars to the road, including the Ferrari 166, Ferrari 375MM, Maserati 5000 GT, BMW 700, Triumph GT6, Triumph Spitfire, Alfa Romeo 2600, and the Prince Skyline Sport for Nissan. Later in life, when asked if he had designed anything other than cars, Michelotti admitted to once designing a coffee maker.

Also on this day: **1954** – The World Motor Sports Show opened in New York City. **1966** – Dan Gurney won his fourth consecutive Riverside 500, setting a NASCAR Grand National record.

January 24, 1860
The internal combustion engine

Patents for internal combustion engines date back as far as 1807, but none were considered commercially successful until engineer Jean Joseph Étienne Lenoir of Mussy-la-Ville, Luxembourg, in modern day Belgium, came up with his own design, for which he received a patent on this day in 1860. His design was the first to burn a mixture of coal gas and air ignited by a 'jumping sparks' ignition system. While the engine was mostly used for stationary equipment, such as power plants, printing presses, water pumps and tooling, Lenoir applied the engines to a few automobiles between 1860 and 1863, most notably his Hippomobile. A 2543cc engine, producing 1.5 horsepower, powered the three-wheeled wagon. In 1863, it was successfully driven from Paris to Joinville-le-Point and back, a total distance of 22km (14 miles).

Michelotti (right) with Enrico Nardi and the 1960 Plymouth Silver Ray. A one off car, built in 1960 on a Nardi chassis, designed by Michelotti.
(Public domain)

1971 Triumph GT6.
(Photo by Riley [21])

Lenoir Gas Engine on display at Quartier Des Arts-Et-Metiers, Paris. (Photo by Daryl Mitchell [22])

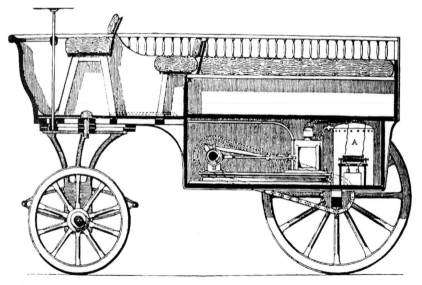

Right: Barney Oldfield and aviator Lincoln Beachey racing.
(Public domain)

Left: 1863 'Hippomobile' by Étienne Lenoir, contemporary depiction.
(Public domain)

Also on this day: **1914** – Automobile racer Barney Oldfield and airplane pilot Lincoln Beachey held their first Championship of the Universe race. **2000** – Jenson Button became the youngest F1 driver to date, at age 20.

January 25, 1905
A Brit sets the land speed record

The sands of Daytona Beach, Florida, have long been notorious for auto racing and speed tests. It was there, on this day in 1905, that British racer Arthur MacDonald drove a Napier six-cylinder racing car named Samson to a new land speed record of 104.65mph (168.42km/h). The L48, as the car was formally known, featured tubular radiators running along each side of the bonnet, giving the car a one-of-a-kind appearance. With an 848 cu in engine, pushing more than 90 horsepower, MacDonald covered five miles in 3 minutes and 17 seconds. The car would be successful in races across Great Britain and France, before its motor was mounted to a boat in Australia.

Also on this day: **1964** – Bruce McLaren won his third straight F1 Tasman Cup.

Napier Samson.
(Public domain)

Arthur MacDonald at the wheel of the Napier at Daytona.
(Public domain)

January 26, 1979
The Dukes of Hazzard premieres

"Ooooh, those Duke boys!" Cousins Bo and Luke Duke and the rest of Hazzard County crashed onto the small screen on this day in 1979 on American broadcast network CBS. *The Dukes of Hazzard* was an action comedy that brought cars into the starlight. Bo and Luke's 1969 Dodge Charger, the 'General Lee,' often stole the show while making their get away from Sheriff Rosco P Coltrane. The Duke boys, on probation for distilling moonshine, aren't allowed to leave Hazzard County, and often find themselves foiling the plots of corrupt county commissioner Boss Hogg. Aside from the General Lee, the show featured Daisy's 1974 Plymouth Road Runner in the first season, before she found herself in 'Dixie,' a white 1980 Jeep CJ-7. Uncle Jesse most often drove a 1973-1977 Ford F-100, while Boss Hogg commonly cruised in a 1970 Cadillac DeVille convertible.

Side view of General Lee #8. It is the only first-season, Georgia-built car to retain its original paint and hand painted graphics. It was built using parts from previously wrecked General Lees, including the roll bar from #1.
(Public domain)

Dashboard view of #8. This car is on display at the Volo Auto Museum just outside of Chicago.
(Public domain)

Also on this day: **1925** – General Motors Brazil was organized.
2014 – Tata Motors Managing Director Karl Slym died after falling out of a 22nd storey hotel window in Bangkok.

January 27, 1965

The Shelby GT350 makes its debut

Sales of the Shelby GT350 launched on this day in 1965. Designed and developed by Carroll Shelby, the GT350 was based on the Ford Mustang fastback, optioned with a 289 V8 that put out 271hp, and was matched to a four-speed manual transmission. The stock vehicles were shipped to Shelby American where they were stripped of weight, including the back seat, and received performance upgrades that included high-riser intake manifolds, a four barrel carburettor and custom exhaust headers, resulting in an output of 306 horsepower. In 1965, Shelby produced 562 examples, all painted Wimbledon White with Guardsman Blue stripes. In 1966 the cars were geared more toward general consumers than racers. They were offered with optional rear vent windows and back seats, and were available in an array of colors. Production of the first generation of Mustang-based Shelbys continued through 1971 with the GT350 and GT500.

Also on this day: 1934 – Chrysler Airflow and DeSoto Airflow debuted at Chicago Auto Show. **1936** – The Cord 810 went into production.

A 1965 Ford Shelby GT350. (Photos by Yahya S [23])

January 28, 1896

The first speeding ticket

In early 1896, the speed limit in London was a blazing 2mph (3km) and every motorist had to have a flag waver walk in front of them to alert people that an automobile was coming through. So when Benz dealer and auto manufacturer Walter Arnold raced through the streets of Paddock Wood, Kent, on this day in 1896, at an astonishing 8mph (13km/h) with no flag waver running in front of him, a local constable was quick to take action. The officer jumped on his bicycle and gave chase for 5 miles before being able to stop the driver. Mr Arnold was issued the world's first recorded automobile speeding ticket and was fined one shilling.

Also on this day: 1911 – Frenchman Henri Rougier won the first Monte Carlo Rally in a Turcat-Mery. **1938** – Rudolf Caracciola drives a Mercedes W125 Rekordwagen to 432km/h (268mph) on a public roadway, a standing record.

1896 Benz Velo, perhaps similar to the car that Mr Arnold was driving when he was pulled over. Arnold licensed the Benz design to build his own cars using his own company's engine design, and between 1896 and 1898, he produced 12 of the vehicles. (Public domain)

Rudolf Caracciola drove the Mercedes-Benz W125 Rekordwagen to a new public road speed record.
(Photo by big-ashb [24])

January 29, 1886

The automobile is patented

Karl Benz received German patent number 37435 when he applied to patent the Benz Patent-Motorwagen on this day in 1886. The vehicle is widely regarded as the world's first automobile, as it was the first carriage designed to be propelled by an internal combustion engine. Benz, who developed stationary engines in his career, utilized his own design of a 954cc single cylinder, four stroke engine, that weighed just 220lb (100kg) and produced ¾ horsepower, to build his auto. While he designed and built the car, it was his wife Bertha who financed the operation and succeeded in marketing it when she took the third Motorwagen built on the first long distance automobile trip. The 121 mile (194km) journey demonstrated its ease of use and durability.

Also on this day: 1929 – General Motors purchased Opel. **1981** – Nissan announced plans to build a UK factory. **1989** – Global Motors, American importer of the Yugo, filed for bankruptcy. **2016** – The last Land Rover Defender was manufactured.

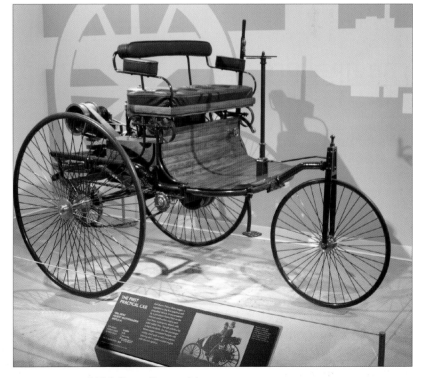

1886 Benz Patent-Motorwagen. (Photo by Brian Corey)

Close up of the engine of a Benz Patent-Motorwagen.
(Photo by LSDSL [25])

January 30, 1920
Mazda is founded

Jujiro Matsuda founded Toyo Cork Kogyo in Hiroshima, Japan on this day in 1920. After the cork manufacturing company had to be saved from bankruptcy by Hiroshima Savings Bank in the late 1920s the business started to reconsider its product offerings. In 1931 Toyo Kogyo

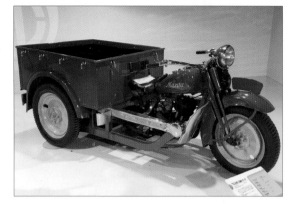

Mazda-Go autorickshaw, first introduced in 1931. (Photo by N A Parish [26])

Mazda R360 coupé. (Photo by Mic [27])

Co, as the company was known by then, introduced the three-wheeled Mazda-Go autorickshaw, beginning its endeavor into automobiles. Mazda's first real car, the R360, was introduced in 1960. At about this time, the company formed a partnership with German company NSU, to further develop the Wankel rotary engine, leading to the introduction of the Mazda Cosmo Sport in 1967. The Mazda name would not be officially adopted until 1984.

Also on this day: **1937** – The Lord Howe circuit in South Africa hosted its first Grand Prix, which was won by Pat Fairfield in an ERA. **1951** – Ferdinand Porsche dies at age 75.

January 31, 1942
The final pre-wars

Under the Lend-Lease act, the US auto industry was to transition from building personal and commercial cars and trucks to war vehicles, machinery and weapons in early 1942 to support US efforts in World War II. It was on this day in 1942 that the last prewar Chryslers, Plymouths and Studebakers would roll off of their respective assembly lines. The last United States civilian car produced was a Ford sedan, which left the factory two days later. Automotive factories were retooled to build tanks, trucks, planes, bombs, boats, guns, ammunition, helmets, and many other items necessary for battle.

Also on this day: **1981** – Elliott Estes retired from his position as president of General Motors. **1994** – It was announced that British Aerospace would sell Rover to BMW for £800 million.

Mazda Cosmo Sport. (Photo by Contri [28])

The auto industry went to war, building tanks, Jeeps, weapons, planes and so much more. This image depicts a Boeing Plant producing B-17Es in December 1942, providing great detail in the large scale of manufacturing that occurred. (Public domain)

February 1, 1907
A steaming pioneer

French inventor and industrialist Léon Serpollet is said to have done more for the steam automobile than anyone else. While experimenting with steam vehicles in the late 1880s, he and his brother Henri built a steam-powered tricycle that helped them convince investors to fund further developments. In 1896 Léon invented and patented the flash boiler, making steam a more viable fuel option. To demonstrate the power of steam, Serpollet set out to break the land speed record, which he did on April 13, 1902, driving a car that he'd built and dubbed Easter Egg. Hitting a top speed of 120km/h (75mph) he became the first driver to hold the land speed record driving a steam vehicle. He would continue development of steam automobiles until his death at age 48 on this day in 1907.

Also on this day: 1947 – Ferrari announced its first model, the 125s. **1970** – Brian Redman finished first and second at the 24 Hours of Daytona after co-driving on two separate teams.

1906 Serpollet Phaéton.
(Photo by Buch-t [29])

1901 Serpollet Vis-a-Vis Typ D. *(Photo by Claus Ableiter [30])*

February 2, 1992
First Japanese winner at Daytona

Endurance automobile racing began at Daytona International Raceway in Florida shortly after the course opened in April of 1959, with the first 24 Hours of Daytona race held in 1966. The inaugural race was won by Ken Miles and Lloyd Ruby driving a Ford GT40 Mk II. The race would be dominated by American and European cars for decades until this day in 1992, when Japanese racers Masahiro Hasemi,

Nissan R91CK, similar to the vehicle used to win the 1992 24 Hours of Daytona. *(Photo by Oli R [31])*

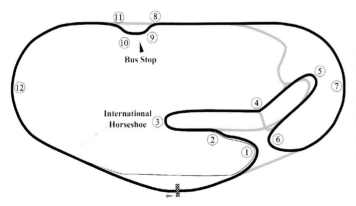

Outline of the road course used for 24 Hours of Daytona.

Kazuyoshi Hoshino and Toshio Suzuki took home the gold driving a Nissan R91CP. They covered 2,712.72 miles (4365.7km) during their monumental victory that brought the trophy to Japan for the first time.

Also on this day: 1926 – Marmon Motor Car Company was established. **1974** – The Bricklin SV-1 was introduced. **2004** – A new 2004 Dodge Ram SRT-10 reached 248.783km/h (154.587mph), a new record for production pickup trucks.

February 3, 1948

Cadillac leads with tailfins

General Motors design chief Harley Earl was an inspired man when he gazed upon the WWII twin-tailed P-38 Lightning fighter plane. Using aesthetic elements of the plane, he and designer Frank Hershey ushered in the tailfin era of the automobile, starting with the 1948 Cadillac, the first of which left the factory on this day in 1948. The style proved popular and quickly spread through American automotive design centers, and then around the world. By the end of the 1950s, fins had grown from small projections to massive wings with sharp edges. After reaching their apex in 1959, the design element was phased out in the first years of the following decade.

1948 Cadillac Sixty Special. (Photo by Alden Jewell [32])

1959 Cadillac Coupe de Ville, the year fins hit their highest point. (Photo by Brian Corey)

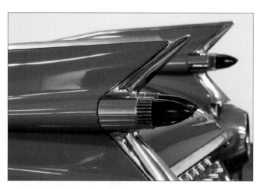

Close up of 1959 Cadillac fins. (Photo by Brian Corey)

Also on this day: **1919** – Cummins Engine Company was incorporated. **1958** – The last stock car race held on Daytona Beach in Florida ended with Paul Goldsmith as the victor. **2016** – Toyota announced Scion would be discontinued.

February 4, 1922

Ford acquires Lincoln

Nearly a decade after selling Cadillac to General Motors, Henry Leland founded Lincoln Motor Company in 1917 to build Liberty aircraft engines under government contract during WWI. Following the armistice Leland began producing automobiles using a V8 based on the Liberty's design, but the company failed to make a profit. Leland, who had created Cadillac out of the failed Henry Ford Company, was forced to sell Lincoln to Ford on this day in 1922 for $8 million, approximately half of what the company was actually worth. A judge blocked Ford's original bid of $5 million, and Henry Ford admitted later that he had 'lowballed' as revenge against Leland.

Also on this day: **1929** – The 1,000,000th Ford Model A was manufactured. **1970** – American Motors received shareholder approval to acquire Kaiser-Jeep. **1971** – Rolls-Royce declared bankruptcy.

1925 Lincoln Model L Berline. The Model L was the first model introduced by Lincoln in 1917. It was discontinued by Ford in 1930 when replaced by the Model K. (Photo by Michel Curi [33])

In 1939 the Lincoln Continental was introduced and quickly became Lincoln's top of the line model. Pictured is a 1941 Continental Cabriolet. (Photo by Jack Snell [34])

February 5, 1878
The birth of André Citroën

The youngest of five children, André-Gustave Citroën was born in Paris on this day in 1878. He developed a passion for engineering as he watched the construction of the Eiffel Tower, which inspired his studies at École Polytechnique in Palaiseau, France. During a visit to Warsaw in 1900 he witnessed a carpenter working on a set of gears; he would later purchase the gear patent to further develop it. This led to the invention of double helical gears, which are used in rear axles, transaxles, camshaft timing gears and other applications. In 1906 Citroën became director of Mors automobiles. After finding success in the automobile industry he founded the Citroën company in 1919, and it would become the fourth largest automobile manufacturer in the world by the early 1930s.

Also on this day: 1919 – The first Voisin automobile was completed. **1954** – Founder of Greyhound Lines bus service, Carl Wickman, died at age 66. **2004** – The Jaguar XK-RS concept car was revealed.

André Citroën (1878-1935).
(Photo from US Library of Congress [US Library of Congress' Prints and Photographs Division, Digital ID ggbain.35699)

1951 Modèle 15 SIX D Traction Avant. The Traction Avant was manufactured from 1934 to 1957. Its development sent Citroën into bankruptcy, but would prove to be an incredibly successful car. (Public domain)

February 6, 1954
Mercedes-Benz 300 SL is born

Mercedes-Benz built a brand new car for the 1952 sports car racing season, dubbed the W194, also known as the 300 SL. The 3-liter straight-six was vicious on the track, taking home the gold at 24 Hours of Le Mans, Bern-Bremgarten, Carrera Panamericana, and other races. Only 10 of the cars were built for racing, but at the suggestion of Daimler-Benz's official US importer Max Hoffman, Mercedes introduced a production version of the car, which was first sold on this day in 1954. The

Schloss Dyck Classic Days 2013. Mercedes Flügeltürer ('Wingdoors').
(Photo by Jorbasa Fotografie [35])

The steering wheel tilted for easier driver access.
(Photo 孝杰 林 [36])

300 SL borrowed the same engine as its racing predecessor but featured direct fuel-injection, opposed to the triple two-barrel Solex carburetors of the racer. The 300 SL was available as a Gullwing coupé or a roadster, of which 1400 and 1858 were built, respectively, between 1954 and 1963.

Also on this day: 1964 – Britain and France agreed to build a channel tunnel. **1995** – The Ferrari 412 T2 Formula One car was introduced.

February 7, 1975

Canada slows down

In 1973 Richard Nixon proposed a maximum speed limit of 50 miles per hour in the United States, following an embargo that banned 11 Arab oil producers from selling to Western countries. Nixon's goal was to conserve gasoline and create a greater oil reserve in the US. What followed was the 1974 Emergency Highway Energy Conservation Act, which limited max speeds to 55mph (90km/h). Aside from saving fuel there was a positive byproduct of the lowered speed limit – a reduction in highway automobile fatalities. Canada, which wasn't heavily reliant on Middle Eastern oil, took notice of the safer roadways and in order to curb its own highway deaths the Canadian government lowered the national speed limit to 55mph on this day in 1975.

Also on this day: 1938 – Harvey S Firestone, founder of Firestone Tire & Rubber Company, died at age 89. **1958** – The 2,000,000th Cadillac, a Sedan DeVille, was produced.

Harvey S Firestone passed away on this day in 1938. (Public domain)

55mph sign. (Photo by KOMUnews [37])

1975-1976 GMC C/K. (Public domain)

February 8, 1993

GM sues NBC

On November 17, 1992, NBC's *Dateline* aired a segment about the dangerous positioning of gas tanks on 1973-1987 GM pickup trucks. The show contained a fiery crash test, demonstrating that when hit in a certain way the tank could rupture and explode. Following an investigation by General Motors, a lawsuit was filed on this day in 1993 on its behalf, suing NBC for defamation. The suit claimed NBC producers staged the test, using remote controlled model rocket engines placed in the fuel tank to ignite the crashes. Just two days after the lawsuit was filed, NBC issued a public apology on air as part of a settlement, acknowledging that it did not inform the viewership of any sort of tampering with the vehicles.

Also on this day: 1936 – General Motors founder William C Durant filed for personal bankruptcy. **1956** – AEC Routemaster double-decker buses went into service in London. **2016** – Jeep celebrated its 75th anniversary with commercials aired during the Super Bowl.

1981 Chevrolet C-10 Silverado LWB.
(Photo by RL GNZLZ [38])

February 9, 1846
Wilhelm Maybach is born

Hailed as the 'King of Constructors' in France during the 1890s for his contributions to the blossoming automotive industry, Wilhelm Maybach was a German inventor, engineer and entrepreneur. Born on this day in 1846, by the end of the 19th century he would partner with Gottlieb Daimler to build automobiles and develop engines for land, sea, and eventually air. Their motors were fitted to the first motorcycle and the first motorboat, and in 1902 they were used in the production of Mercedes automobiles. Maybach left DMG in 1907, and two years later founded Luftfahrzeug-Motorenbau GmbH to build aircraft engines. In 1912 the name was changed to Maybach-Motorenbau GmbH. The company produced engines for Zeppelins and, following the Versailles Treaty in 1919, the company began producing large luxury vehicles under the name Maybach.

Wilhelm Maybach.
(Public domain)

Also on this day: **2001** – The 100th annual Chicago Auto Show opened. **2006** – Former Formula One driver Gerhard Berger bought 50 per cent of Toro Rosso.

Maybach Zeppelin DS 8, 1938-39, exhibited in the Zeppelin Museum Friedrichshafen, Seestraße 22, Friedrichshafen, Germany. (Public domain)

February 10, 1966
Ralph Nader takes the stand

Consumer activist and lawyer Ralph Nader's 1965 book *Unsafe at Any Speed: The Designed-In Dangers of the American Automobile* accused automakers of resisting the introduction of proven safety measures, such as seat belts, because of the reluctance to spend money on safety. Nader would go before congress for his first time on this day in 1966, to testify about poor safety practices within the automobile industry. In his book he famously used the example of the first generation Chevrolet Corvair, stating the General Motors (GM) built rear engine sedan was prone to rollover accidents. Following his testimony, Nader accused GM of prying into his personal life, in an effort to discredit him. He filed a lawsuit against the company and was later awarded a settlement in the case. Nader's activism played a large role in the passing of the 1966 National Traffic and Motor Vehicle Safety Act, which allowed the federal government to set safety standards for automobiles and highways.

Ralph Nader in 1975.
(Public domain)

A first generation 1963 Corvair,
(Photo by Don O'Brien [39])

Also on this day: **1885** – First US patent for a seatbelt was issued to Edward Claghorn. **1953** – Volkswagen began using an oval rear window on the Type 1. **1989** – The Mazda MX-5 Miata was introduced.

February 11, 1959

A deadly record attempt

Marshall Teague walked unannounced into the Detroit offices of Hudson Motor Car Company, and left with a sponsor for his new NASCAR racing career. For the 1951 and 1952 seasons he drove the 'Fabulous Hudson Hornet' stock cars. Teague won seven of his 23 NASCAR entries, before dropping out in 1953 following disputes with NASCAR founder Bill France Sr. The King of the Beach, as Teague was known, joined other racing circuits, including Formula One. It was on this day in 1959 that Teague pushed to top 177mph (285km/h) for a closed course speed record, driving a Sumar Special Streamliner. At about 140mph (225km/h) Teague's car spun and rolled, ejecting and killing him almost instantly. He would later be posthumously inducted into several halls-of-fame, including the National Motorsports Press Association's Hall of Fame. Teague also served as inspiration for Doc Hudson in the film *Cars*.

Restored 1952 Hudson Hornet 2 door coupé raced by Marshall Teague.
(Photo by Sicnag [40])

Also on this day: 1899 – A motorcycle accident in Exeter, Devon would cause rider George Morgan to die of his injuries 12 days later, the first recorded motorcycle fatality. **2005** – Samuel Alderson, inventor of the crash test dummy, died at age 90.

February 12, 2014

Sinkhole swallows Corvettes

The Chevrolet Corvette has been built at GM's Bowling Green Assembly Plant in Kentucky since 1991. Just a quarter of a mile away from the plant is the National Corvette Museum, home to some of the rarest and most iconic Corvettes ever built. Mother Nature tried to start her own collection of Corvettes on this day in 2014 when a sinkhole opened up inside the museum, swallowing eight of the prized cars. The damaged Corvettes were a 1962 Corvette, 1993 ZR-1 Spyder, 2009 ZR-1 prototype 'Blue Devil,' 1992 1,000,000th Corvette, 1984 PPG pace car, 1993 40th Anniversary Ruby Red, 2001 Mallett Hammer Z06, and the 2009 1,500,000th built Corvette. Chevrolet meticulously restored the 'Blue Devil' and the 1,000,000th Corvette, as well as funded the restoration of the 1962 Corvette, which was overseen by the museum. The other vehicles remain on display in their recovered state.

Also on this day: 1902 – The first Studebaker automobile was sold. **1957** – Jaguar's Browns Lane factory, along with several hundred cars in various states of finish, were destroyed in a fire.

1993 Chevrolet Corvette 40th anniversary Ruby Red. Just 6749 of this special edition were built. (Photo by zombieite [41])

This 2009 Corvette, the 1,500,000th produced, suffered some of the worst damage in the sinkhole. *(Photo by zombieite [42])*

This 1993 ZR-1 Spyder was on loan to the museum from GM at the time of the sinkhole. The car featured a unique hood, front quarter panel vents and a lower windshield and lowered side glass. In the background is a 1962 tuxedo black Corvette, and a one of a kind 1984 PPG Pace Car. *(Photo by zombieite [43])*

February 13, 1953
Founder of Mack Trucks dies

The Mack Brothers Company was established in 1900 when John M, Augustus F, and William C Mack delivered their first successful vehicle – a four-cylinder, 24 horsepower, 13 passenger bus, dubbed 'Manhattan.' The bus would take sightseers around Brooklyn, New York's Prospect Park for eight years, and rack up more than 1,000,000 miles before being retired. The success of the bus solidified the company as a reputable source for heavy-duty vehicles. In 1922, the name was officially changed to Mack Trucks, Inc, and the bulldog was approved as the company logo. William C Mack, one of the original three brothers to start the company, passed away on this day in 1953 after watching the family business participate in some of America's toughest jobs, including surveying for and building highways, the construction of the Hoover Dam, and participating in World War II.

A Mack Truck at Naval Station Key West on June 18, 1917.
(Public domain)

Also on this day: **1946** – Donald Healey Motor Company Limited was founded in Warwick, England. **1958** – The first four-seat Ford Thunderbird was introduced. **2004** – Polish rally champion Janusz Kulig was killed, at age 33, in a non-racing accident when his car was struck by a train.

The Bulldog that adorns Mack Trucks. *(Photo by John Lloyd [44])*

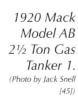

1920 Mack Model AB 2½ Ton Gas Tanker 1.
(Photo by Jack Snell [45])

February 14, 1867
Toyota patriarch is born

The 'King of Japanese Inventors' and patriarch of Toyota was born on this day in 1867 in Kosai, Shizuoka, Japan. Sakichi Toyoda was the inventor of a variety of weaving machines, including the automatic power loom, which led him to found Toyoda Automatic Loom Works. By the late 1920s Sakichi offered his support to his son Kiichiro who wanted to develop an automobile. Sakichi was unfortunately not able to see the project through to fruition, as he passed away in 1930. Kiichiro would take over the family business, establishing an automotive division in 1933 that would lead to the formation of Toyota Motor Corporation four years later.

Sakichi Toyoda. (Public domain)

1936 Toyoda AA replica. The name was officially changed to Toyota in 1937. (Photo by Iwao [46])

Also on this day: **1960** – Junior Johnson won the second running of NASCAR's Daytona 500. **1974** – Mark Donohue won the final race of the inaugural International Race of Champions (IROC). **2000** – The Chrysler PT Cruiser began production in Toluca, Mexico.

February 15, 2002
Prowler becomes extinct

Chrysler rolled out the Plymouth Prowler concept in 1993 as a follow up to Dodge Viper, which had gone into production the year prior. The concept's design, influenced in part by famed hot rod builder Chip Foose, garnered enough attention that it was put into production in 1997. The first year Prowler featured a V6 engine that produced 214 horsepower. Following a one-year hiatus the Prowler returned for 1999 with an upgraded V6 putting out 253hp that was coupled to a four-speed, rear-mounted semi-automatic transmission. When Plymouth went defunct in 2001, the model was rebadged as a Chrysler until the last one rolled off the assembly line on this day in 2002, bringing total production to 11,702.

A pair of 1999 Plymouth Prowlers. (Photos by Greg Gjerdingen [47], [48])

Also on this day: **1935** – BMW launched the 326. **1963** – Studebaker announced all of its new cars would have front seat belts. **1968** – The AMC AMX debuted.

February 16, 1843
Henry Leland, founder of Cadillac and Lincoln

Henry Leland, born on this day in 1843, began his engineering career in the firearms industry, including time spent at Colt. He learned many valuable lessons in tool making, manufacturing and part interchangeability early in his professional life. He would use this knowledge extensively at his firm Leland & Faulconer Manufacturing Co in Detroit, which he founded with Robert Faulconer. When Leland was approached by partners of the failed Henry Ford Company to conduct an appraisal of its equipment for liquidation, Leland convinced them to use it to start a new company. They accepted and Cadillac was born in 1902. After selling Cadillac to GM, Leland would go onto start Lincoln in the midst of World War I. The company was not profitable, however, and in 1922 he sold Lincoln to Ford (see February 4).

Henry Leland (right) and Robert Faulconer (left), in the office at Leland & Faulconer Manufacturing Co, Detroit, Michigan. (Public domain)

Also on this day:
1967 – Mario Andretti won the Daytona 500 with only one other driver finishing on the lead lap. **2001** – The 4000th Aston Martin DB7 was manufactured.

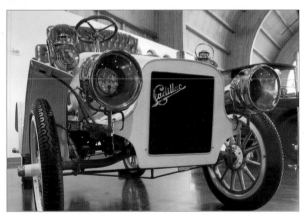

1906 Cadillac featuring a Leland-designed single cylinder engine. (Photo by Brian Corey)

February 17, 1972
A new best seller

Introduced in 1908, the Ford Model T held the record for the best selling car of all time for 45 years after its production ceased in 1927. It was finally overtaken on this day in 1972 when the 15,007,034th Volkswagen Beetle left the factory. Developed in Nazi Germany by Dr Ferdinand Porsche in the 1930s, the Beetle would go into full-scale production following WWII. Dismal US sales led to a massive marketing campaign launched in 1959 by advertising agency Doyle Dane Bernbach to promote the advantages of the small car. The Bug, as it is informally known, underwent very little redesign throughout its production life. After more than 60 years, and more than 21 million Beetles built, the final Type 1 rolled off the assembly line in Peubla, Mexico in 2003.

Also on this day: **1920** – It was announced the London Metropolitan Police would replace its horses with cars, the first department in Britain to officially do so.

Above: VW Beetle/bug parked parallel to the former Berlin Wall (bricks on the road) in Berlin, Germany.
(Photo by Ben Garrett [49])

1927 Ford Model T.
(Photo by F D Richards [50])

February 18, 2001

Racing legend dies in action

NASCAR superstar Dale Earnhardt Sr was killed in an accident on the final lap of the Daytona 500 on this day in 2001. Earnhardt's career in NASCAR began in 1975 at the World 600. During his time on the track he racked up 76 Winston Cup Series wins and seven NASCAR Winston Cup Championships, a feat only Richard Petty had accomplished previously, and not done again until Jimmie Johnson won his seventh. At the 2001 Daytona 500 a three car crash sent Earnhardt's #3 car into the outside wall head on. An autopsy revealed he died instantly of blunt force trauma. In the aftermath of the crash NASCAR mandated numerous safety measures.

Also on this day: **1900** – Léonce Girardot won the first circuit race at Course du Catalogue driving a Panhard. **1940** – Buick debuted the Town Master model. **1965** – The Mercury Cougar was approved for production.

February 19, 1954

Thunderbird prototype emerges

When Chevrolet rolled out the Corvette prototype in January 1953, Ford knew it would need a response, and fast. The idea for the Thunderbird was born the very next month. From idea to rolling reality in just one year, the Ford Thunderbird prototype was completed on this day in 1954, and would debut the following day at the Detroit Auto Show. The car would go into production that fall, officially going on sale as a 1955 model on October 22. The Thunderbird, billed as a personal luxury car and not a sports car, was a smashing success in its first year, outselling Corvette with 16,155 sales compared to 700. From 1955 to 1957 the Thunderbird remained relatively unchanged, but in 1958 it was completely redesigned and included a backseat.

Also on this day: **1932** – Ford unveiled its first model specifically designed for the British market, the Model Y. **1989** – Driving number 17 Darrell Waltrip won the Daytona 500 on his 17th attempt. **2015** – Engineer and designer, and Nissan's first president, Yutaka Katayama, passed away.

Earnhardt in the No 3 car.
(Photo by Darryl Moran [51])

Dale Earnhardt 10th Anniversary Daytona 500 win Chevy Impala COT.
(Photo by Freewheeling Daredevil [52])

1936 8hp Ford Model Y.
(Photo by Thomas's Pics [53])

1955 Ford Thunderbird. *(Photo by Staffan Andersson, public domain)*

February 20, 1909

Hudson is founded

When department store founder Joseph L Hudson was approached by eight men requesting an investment for a new automobile company, he liked what he heard, and provided the necessary capital to get the operation up and running. For his contribution the eight Detroit businessmen requested to use his name for their new auto, leading to the Hudson Motor Car Company being founded on this day in 1909. The company made its first home in the old Aerocar factory on the intersection of Mack Avenue and Beaufait Street in Detroit, Michigan. The first Hudson rolled off the production line less than five months after the company was officially formed.

Also on this day: **1986** – Hyundai began selling cars in the USA. **1993** – Ferruccio Lamborghini died at age 76.

A 1909 Hudson Model 20 (red) next to a 1909 Hupmobile (blue). (Photos by Brian Corey)

February 21, 1948

NASCAR founded

The roots of NASCAR can be traced to smuggling moonshine during America's prohibition era. Drivers delivering the illegal alcohol needed fast cars to outrun police so they found themselves regularly tuning their vehicles for more power and better handling. Following the end of prohibition, organized races of the hopped-up cars began taking place for profit. Daytona Beach mechanic and auto racer William "Bill" France Sr wanted to see a set of standardized rules, racing schedules and a points system for stock car racing. He began talking with influential racers and race promoters to create a governing body for the sport. France, with the assistance of several other drivers, founded NASCAR (National Association for Stock Car Auto Racing) on this day in 1948. The original points system was written on a bar room napkin.

Also on this day: **1916** – The Dixie Flyer made its debut. **1944** – Famous Italian coachbuilder Giacinto Ghia died at age 56.

1949 Oldsmobile Rocket. A NASCAR race car from the sport's early days.
(Photo by Supermac1961 [54])

February 22, 1959

A most prestigious race

Since the inaugural running of the Daytona 500 on this day in 1959, the race has been widely regarded as the most important event on the annual NASCAR calendar. It has been the season opener since 1982, and it carries the largest prize purse of any race in the sport. The first running of the race, originally named, "First Annual 500 Mile NASCAR International Sweepstakes at Daytona," coincided with the opening of Daytona International Speedway, which was built by NASCAR founder Bill France Sr. The race came down to the final 30 laps as Johnny Beauchamp, driving a 1959 Ford, and Lee Petty, with his 1959 Oldsmobile, duked it out, resulting in a literal photo finish. When the race was over, NASCAR officials declared Beauchamp the winner, but Petty protested. After three days of reviewing photos and newsreel footage, Bill France declared Petty the actual winner of the first Daytona 500.

Also on this day: **1907** – The first cabs with automated taxi meters began operating in London. **1944** – The first Saxon automobile was built. **1970** – Pete Hamilton won the Daytona 500 driving a Plymouth Superbird.

The start of the 2015 Daytona 500. (Photo by Nascarking [55])

Harley J Earl Trophy, won by Daytona 500 winner Jimmie Johnson.
(Photo by GabboT [56])

February 23, 1958

F1 driver kidnapped

Juan Manuel Fangio.
(Public domain)

Argentinian race car driver Juan Manuel Fangio dominated the first decade of Formula One, winning the World Drivers' Championship five times in the 1950s, a record which stood for 47 years. But he wasn't in the driver's seat when he made headlines on this day in 1958. It was the day before the Cuban Grand Prix, when two men associated with Fidel Castro's 26th of July Movement entered the Lincoln Hotel in Havana, and kidnapped Fangio at gunpoint. Their goal was to cancel the race and raise awareness of Castro's cause. The race went on, and the captors allowed Fangio to listen to the radio and view race reports. After a friendship developed between the captors and Fangio he was released unharmed the next day.

Also on this day: **1967** – The Chevrolet Camaro counterpart, the Pontiac Firebird, debuted. **1971** – Beatle George Harrison was fined for speeding and received a one-year driving suspension.

Juan Manuel Fangio driving a Mercedes-Benz W196 in the 1986 Oldtimer Grand Prix at the Nürburgring.
(Photo by Lothar Spurzem [57])

February 24, 1955
Alain Prost is born

Four-time Formula One Drivers' Champion Alain Prost was born on this day in 1955. The French race car driver is tied with Sebastian Vettel for third most F1 Championships, and falls behind Juan Manuel Fangio with five, and Michael Schumacher, who holds the record with seven trophies. Prost began his racing career in karting at the age of 14, after discovering the sport on a family holiday. By age 24 he had worked his way up from Formula Three to join McLaren's Formula One team in 1980. Between his rookie year and 1993 Prost racked up 51 wins, including his championships in 1985, 1986, 1989 and 1993. Known for a smooth and relaxed driving style, Prost earned the nickname 'The Professor' for his intellectual approach to racing.

Prost practicing for his first event for Ferrari, the 1990 United States Grand Prix. (Photo by Stuart Seeger [58])

Alain Prost driving a Renault RE40.
(Photo by Jake Archibald [59])

Also on this day: **1932** – Malcolm Campbell set a land speed record of 253.96mph. **2003** – Triumph announced its return to sponsored motorcycle racing. **2005** – The MINI debuted in Korea.

February 25, 1899
First death of a driver

Edwin Sewell just wanted to sell Major James Richer a new Daimler automobile when they went for a demonstration drive in West London on this day in 1899. Instead, he ended up killing himself and the major after losing control of the vehicle while descending Grove Hill. One wheel collapsed causing both driver and passenger to be thrown from the auto. Sewell died instantly, earning a spot in history as the first recorded death of an automobile driver in Britain as the result of a road accident. Major Richer was taken to a hospital but died four days later due to a fractured skull. A plaque marks the location of the incident.

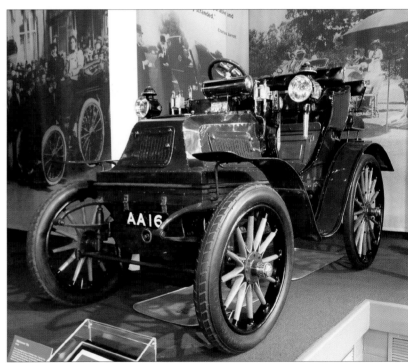

An 1899 12hp Daimler, perhaps similar to the vehicle involved in the incident. (Photo by Przemysław JahrAutorem [60])

Also on this day: **1919** – Oregon became the first US state to impose a tax on gas. The tax was used for road maintenance and construction. **1979** – Christie's, a London Auction House, held its first collector car auction. A 1936 Mercedes-Benz 500K roadster sold for $400,000.

February 26, 1725
The father of self-propulsion

The first self-propelled, land-based vehicle is credited to French inventor Nicolas-Joseph Cugnot, who was born on this day in 1725. Cugnot was a captain in the French army who relied on two-wheeled horse-drawn fardiers to carry heavy equipment such as artillery and arms across long distances. He developed a way to turn the reciprocating motion of a steam piston into rotary motion by means of a ratchet system. Using this design he built a less than full-scale "fardier à vapeur," a steam powered fardier, in 1769, which had three wheels, the third in place of the horses. The next year he built a full-size version. In 1771 a second full-scale fardier is said to have run into a wall after its driver lost control, the first recorded automobile accident.

Also on this day: **1936** – The first Volkswagen manufacturing factory, located in Saxony, was opened by Adolf Hitler. **1968** – London's first bus lane opened across the Vauxhall Bridge.

February 27, 1951
A life by design

At just 21 years old, Italian Walter de Silva was hired by Fiat as an automotive designer in 1972. Born on this day in 1951, de Silva would go on to lead design for Alfa Romeo, SEAT, Audi brand Group and Volkswagen Group, of which he held the reins from 2007 until 2015. During his career he would craft and sign off on a number of important designs for numerous automakers. Some of the autos he is responsible for include the 1997 Alfa Romeo 156, 2004 Audi A6, 2006 Audi TT and R8, 2006 Lamborghini Miura concept, 2010 Volkswagen Jetta, 2011 Volkswagen Beetle, 2013 Lamborghini Egoista concept, and 2015 Volkswagen Touran, among many others. After leaving Volkswagen he started a women's shoe company named Walter de Silva Shoes.

Also on this day: **1892** – Rudolf Diesel filed for a patent for his new engine type.

Cugnot's 1770 fardier à vapeur, as preserved at the Musée des Arts et Métiers, Paris. (Photo by Joe deSousa, public domain)

Second view of Cugnot's vehicle. (Photo by Andrew Duthie [61])

1999 Alfa Romeo 156.
(Photo by BiTurbo228 [62])

2015 VW Touran. (Photo by TuRbO_J [63])

2006 Lamborghini Miura concept. (Photo by NAParish [64])

February 28, 1940
Mario Andretti is born

Mario Andretti, one of the most decorated auto racers of all time, was born on this day in 1940. After moving from Italy to the US, Mario and his twin brother Aldo purchased a 1948 Hudson Commodore, and in 1959 Mario won two of his first four races. He has since become one of only two drivers to have won races in Formula One, IndyCar, NASCAR and the World Sportscar Championship, the other being Dan Gurney. He is also the only driver ever to win the Daytona 500 (1967), Indianapolis 500 (1969), and the Formula One World Championship (1978). His records also include being the only person to win United States Driver of the Year in three different decades (1967, 1978 and 1984). With his final IndyCar win in 1993, Andretti became the first driver to have won an Indy race in four separate decades, and any kind of professional automobile race in five.

Mario Andretti at the 1991 Monterey Grand Prix, CART. (Photo by Stuart Seeger [65])

Also on this day: **1921** – The first Rolls-Royce to be built in the US was completed. **1975** – AMC introduced the Pacer. **1990** – Ford purchased Jaguar for $2.5 billion.

February 29, 1932
Racing into the Hall of Fame

Masten Gregory was born in Kansas City, Missouri, on this day in 1932. He used his inheritance to purchase a Mercury-powered Allard, which he entered in his first race in 1952. Throughout his career he would participate in more than 40 World Championship Formula One races, earning a best second place at the 1959 Portuguese Grand Prix. His career was riddled with injuries, but it didn't stop him from taking two first-in-class finishes at the 24 Hours of Le Mans in 1961 and 1965, the latter also being a best overall finish. In August 2013, nearly 30 years after passing away due to a heart attack, he was inducted in the Motorsports Hall of Fame of America.

Masten Gregory in 1965. (Photo by Lothar Spurzem [67])

Andretti driving at Laguna Seca Raceway in 1991. (Photo by Stuart Seeger [66])

A Ferrari driven by Mario Andretti. (Public domain)

March 1, 1981

The man who built a home for the US Grand Prix

Cameron Argetsinger, born on this day in 1921, is the man who put Watkins Glen, New York, on the racing map. In 1947 Argetsinger's interest in auto racing led him to buy an MG TC before becoming a member of the Sports Car Club of America. The next year he organized the Watkins Glen Sports Car Grand Prix, which was held on a circuit made up of public roads. The event became widely popular, but due to the deaths of drivers and spectators it was stopped after eight years. In 1956, as Executive Director of the Watkins Glen Grand Prix Corporation, he signed off on the purchase of 550 acres in Watkins Glen, and a 2.3 mile racing course designed to imitate the winding country roads of the area was built. In 1961, the track hosted its first Formula One United States Grand Prix.

Ford GT40s race around Watkins Glen in 2006.
(Photo by Nathan Bittinger [69])

Formula One at Watkins Glen, circa 1974.
(Photo by Christian Sinclair. [68])

Also on this day: **1931** – Bridgestone Tire Company was founded in Japan. **1941** – Ford built its first production GP for the military, later to become known as the Jeep. **1974** – The Honda Civic was introduced in America.

March 2, 1966

One millionth Ford Mustang

Before the Ford Mustang went on sale, a number of them were shipped to dealers to entice buyers. In a lapse, Ford shipped a white convertible Mustang with serial number 5F08F100001 to George Parsons Ford in Canada. This wasn't just any Mustang; it was what is widely assumed to be the first production Mustang built. The day the cars went up for sale, Captain Stanley Tucker talked the dealer into accepting a check for the car, even though it wasn't supposed to be sold. Ford tracked the car to Tucker, who refused to sell it back. Tucker was later presented with an offer he couldn't refuse. In return for the first Mustang he would be given the one millionth Mustang, which rolled off the assembly line on this day in 1966. The first Mustang made its way to the Henry Ford Museum, while the one millionth Mustang was reportedly crushed after a decade of hard use.

Also on this day: **1903** – The Standard Motor Company of Britain was registered. **1926** – Woolf Barnato becomes chairman of Bentley.

1910 Standard Motor Company Thirty. The company was founded on March 2 1903 in Coventry, England. *(Photo by Peter Turvey [70])*

1966 Ford Mustang, similar to the one millionth Mustang produced.
(Photo by Gilberto Gonzales)

March 3, 2009
Maybach Zeppelin hits the market

Wilhelm Maybach founded Luftfahrzeug-Motorenbau GmbH in Germany in 1909, the literal translation of the name being Aircraft Engine Building Company. The business was originally aimed at producing engines for Zeppelins, and then other aircraft during WWI. Following the war, the company built its first experimental car, the W1, which it introduced in 1919. Its first production model, the W3, would roll out of factories two years later. In 1930 Maybach introduced in the DS7 Zeppelin; the name paid homage to the company's history. Daimler-Benz purchased Maybach in 1960, using the company to produce special edition Mercedes. Daimler-Chrysler would reintroduce a car with a Maybach badge in 2002, and on this day in 2009 the Maybach Zeppelin went on sale, again using the name to pay tribute to the company's beginnings.

Also on this day: **1932** – Alfieri Maserati died at age 44. **1972** – Sir William Lyons, the founder of Jaguar, retired from his post as Chairman. **1980** – The Audi Quattro coupé debuted.

Maybach 57 Zeppelin front and rear views, with interior.
(Front and rear view photos by Ben [71], [72]; interior photo by Jay Clark [73])

March 4, 1932
'Big Daddy' Roth is born

Iconic American hot rod builder Ed 'Big Daddy' Roth entered the world on this day in 1932 in Beverly Hills, California. Growing up, Roth attended Bell High School where he took auto shop and art classes, setting the scene for a career filled with grotesque characterizations and one of a kind hot rods. He would open a custom car shop in Maywood, California, in 1959, and the next year he had one of his custom cars, The Outlaw, featured in *Car Craft* and *Rod & Custom* magazines. He began producing outlandish vehicles and found himself leading the 'Kustom Kulture' movement of the late 1950s and 1960s, during which time he introduced Rat Fink. Some of his vehicles include the Beatnik Bandit (1961), Mysterion (1963), The Orbitron (1964), and a 1920 Ford named Tweedy Pie. In 1994, just five years before his death he created the Beatnik Bandit II.

Also on this day: **1902** – The American Automobile Association was founded. **1966** – Studebaker built its last automobile, a Cruiser. **2009** – Briggs Automotive Company was founded in Britain.

Left: 1961 Beatnik Bandit; right: 1963 Mysterion; far right: 1920 Ford T Bucket, "Tweedy Pie," with Rat Fink sculpture back left. (Photos by Sicnag [74], [75], [76])

March 5, 1929

Buick founder passes away

David Buick sold his plumbing company to start the Buick Auto-Vim and Power Company in 1899, which manufactured engines for agricultural use. After creating a revolutionary 'valve in-head' engine, he turned to complete automotive development, founding the Buick Motor Company in 1903. Three years later he accepted a severance package from Buick, leaving him with one share of the company that he'd started. The new president of Buick, William C Durant, purchased this share for $100,000 (approximately $2.6 million in the present day, when adjusted for inflation). Following more than two decades of unsuccessful investments, Buick died with nearly no money to his name on this day in 1929.

Also on this day: **1927** – General Motors announced LaSalle, a companion brand to Cadillac. **1929** – More than 320 new cars were destroyed when fire broke out at the Los Angeles Automobile Show. **1955** – The BMW Isetta was shown to the press. **1967** – Richard Petty won his 50th NASCAR Grand National race.

A 1906 Buick Touring – from the year David Buick left the company that he started. Inset: Pedals of 1906 Buick.
(Photos by F D Richards [77], [78])

March 6, 1900

Daimler dies

Gottlieb Daimler was a German industrialist and internal combustion engine pioneer. He and his longtime business partner Wilhelm Maybach aimed to produce high speed engines that could be applied to a variety of locomotive devices for land and water. They developed a horizontal cylinder engine that could be throttled in 1883, making it useful for numerous types of transportation vehicles; it was named Daimler's Dream. Daimler also invented the first internal combustion motorcycle in 1885, and the next year

Gottlieb Daimler. (Public domain)

developed a four-wheel vehicle, at about the same time as, and just 60 miles from where Karl Benz built his in Germany. In 1890 the pair converted their partnership to a stock company known as DMG, which sold its first car in 1892. Daimler died eight years later on this day in 1900.

Also on this day: **1896** – Charles Brady King test drove a car he built in Detroit, the first car to be driven in what would become the Motor City. **1927** – Emilio Materassi won the Tripoli Grand Prix. **1995** – The Ferrari F50 debuted at the Geneva Motor Show.

Daimler MotorKutsche of 1886. (Photo by big-ashb [79])

March 7, 1938
First female in the Indy 500

Janet Guthrie, born on this day in 1938 in Iowa City, Iowa, raced her way into the history books when she became the first woman to compete in a top tier NASCAR Winston Cup race, finishing in 15th place at the 1976 World 600. After graduating from the University of Michigan she became an aerospace engineer but she found a new love when she began racing a Jaguar XK 140 in 1963. A decade later racing became her full time profession. Apart from becoming the first woman to race at the highest levels of NASCAR, she was the first woman to compete in the Daytona 500, which she first qualified for in 1977. The same year she also became the first woman to race in the Indianapolis 500, finishing 29th with engine trouble.

Also on this day: **1929** – General Motors initiated the purchase of 80 per cent of Opel.

Janet Guthrie at the Indianapolis Motor Speedway in 2011.
(Photo by Tim O'Brien [80])

Below: Janet Guthrie's Wildcat 3-DGS, which she drove to ninth place in the 1978 Indianapolis 500. *(Photo by Dan Wildhirt [81])*

March 8, 1950
VW Bus begins production

Ben Pon may not be a familiar name, but he is credited for the introduction of the Volkswagen Type 2 Transporter van, which began production on this day in 1950. Pon visited Wolfsburg in 1946, intending to import the Beetle to the Netherlands after it went back into production following WWII. The next year Pon sketched out a concept for a small bus that was designed to use the same pan as the Type 1. Volkswagen developed his idea, but realized a new pan would be needed. It launched the Type 2, also known as the Transporter, and it affectionately became known as the VW Bus, Camper and a myriad of other names. An icon of '60s hippiedom, the Type 2 was produced in factories all over the world with the final one leaving a Brazilian production facility on December 13, 2013.

Also on this day: **1929** – The one millionth Oakland came off the assembly line. **1946** – Pioneering British automobile engineer Frederick Lanchester died at age 77.

1955 Type 2 Splitscreen Camper. *(Photo by Karen Roe [82])*

A now retired VW van dressed from its days as a hippie. *(Photo by Mac H [83])*

March 9, 1901

Olds Motor Works burns to the ground

By 1901 Ransom E Olds had built as many as six horseless carriage prototypes, all of which were stored inside the Olds factory in Lansing, Michigan. A number of the cars were set to go into production when fire broke out at the factory on this day in 1901, destroying the facility and all but one of the prototypes, the Curved Dash. A new factory was built and with only one prototype to work off of the Curved Dash went into production as Olds' sole model. Olds produced 425 of them by the end of 1901; leading to Olds often being credited as the first automobile company to mass-produce an internal combustion engine powered vehicle. The Curved Dash continued to roll off production lines through 1907 and Oldsmobile, as it was called by then, would be sold to General Motors the following year.

Also on this day: **1955** – The Fiat 600 debuted in Geneva.

Caption on back of original photograph reads, "Oldsmobile, 1897. First gasoline powered model." (Public domain)

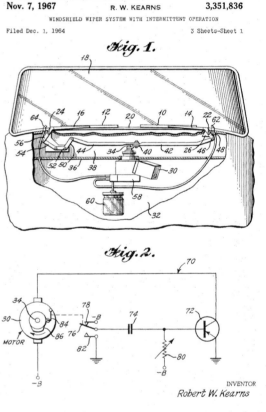

1903 Olds Curved Dash. (Photo by Brian Corey)

One page of original patent paperwork for intermittent windshield wipers, filed Dec 1, 1964, awarded, Nov. 7, 1967. (Public domain)

March 10, 1927

Inventor Robert Kearns is born

When Robert Kearns approached automakers about licensing the technology for the intermittent windshield wiper system, for which he received a patent in 1967, they all passed. Yet, beginning in 1969, a similar system began to show up as an option in new vehicles. Kearns, born on this day in 1927, would go after the Big Three for patent infringement, starting with Ford in 1978 and Chrysler in 1982. The Ford case came to a close in 1990 when the automaker was ordered to pay Kearns $10.1 million in damages. Following the success of the case Kearns acted as his own lawyer against Chrysler, with the verdict coming down as a victory for Kearns in 1992. By 1995 he would receive approximately $30 million in compensation from Chrysler. Subsequent cases against GM were dismissed due to missed deadlines for filings.

Also on this day: **1983** – The Ford Bronco II went on sale. **2017** – The only man to win Grand Prix World Championships on both two wheels and four, John Surtees, died at age 83.

The Ford Bronco II went on sale on this day in 1983. (Photo by Marion Doss [84])

March 11, 2009
One millionth Toyota hybrid

Toyota was the first company to mass-produce a hybrid vehicle that was successful in the United States. The gas-electric Prius launched in Japan in 1997, and made its way to America by July 2000, but it wasn't the only hybrid from the auto giant. On this day in 2009 Toyota announced that it had sold its one millionth hybrid in the US under its six Toyota and Lexus brands, more than 700,000 of them being Priuses. Other hybrid models included the Lexus RX 400h, the world's first hybrid luxury vehicle, and the Toyota Highlander hybrid, which launched in June 2005. Just more than two years later, on April 6, 2011, Toyota announced it had sold its one millionth Prius in the United States.

Also on this day: 1929 – Henry Segrave raised the landspeed record to 231.446 mph driving the Napier 'Golden Arrow.' **1971** – The Maserati Bora was shown at the Geneva Motor Show.

First generation Toyota Prius (2000-2003). (Public domain)

Lexus RX 400h.
(Photo by Luftfahrrad [85])

March 12, 1831
Studebaker founder is born

Clement Studebaker, born on this day in 1831, was a skilled blacksmith by age 14 after apprenticing under his father. Clement and his older brother Henry would go on to found H&C Studebaker Company in 1852 in South Bend, Indiana, to build wagons and provide additional blacksmithing services. Henry sold his interest in the company to their younger brother John in 1858, when the business was busy building wagons for the US Army. This was likely a conflict of interest for Henry, who was a Dunkard, a committed pacifist. When the remaining Studebaker brothers joined the company, the name was changed to Studebaker Brothers Manufacturing Company. The business became the world's largest wagon manufacturer, and the only producer of horse-drawn vehicles to successfully transition to building automobiles, which it began to do in 1897.

Portrait of Clement Studebaker.
(Public domain)

Portrait of Studebaker brothers. Left to right, (standing) Peter and Jacob, (seated) Clement, Henry, and John. (Public domain)

Also on this day: 1928 – The British Racing Drivers' Club was founded. **1952** – Mercedes introduced the 300SL race car to the press. **1982** – Ford introduced the Ranger pickup truck.

March 13, 1969
The Love Bug hits theaters

The Love Bug made its official debut on this day in 1969. Starring a pearl white 1963 Volkswagen Beetle named Herbie, the movie follows the adventures of Jim Douglas, a racing driver who can't catch a break. When Jim finds himself in need of a car he heads into town, and is caught off guard by an attractive mechanic and sales associate, Carole Bennett, working inside a European auto showroom. There he also meets the showroom owner, Peter Thorndyke, who is rude to Herbie. After defending the car Herbie winds up in Jim's driveway unannounced the next morning. To prevent Thorndyke from pressing charges Jim agrees to buy it. Jim soon discovers the car has a mind of its own, and was out to win the big race while helping Jim land the lady. The movie took home $51,264,000 at the box office.

A 1963 Volkswagen Bug that was used to make Herbie: Fully Loaded, the 2005 sequel to The Love Bug, starring Lindsay Lohan.
(Photos by Brian Corey)

Also on this day: **1944** – Long time Ford executive Charles Sorensen retired from his Vice President position. **1947** – Maserati's first production car, the A6 1500, was unveiled.

March 14, 1914
A legend is born

The patriarch of the Petty racing family, Lee Arnold Petty, was born on this day in 1914. Petty would begin his racing career at age 35, going on to participate in the first NASCAR race at Charlotte Motor Speedway, and eventually winning the first Daytona 500 in 1959, launching him into celebrity status as one of NASCAR's first superstars. He was father to Richard Petty, grandfather to Kyle Petty and Ritchie Petty and great grandfather to Adam Petty, who was the first fourth-generation driver in NASCAR. Richard Petty passed away just three days after Adam's Winston Cup Series debut at the age of 86.

Lee Petty's 1956 Dodge Coronet, number 42. (Photo by Freewheeling Daredevil [86])

Also on this day: **1954** – Fiat tested the Turbina, its gas-turbine prototype, for the first time. **1957** – Ford introduced its retractable hardtop convertible, the Skyliner.

March 15, 1968
The highest automobile tunnel

At the time of its completion, the Eisenhower-Johnson Memorial Tunnel, about 60 miles west of Denver, Colorado, was the world's highest tunnel, with a maximum elevation of 11,158ft (3401m). The 1.69 mile (2.72km) tunnel, a part of Interstate 70, broke ground on this day in 1968, starting with the westbound bore named after President Dwight D Eisenhower. The eastbound bore, named for Edwin C Johnson, a Colorado governor who lobbied for a highway to be built through Colorado, was begun in August 1975, a year and a half after the first bore opened to traffic. The tunnel remains the highest tunnel in the United States, but higher tunnels have since been constructed. The world's highest tunnel to date, completed in 2016, sits at an astonishing 20,236.22ft (6168m) above sea level, connecting Chengdu, China to Nagqu in Tibet.

Also on this day: **1954** – Porsche built its 5000th car. **1961** – The Jaguar E-Type debuted.

West portal, named for Dwight D Eisenhower, in 1978. (Photo by Seattleretro [87])

Eastern portal, named for Edwin C Johnson. (Photo by Patrick Pelster [88])

March 16, 1958
Ford's 50 millionth car

Founded in 1903, Ford Motor Co soon began producing hundreds of thousands of cars per year after the introduction of the moving assembly line in 1913. Less than a decade later, in 1921, the company hit the million cars per year mark for the first time. Just 55 years after the company's beginning, the 50 millionth Ford rolled off a Dearborn, MI, assembly line on this day in 1958. The special car was a 1958 Thunderbird.

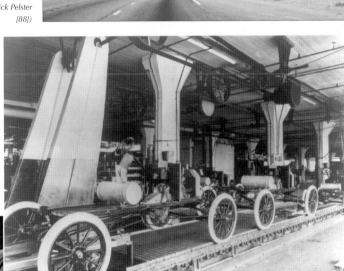

Assembly line at Ford Motor Company's Highland Park plant, circa 1913. (Public domain)

1958 Ford Thunderbird. (Photo by Greg Gjerdingen [89])

Also on this day: **1928** – The first permanent traffic lights were installed in Leeds, West Yorkshire, UK. **1934** – The Chrysler Airflow made its European debut. **2013** – The MINI Paceman went on sale in the USA.

March 17, 1948
Hells Angels' first ride

The Bishop family in Fontana, California formed the Hells Angels Motorcycle Club on this day in 1948. Composed of members from a number of other area clubs, the Angels' took a name inspired by WWII fighter pilots, as well as Howard Hughes' 1930 film *Hell's Angels* about WWI pilots. Early chapters of the club were started in San Francisco, Fontana and Oakland, CA. By the 1960s, the club took a leading role in the counterculture movement after establishing connections with many of the movement's key figures, including The Beatles, The Rolling Stones and Ken Kesey. The HAMC is now considered an organized crime syndicate by the US Department of Justice.

Also on this day: 1972 – The Japanese-built Ford Courier mini pickup went on sale in the US. **1977** – The Lamborghini Cheetah off road vehicle was shown at the Geneva Motor Show. **2005** – BMW built its three millionth vehicle at its Regensburg plant.

English Hells Angels MC member in South Queensferry, Scotland.
(Photo by Tee Cee [90])

Below: Street scene featuring a Hells Angels member from Illinois, USA.
(Photo by Mario Mancuso [91])

March 18, 1933
Studebaker goes under

In 1920, under the leadership of Albert Erskine, Studebaker fully committed to the auto industry after building its last horse-drawn wagon, the main product of the company since it was founded more than 60 years before. In the 1920s Erskine led Studebaker through the acquisition of luxury automaker Pierce-Arrow, and the launch of two short lived, more affordable automobile lines, Erskine and Rockne. When the Great Depression hit in October 1929 Studebaker fell into a financial tailspin, and on this day in 1933 the company was forced into bankruptcy. Riddled with personal debt, ousted from his position at Studebaker, and suffering from health issues Erskine killed himself on July 1, 1933. New management dropped the Rockne brand and sold Pierce-Arrow in order to get things back on track, and in January 1935 the new Studebaker Corporation was incorporated.

Also on this day: 1970 – Bobby Unser won the USAC Championship race at Phoenix International Raceway.

Ad for an Erskine automobile printed in February 1927 Country Gentleman publication.

At Last—The Farmer's Ideal Car

Beautiful—Sturdy—Dependable—Economical

Erskine Six Custom Sedan

$985

f. o. b. factory

1935 Studebaker Commander. Studebaker was reorganized as the Studebaker Corporation in 1935 after falling into bankruptcy two years prior. (Photo by Jack Snell [92])

March 19, 2005
DeLorean's death

American automotive engineer and industry executive John Z DeLorean passed away on this day in 2005, at the age of 80. While he is most remembered for building the iconic DeLorean DMC-12, he worked for a number of other automakers prior to starting his own venture. He began his automotive career with Chrysler in 1952. Less than a year later he would move to Packard, and then onto Pontiac, where he made sizeable contributions, including designing the GTO, which is widely considered the first muscle car. He is also credited with designing the Pontiac Firebird and Grand Prix cars, before moving to Chevrolet in 1969. His rambunctious lifestyle often led to clashes with fellow General Motors executives, but President Ed Cole believed in DeLorean's managerial capabilities. He left GM in 1973 to start the DeLorean Motor Company.

Also on this day: **1900** – Fiat's new plant in Turin is opened. 1952 – The one millionth Jeep is produced. **1999** – Ford established the Premier Auto Group, made up of Lincoln, Jaguar and Aston Martin.

John DeLorean with the DMC-12 above and 1964 Pontiac GTO below.
(Illustration by Brian Corey)

March 20, 1928
James Packard dies

Born in Warren, Ohio on November 5, 1863, James Ward Packard founded the Packard Electric Company with his brother William in 1890. Three years later the brothers formed a partnership with George L. Weiss, who also invested in Winton Motor Carriage Company, leading to the release of the first Packard automobile in 1899. The next year the company incorporated as the Ohio Automobile Company before being renamed Packard Motor Car Company in 1902. Following James Packard's death on this day in 1928, GM acquired the Packard Electric Company and the high-end automaker merged with Studebaker Corporation to fight financial difficulties in 1954. The merger failed to save the company, and 1958 saw the production of the last Packard.

James Packard and Elizabeth Packard (Gillmer) on their honeymoon driving a Packard in New York following their August 1904 wedding.
(Photo courtesy of the New York Historical Society.)

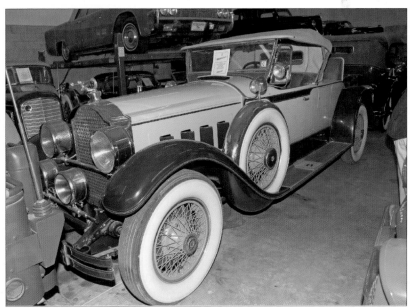

1928 Packard. (Photo by mark6mauno [93])

Also on this day: **1936** – The BMW 326 made its world debut. **1988** – The final Pontiac Fiero leaves the assembly line.

March 21, 1920

A NASCAR Hall of Fame star is born

Truman Fontello "Fonty" Flock – brother of NASCAR pioneers Tim Flock, Bob Flock, and Ethel Mobley (the second female NASCAR driver) – was born on this day in 1920. Falling in line with his siblings, he became an early great on the young circuit. Flock grew up in Alabama, and like many early NASCAR racers, his need for speed developed while delivering moonshine. "I used to deliberately seek out the sheriff and get him to chase me," he later recalled. He started his racing career in 1940, and on July 19, 1949 all four siblings participated in a NASCAR race at Daytona Beach Road Course, making it the first NASCAR race to feature a brother and sister, and a total of four siblings. Fonty won 11 features, and the NASCAR National Modified championship in 1949. He retired in 1957 with 19 wins and 83 top tens.

Also on this day: **1926** – Alessandro Consonno won a Grand Prix in Verona, Italy behind the wheel of a Bugatti T35. **2000** – DaimlerChrysler announced that it had purchased a 34 per cent share of Mitsubishi Motors.

1955 Ford raced by Fonty's brother Tim. (Photo by Freewheeling Daredevil [94])

March 22, 1983

A Hummer of a contract

In 1979, the US Army drafted specifications for a High Mobility Multipurpose Wheeled Vehicle, or HMMWV for short, better known as Humvee. These specs called for a performance off-road vehicle that would replace existing military transport vehicles. Among its many requests the Army asked that it had the ability to ford five feet of water. More than 60 companies showed interest in the project, but only three ended up submitting prototypes, Chrysler, Teledyne Continental and AM General. After extreme evaluation of the prototypes, which amounted to more than 600,000 miles of testing in conditions ranging from arctic to desert, AM General was awarded the government contract on this day in 1983.

Also on this day: **1926** – Ford renamed its River Rouge facility the Fordson Plant.

Salah Ad Din Province, Iraq (March 22, 2006) – US Army soldiers assigned to the Bravo Battery 3rd Battalion 320th Field Artillery Regiment, along with Iraq Army soldiers from the 1st Battalion 1st Brigade 4th Division, perform a routine patrol. (Photo by Shawn Hussong, US Navy)

March 23, 1921
By land and by sea

English daredevil Malcolm Campbell snagged 13 land and water speed records in the 1920s and 1930s, driving the famous Bluebird cars and boats. Malcolm's son Donald, born on this day in 1921, followed in his father's footsteps, at a bit quicker pace. Donald would achieve what no person had done before; set the land speed record and the water speed record in the same year. On July 17, 1964 near Lake Eyre in Australia he posted a new land speed record of 403.1mph (648.73km/h) driving the Bluebird-Proteus CN7, designed to go 500mph (805km/h). Then, on the last day of 1964, piloting the Bluebird K7 he earned his seventh water speed record at 276.33mph (444.71km/h) on Lake Dumbleyung near Perth, Western Australia. Campbell died while attempting a new water speed record in the same boat on January 4, 1967.

Also on this day: **1901** – The first Chicago Auto Show opened. **1958** – DAF began production. **2009** – Tata Motors launched its $2000 Nano in Mumbai.

Bluebird CN7 on display at the National Motor Museum in Beaulieu.
(Public domain)

March 24, 1999
Mont Blanc Tunnel fire

The Mont Blanc Tunnel connects Chamonix, Haute-Savoie, France with Courmayeur, Aosta Valley, Italy, via European route E25 through the Alps. This tunnel was the scene of a fatal fire that took the lives of 38 people on this day in 1999. A cargo truck carrying flour and margarine caught fire while passing through the tunnel, and when the driver stopped his truck to try and extinguish the flames the heat quickly overwhelmed him. Authorities stopped additional traffic from entering the tunnel once the emergency was reported, but as many as 10 personal vehicles and 18 trucks were stuck inside. The toxic fumes prevented people from escaping and the intense heat melted wiring, turning the tunnel into a dark, smoke-filled void that made fighting the flames nearly impossible. After 53 hours the fire was extinguished.

French entrance to the Mont Blanc Tunnel. (Photo by Kristoferb [95])

Also on this day: **1948** – The last Lincoln Continental Mark I was manufactured. **2003** – The Vauxhall VX220 supercar goes on sale.

Driving through the Mont Blanc Tunnel.
(Photo by James Stewart [96])

March 25, 1982

Happy birthday Danica Patrick

The most successful woman in open wheel racing was born on this day in 1982. Danica Patrick has raced in numerous series, including Indy and NASCAR, in both of which she found success. Her win at the 2008 Indy Japan 300 is the only victory held by a woman in IndyCar Series racing, and she is the only woman to score the pole position for a NASCAR race, which she did for the 2013 Daytona 500. Patrick got her start in racing at age 10, after taking the wheel of a competition go-kart. She made her IndyCar debut in 2005, and raced in top tier NASCAR for the first time in 2012.

Also on this day: **1984** – Ayrton Senna made his F1 debut in Jacarepagua, Brazil. **2005** – The Saturn Sky was introduced to the media. **2015** – The BBC announced it would not renew Jeremy Clarkson's *Top Gear* contract after he physically and verbally attacked one of the show's producers.

Danica Patrick at Dover in 2016. (Photo by Zach Catanzareti [97])

Left: Danica Patrick at Infineon in 2008. (Photo by dodge challenger1 [98])

2008 Jaguar XF.
(Photo by Michael Kumm [99])

2008 Land Rover Range Rover.
(Photo by Michael Kumm [100])

March 26, 2008

Ford offloads Jaguar and Land Rover

Tata Motors, a part of Indian conglomerate Tata Group, closed a deal to purchase Jaguar and Land Rover from Ford Motor Company on this day in 2008 for $2.3 billion. Under the terms of the deal Ford was to pay Tata another $600 million once the sale closed, to make up for shortfalls in the two brands' pension plans. Tata Group, which at the time of the sale was on an acquisition spree of everything from coffee companies to manufacturing businesses, had no intention of making any major changes to either brand, nor would it affect the jobs of the 16,000 people employed by the automakers. Ford offloaded the brands during a major company overhaul, following a two-year loss of $15 billion.

Also on this day: **1903** – The first speed trials were held at Daytona Beach, Florida. **1932** – Henry Leland, founder of Cadillac and Lincoln, died at age 89.

March 27, 1863
Half of Rolls-Royce is born

For a boy whose professional career began as a newspaper salesman and telegram deliverer, it may have never crossed his young mind that he would eventually co-found one of the world's most luxurious automotive brands. But that is exactly what happened to Henry Royce, who was born on this day in 1863. He would go on to complete an apprenticeship with the Great Northern Railway Company, before starting an electrical and machine shop with a friend in Manchester in 1884. Two decades later he built his first cars, one of which was sold to a friend of Charles Rolls, who ran a London car dealership. After Rolls viewed the car a subsequent meeting was arranged between the two men and Rolls-Royce was born.

Henry Royce portrait.
(From The National Archives, United Kingdom, artist unknown)

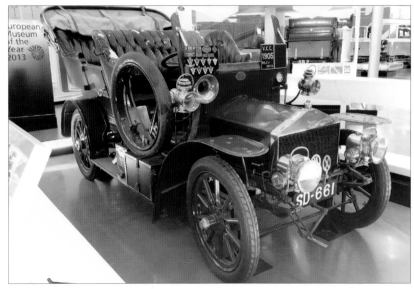

1905 Three-Cylinder 15hp. (Photo by Michel Curi [101])

Also on this day: **1907** – Vauxhall Motors Ltd registered in Great Britain. **1982** – Porsche tested the 956 for the first time. **2002** – The Toyota Scion debuted at the New York Auto Show.

March 28, 1941
Willow Run begins construction

Ford Motor Company's Willow Run manufacturing plant began construction on this day in 1941. The facility was built with the intention of manufacturing aircraft for the Allies in WWII, a war the United States would join in December of the same year. The plant, located between Ypsilanti and Belleville, Michigan, primarily produced B-24 Liberator bombers. Once complete production of the Liberator started in October of 1941, it did not stop until May of 1945. More than half of these particular planes were produced at Willow Run. Ford built the plant and sold it to the government, then leased it back for

Right: Men and women work side by side producing parts and aircraft at Willow Run.
(Public domain)

the remainder of the war. When the war ended, Ford declined to purchase the plant back, and Kaiser-Frazer took ownership. In 1953, General Motors purchased the plant, and operated it as Willow Run Transmission until 2010.

Also on this day: **1900** – The British Royal family, headed by King Edward VII, received its first automobile, a Daimler Mail Phaeton.

B-24 production at Willow Run.
(Public domain)

March 29, 1927

200 miles per hour

March 29, 1927, was a clear, sunny day at Daytona Beach, Florida, with temperatures reaching 85 degrees Fahrenheit. It was perfect weather for setting a new land speed record, which is just what

Henry Segrave in 1921.
(Public domain)

British race car driver Henry Segrave intended to do. His vehicle, the Sunbeam 1000 HP, was powered by two Sunbeam Matabele aircraft engines, one that sat in front of the driver and one behind. Segrave, who set his first land speed record in 1926, was anxious to earn the top spot once again driving the Sunbeam, and he did so in quality fashion. During his record run on this day in 1927, Segrave recorded a speed of 203.79mph (327.97km/h), making him the first person to ever drive any automobile faster than 200 miles per hour.

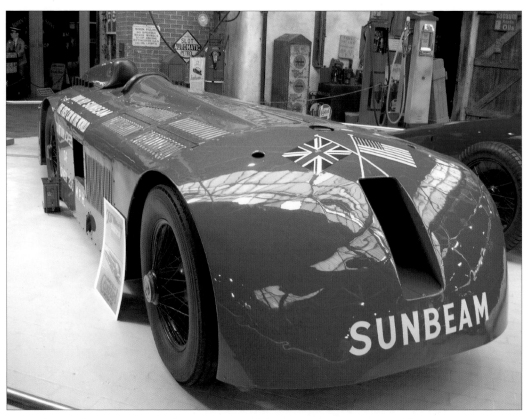

The Sunbeam 1000 HP, the first automobile to reach 200 miles per hour. (Public domain)

Also on this day: **1971** – The Jaguar E-type Series III was introduced, featuring the new Jaguar 5.3-litre V12.

March 30, 1948

Jordan Grand Prix

Eddie Jordan in 2009.
(Photo by Lutz H [102])

Jordan Grand Prix was a Formula One constructor that operated from 1991 until 2005, founded by former Irish racer Edmund 'Eddie' Jordan, who was born on this day in 1948. At one point or another the team included Michael Schumacher, Heinz-Harald Frentzen, Damon Hill, and Andrea de Cesaris, among others. The team never reached the top of the podium, but did earn bronze in the 1999 Constructors' Championships and Drivers' Championships with Frentzen. In early 2005 the team was sold to the Midland Group. It remained as Jordan for 2005, before being renamed as MF1 Racing for

Bertrand Gachot giving Jordan its F1 début at the 1991 United States Grand Prix. (Photo by Stuart Seeger [103])

the next season. Eddie Jordan went on to be an F1 commentator for multiple TV networks, and became a presenter for the BBC TV show *Top Gear.*

Also on this day: **1909** – New York's Queensboro Bridge opened, connecting Long Island and Manhattan. **1998** – Porsche delivered the last air-cooled model to its new owner, TV star and Porsche enthusiast Jerry Seinfeld.

Tiago Monteiro at the United States Grand Prix in 2005, Jordan's last year as an F1 team. Monteiro placed 3rd in the race. (Photo by Dan Smith [104])

March 31, 1932
The Ford V8

The Ford Flathead V8 was unveiled to the general public on this day in 1932. While the V8 itself was not new, the way that Ford manufactured it, as a single cast block, and made it affordable to the masses in the Ford Model 18 was – and it ushered private motoring into a new era.

1932 Ford V8. (Photo by Joe Ross [105])

It is said that Ford tried to develop a six-cylinder engine to compete with Chevrolet, but ran into numerous problems, so Henry Ford instead pushed for an affordable V8, framing Ford as an industry leader, not a follower. The original Flathead was a 221cu in (3.6-litre) that produced 65 horsepower. The final Ford flatheads were produced in 1954, but the engines remain a favorite of hot rodders.

Also on this day: 1949 – Carlo Abarth founded race car manufacturer Abarth & C.

1932 Ford V8 Cabriolet. (Photo by Riley [106])

April 1, 1970

Hello, Gremlin

Word on the street was Ford and General Motors were going to release new subcompact cars in 1971 – AMC needed a response, and quick. By essentially cutting down the existing AMC Hornet and adding an almost vertical hatchback, the AMC Gremlin was born nearly a year before the suspected launch from the competition. Introduced to the general public on this day in 1970, the new economy car would compete with the Chevrolet Vega, Ford Pinto, Toyota Corona and the VW Beetle, which was only two inches shorter. It originally featured a 199 cu in (3.3-liter) in-line 6, and was available with or without a back seat. Production of the iconic Gremlin lasted through 1978, with 671,475 units leaving the assembly line, before being replaced by the AMC Spirit.

Also on this day: **1932** – Franklin automobiles introduced its V12. **1961** – The first mass produced amphibious automobile, the Amphicar, was introduced in New York. **1995** – Daewoo began selling cars in the UK.

1974 AMC Gremlin front and rear views.
(Photos by Greg Gjerdingen [107], [108])

April 2, 1875

Walter Chrysler is born

While working as a railroad mechanic and machinist, Walter Chrysler, born on this day in 1875, caught the eye of General Motors executive James J Storrow in 1911. Following a meeting with Buick president Charles Nash, Chrysler became works manager at Buick, tasked with production cost reduction. When William Durant re-took over GM, Chrysler planned to resign with many coworkers, but Durant visited Chrysler in person and offered him an incredible salary of $10,000 (US $165,000 adjusted for inflation) per month for three years, with a US $500,000 stock bonus at the end of each year, to run Buick. Chrysler accepted immediately. Following the three years Chrysler resigned, and was paid $10 million for his stock. He started at Buick making $6,000 per year, and left one of the richest men in America. He used his capital to acquire Maxwell Motor Company, which he reorganized into Chrysler Corporation.

Walter Chrysler during a White House visit 1937. (Public domain)

Also on this day: **1956** – Alfred P Sloan stepped down as chairman of General Motors. **1995** – Emilio Scotto finished his record-setting motorcycle journey of 735,000km (457,000 miles). He visited 214 countries and territories during his ten years on the road.

The New Chrysler Six, with Startling New Results

1925 Chrysler advertisement. (Public domain)

April 3, 1885
The grandfather clock engine

Gottlieb Daimler and Wilhelm Maybach started developing what would become known as the grandfather clock engine in the early 1880s in a garden shed behind Daimler's home in Cannstatt, Germany. The upright 0.5hp engine, which featured a single horizontal cylinder, air cooling, hot tube ignition, and cam operated exhaust valves, weighed in at approximately 50kg (110lb) and had a height of 76cm (30in). The engine, patented on this day in 1885, was fitted to a vehicle dubbed the Reitwagen, which earns credit as the first modern motorcycle, although it had stabilizers similar to a child's bike with training wheels. Daimler did not intend to build a motorcycle, but wanted to learn what his engine was capable of, and he did not believe the 0.5hp engine was powerful enough to move a full size carriage. The Reitwagen was taken for its first ride on November 18 of that year.

The 1885 Grandfather clock engine. *(Photo by Morio [109])*

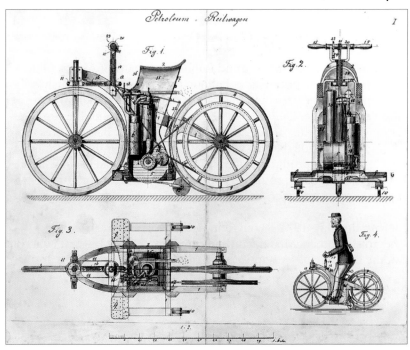

Plans for the Reitwagen. *(Public domain)*

Also on this day: 1934 – Percy Shaw applied for a British patent for the cat's eye road marker. **1966** – Battista Farina, founder of Pininfarina coachbuilders, died at age 72.

April 4, 1996
Here, kitty, kitty

Jaguar introduced a new kitten to their litter on this day in 1996 at the New York Auto Show. The Jaguar XK8 was a grand touring model and the first car of the new XK series, although it borrowed lettering from earlier models such as the original XK150 and XK-E. The XK8, replacing the aged XJ-S, was available as a coupé or convertible and featured Jaguar's new AJ-V8 4.0-liter engine. While the XK8 was only manufactured through the 2006 model year, the XK series wouldn't meet the end of production until July of 2014.

Jaguar X100. *(Photo by Rudolf Stricker [110])*

Also on this day: 1929 – Karl Benz passed away. **1959** – The V8 Daimler Dart launched at the New York Motor Show. **1993** – Mario Andretti won his final Champ Car victory at a race in Phoenix, Arizona.

XKR (X150) Coupé. The last of the XK series. *(Photo by S 400 HYBRID S [111])*

April 5, 1923

Firestone balloons

Today in 1923, Firestone Tire and Rubber Company of Akron, Ohio, began balloon-tire production. Balloon tires had been previously developed, but the tire company improved upon the design, which allowed for a larger contact area between the ground and the tire, thus providing better handling and a smoother ride. Balloon tires use an inner tube inside the tire, which is inflated with air. By the time Firestone started production of this new tire type it had become the United State's largest producer of tires, having received the contract to supply Ford with rubber for the Model T.

Also on this day: **1921** – Louis and Arthur Chevrolet started the Chevrolet Brothers Manufacturing Company. **1940** – The first concept car, the Buick Y-Job, was introduced to the press.

The Buick Y-Job concept car was introduced in 1940. (Public domain)

Henry Ford, Thomas Edison and Harvey Firestone circa 1930. (Public domain)

Mercedes Adrienne Ramona Manuela Jellinek, born on September 16, 1889.
(Photo by Skblzz1 [112])

April 6, 1853

The man who took his daughter's name

Emil Jellinek may not ring any bells, but add Mercedes and it sure does. Born on this day in 1853 in Leipzig, Germany, Emil found success in the auto industry after partnering with DMG to build a car not for today or tomorrow, but the day after tomorrow, as he put it. The cars he built were named after his daughter, Mercedes. This led Emil, at the age of 50, to add her first name to his surname, saying, "This is probably the first time that a father has taken his daughter's name." From then on, he was known as Emil Jellinek-Mercedes, and signed his name as E J Mercedes. The success of the 1900 35hp Daimler-Mercedes, often regarded as the first modern automobile, sent DMG sales soaring, and on September 26, 1902 Mercedes was trademarked by DMG to be used on their entire automobile line.

Emil Jellinek driving his Phoenix Double-Phaeton.
(Public domain)

Also on this day: **1908** – Cartercar founder Byron Carter died at age 44 from complication with injuries he received when a vehicle's starting crank kicked back and broke his jaw. **1934** – Ford introduced white wall tire options. **1983** – SEAT manufactured its first Marbella model.

April 7, 1947
The death of Henry Ford

Henry Ford circa 1919.
(Public domain)

Henry Ford's career, and his life, came to an end on this day in 1947 when he passed away at his estate in Dearborn, Michigan, of a cerebral hemorrhage at the age of 83. Henry's professional life started as an engineer for the Edison Illuminating Company, where he began work in 1891. After a promotion in 1893 he found himself with enough time and money to begin experimenting with automobiles and gas engines. In 1896, his work led to the development of the quadricycle. After founding Ford Motor Company in 1903 Henry achieved great success in the development of automobiles, the automobile manufacturing process, and his pursuits to better the workplace.

Also on this day: **1902** – Texaco was founded. **1936** – The Fiat 500, AKA Topolino, was introduced.

April 8, 1916
Safety born from death

Bob Burman participated in many significant races in the early 20th century, including winning the Prest-O-Lite Trophy Race in 1909 at Indianapolis Motor Speedway, the precursor to the Indy 500. In the truest sense of the statement, he died doing what he loved. Burman was killed on this day in 1916 when his open-cockpit Peugeot rolled over during a race in Corona, California, also taking the lives of three spectators and seriously injuring five others. Following his death, two of Burman's friends, Barney Oldfield and Harry Arminius Miller, were inspired to build a safer race car. The pair are credited with inventing what is now referred to as the roll cage. Taking it a step further they built a fully enclosed race car in 1917, which they dubbed the Golden Submarine.

Also on this day: **1971** – Automobile producer Fritz von Opel, the grandson of Opel car company founder Adam Opel, died at age 72. **1998** – Ford announced plans to use side-impact airbags on all US models. **2004** – The one millionth Skoda Fabia left the assembly line.

Henry Ford leaving the White House on April 27, 1938, following a meeting with President Roosevelt. He is accompanied by Major Henry M Cunningham, Manager of the Alexandria, VA branch of the Ford Motor Co. (Photo courtesy of US Library of Congress, call number LC-H22-D- 3829 [P&P])

Bob Burman on May 25, 1911.
(Photo by Bain News Service, US Library of Congress, Prints and Photographs division, digital ID ggbain.09237)

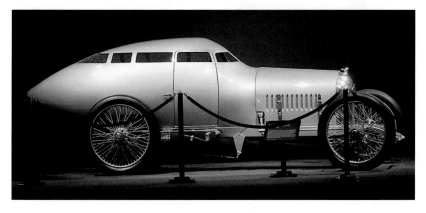

The Golden Submarine in 2012 at the Petersen Automotive Museum.
(Photo by Raynardo [113])

April 9, 2009

A green car

The Honda FCX Clarity went into production in June 2008 with Honda calling it the world's first hydrogen-powered fuel-cell vehicle intended for mass production. During its appearance at the New York Auto Show it took home the World Green Car award on this day in 2009, after more than 15 years of development. Fuel-cell vehicles work by combining hydrogen and oxygen to generate electricity, resulting in emissions of only water and heat. In July 2008, when the Clarity was ready for the market, Honda chose to lease them to consumers for some $600 per month, as the retail price would be in the $200,000 range due to the high production costs.

Left and above: Honda FCX Clarity. (Photos by Joseph Brent [114], [115])

Also on this day: **1930** – The first Bridgestone tires were manufactured. **1961** – Australian Jack Brabham won the Brussels Grand Prix in a Cooper T53.

April 10, 1879

A rental car empire

John Hertz, Sr, born Sándor Herz, was born on this day in 1879 in modern Slovakia. In 1910 he was working as a car salesman in Chicago, Illinois, when he partnered with Walden W Shaw to found the Shaw Livery Company to offer taxi services. After finding success in painting their cabs yellow to attract would-be riders, the name was changed to the Yellow Cab Company. Hertz incorporated the business in Chicago in 1915 with 40 cabs, and soon franchised out in other large cities, including New York City. Hertz would then found the Yellow Cab Manufacturing Company to build his own cars, and the Yellow Coach Manufacturing Company to build buses and other large transport vehicles. In 1923 he acquired a rental car company, and renamed it Hertz Driv-Ur-Self Corporation, leading to his name becoming synonymous with rental vehicles.

John Hertz Sr with a 1920s advertisement for Hertz car rentals

Also on this day: **1922** – Horsedrawn fire-fighting rigs were used for the last time by Detroit firemen. **1972** – Fiat executive Oberdan Sallustro was executed by Argentine Communist guerrillas at age 56. **1978** – The first US built Volkswagen leaves a Pennsylvania assembly line.

April 11, 1888
Holy matrimony

Clara Jane Bryant and Henry Ford tied the knot on this day in 1888, Clara's 22nd birthday. The ceremony took place at her parents' home in Greenfield Township, Michigan. Over the next 50 years Clara offered her support to Henry's ever growing company, and regularly traveled with him on business trips. The couple originally met at a New Year's dance in 1885 and were engaged the next year. Clara's mother said she was too young to marry, and made them wait two more years. In 1891 the couple moved from the farmland that Henry received from his father to Detroit when Henry began work for the Edison Illuminating Company. The couple had one child, Edsel, and remained married until Henry's death in 1947.

Also on this day: **1928** – The Opel RAK 1 rocket car was publicly demonstrated for the first time. **1993** – Ayrton Senna set a fastest lap record at Donington Park, England during the Grand Prix of Europe, which he won.

Henry Ford with his wife Clara in Ford's first car, the Ford Quadricycle.
(Public domain)

April 12, 1888
Founder of MG is born

On April 12, 1888 a boy by the name of Cecil was born in London, to Henry and Fanny Kimber. Just 40 years later, in 1928, he would be responsible for the founding of MG. Cecil Kimber's interest in automobiles started with a love of motorcycles, but following a riding accident he took to four wheel vehicles, first purchasing a 10 hp Singer in 1913. A year later he took a job with Sheffield-Simplex, a British car and motorcycle maker, as assistant to the chief designer. He bounced around a few different automakers before he landed a long-term position with Morris Motors Limited.

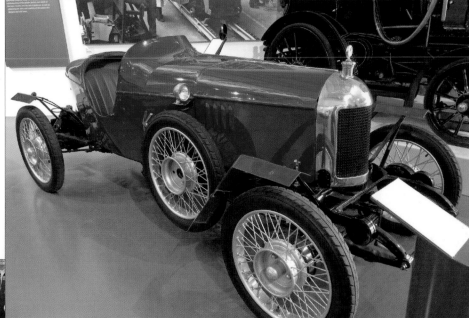

The 1925 MG is dubbed "Old Number One," but it wasn't the first MG produced, rather the first manufactured specifically for racing competition. It made its debut at the 1925 Lands End Trial. (Photo by Karen Roe [116])

1925 MG Morris Oxford 4-seater tourer.
(Photo by rhino not for sale [117])

His job was to develop specialized bodies for the cars, focusing on sports car styling. This role led him to become the driving force in the official founding of MG, which stands for Morris Garages, in 1924.

Also on this day: **1902** – King Edward VII became the first British monarch to travel by automobile when he was driven in a 24 hp Daimler. **1992** – Italian car builder and racing driver Ilario Bandini passed away at age 80.

April 13, 1931

Daniel Gurney, superstar

On this day in 1931 American race car driver Daniel Sexton Gurney was born in Port Jefferson, New York. Gurney moved to California as a teenager, and quickly got caught up in the hot rod culture that had taken the state by storm. By 1958 he was on the fast track to the racing hall of fame, as he competed successfully in multiple disciplines of auto racing. He took home first-place trophies in Sports Cars in 1958, Formula One in 1962, NASCAR in 1963, and IndyCar in 1967. He was the first of only three drivers to accomplish such a feat to date.

Dan Gurney at the 1970 Grand Prix of the Netherlands.
(Photo by Joost Evers [118])

Also on this day: 1904 – Cadillac's Detroit manufacturing facility caught fire, resulting in massive damage. **1907** – The Rolls-Royce Silver Ghost, under the name 40/50, made its press debut. **1965** – The 10 millionth Pontiac, a 1965 Catalina, came off the assembly line.

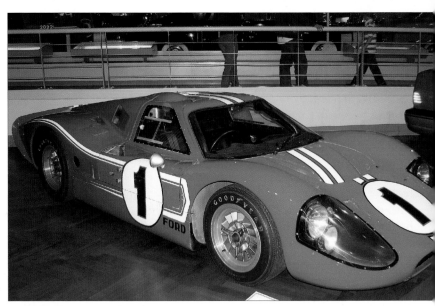

The Ford GT40 Mk. 4, which won the 1967 24 Hours of LeMans with AJ Foyt and Dan Gurney at the wheel. (Photo by Dave Hogg [119])

April 14, 1912

A Renault sinks with the Titanic

There are probably very few, if any, remnants left of a certain 1912 Renault Type CB Coupé de Ville that sank to the bottom of the North Atlantic Ocean, after the famous ocean liner it was being shipped on hit an iceberg on this day in 1912. William Carter had bought the vehicle and planned to transport it to New York City on board the RMS Titanic, but by early the next morning the cruise liner, along with the Renault, sank beneath the waves on the unsinkable ship's maiden voyage. Carter and his family were rescued but the vehicle has never been located, despite many excursions seeking Titanic artifacts.

A 1912 Renault 9hp. This car is smaller than the Type CB Coupe de Ville that sank on the Titanic, but had a similar appearance. (Public domain)

The Titanic on April 2, 1912.
(Public domain)

Also on this day: 1926 – Maserati manufactured its first Tipo 26 race car. **1927** – The first production Volvo left the assembly line in Goteborg, Sweden.

April 15, 1924
Launching a road map empire

Founded in 1868, Rand McNally & Co was one of the largest printing operations in Chicago, pumping out newspapers for the *Chicago Tribune*, as well as timetables and tickets for the blossoming railroad industry in the area. It would print its first map in 1872, which appeared in the December edition of *Railroad Guide*. Its first road map, the *New Automobile Road Map of New York City & Vicinity*, would appear in 1904, and two decades later, on this day in 1924, the first edition of the *Rand McNally Auto Chum*, was published. This annually updated and digitized map is now known as the *Road Atlas*. The first publication featured hand-drawn maps of the 48 US states printed in blue and red. It only included paved roads and showed zero miles of interstate. Modern US editions now include more than 47,000 miles of interstate and 160,000 miles of highway.

Also on this day: **1931** – Ford closed its auto plant in Berlin, Germany. **1961** – The Jaguar E-Type made its racing debut at Oulton Park, England. **1964** – Gail Wise, a 22 year old school teacher, became the first person to purchase the brand new Ford Mustang, two days before they were supposed to go on sale.

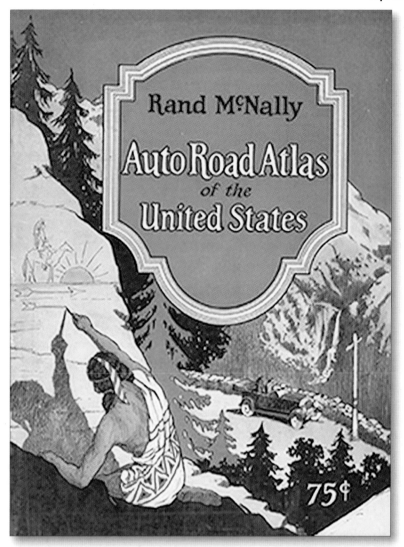

The cover of the 1926 Rand McNally Road Atlas.

April 16, 1946
Arthur Chevrolet commits suicide

Arthur Chevrolet is better known for his racing career than his participation in creating the brand that bears his name. Louis Chevrolet, Arthur's brother, gets most of the credit for that. Arthur, who participated in the inaugural Indianapolis 500 in 1911, suffered major injuries in 1920, after being involved in an accident while practicing for the Indy 500. The bodily damage was severe enough that it ended his racing career. He continued to dabble in the auto industry with his brother, and even filed for, and received, a patent for an overhead valve engine. The brothers founded Chevrolet Brothers Aircraft Company in 1929, but it proved unsuccessful. On this day in 1946 Arthur hung himself following severe issues with depression. His final resting place is now in question. It was believed he was buried next to his brother, but an investigation found those remains to be those of his son, who died 15 years prior.

Also on this day: **1908** – The first sale of an Oakland car was made. **1954** – The first stock car race in Great Britain took place in front of an audience of 26,000 at New Cross Stadium in London.

Arthur Chevrolet lying next to his Marquette-Buick at the 1910 Vanderbilt Cup Race after the drive chain broke during the 8th lap.
(Image courtesy Howard Kroplick; www.vanderbiltcupraces.com)

April 17, 1964

The Mustang debuts

The Ford Mustang stole the show when it debuted on this day in 1964 at the New York Auto Show, officially going on sale the same day at Ford dealers across the world. The day that Henry Ford II introduced legendary auto executive Lee Iacocca's latest creation to the masses, more than 22,000 of them sold, and, within 18 months, more than

Front end of a first generation Mustang. (Photo by Yasser Alghofily [120])

1,000,000 Mustangs had been bought up, smashing Ford's projection of moving 100,000 of the cars in its first year on the market. Iacocca first dreamed up the idea for a car that mixes American power with the sex appeal of European style in 1960. The Mustang would become the greatest selling Ford since the Model T.

Interior and dashboard of a 1964½ (1965) Mustang. (Photo by FD Richards [121])

Also on this day:

2013 – On the Mustang's 49th anniversary Ford celebrated the production of the one millionth Mustang to be built at its Flat Rock, Michigan plant.

1969 Ford GT40. (Photo by Michel Curi [122])

April 18, 1964

Ford GT40 makes a public appearance

The American-powered, British-bodied, Ford GT40 was developed to outperform Ferrari in endurance races, after Henry Ford II grew angry with Enzo Ferrari for not selling Ferrari to Ford. The first of the cars, the Mk1 chassis 101 and 102, made their first public appearance on this day in 1964 at LeMans, during a test weekend. The vehicles were found to suffer from aerodynamic issues, a problem that caused one of the cars to become airborne and crash on the Mulsanne straight. The GT40 would make its official race debut a month later at the Nürburgring 1000km. The car had to be retired due to suspension issues after holding second place early in the race. The GT40 would go on to become the Ferrari beater that Henry Ford II envisioned, winning 24 Hours of LeMans four years in a row, starting in 1966.

Also on this day: **1934** – Citroën showed off the Traction Avant (front-wheel drive) in Paris. **1958** – The Corvette Stingray debuted at Maryland's Marlboro Raceway.

Ford GT40 at the Goodwood Festival of Speed.
(Photo by Nic Redhead [123])

April 19, 1953
More than 100 beautiful automobiles

The first annual Pebble Beach Concours d'Elegance was held in 1950 in conjunction with the first Pebble Beach Road Race, in Monterey, California. The Concours drew the finest automobiles from all around the world. In its inaugural year the judges awarded the Best of Show trophy to a custom built 1950 Edwards R-26 Special Sport Roadster. On this day in 1953 the show opened with more than 100 entries for the first time. Best of show went to Peter Clowes and his 1953 Austin Healey 100.

Also on this day: **1932** – Austin launched the Ten, the company's best selling car in the 1930s. **1951** – Mercedes introduced the 220 at the International Motor Show in Frankfurt. **1979** – Chevrolet began production of its first mass-produced front-wheel drive car, the Citation. **2005** – a Bugatti Veyron hit a top speed of 253.8mph, making it the fastest production car to date.

A scene from the 2007 Pebble Beach Concours d'Elegance.
(Photo by Simon Davison [124])

April 20, 2008
First woman to win an IndyCar race

Following a 22 hour weather delay that canceled qualifying, and resulted in a starting field set by points, the green flag finally dropped at the Indy Japan 300 on this day in 2008. Hélio Castroneves started in pole position and led the fastest lap at Twin Ring Motegi, in Japan, but he would fall to second place by the time the checkers flew. Ahead of him by 5.85 seconds was Andretti Green Racing team member Danica Patrick, who crossed the finish line to become the first woman to win a race in the IndyCar Series.

1953 Austin Healey 100, similar to the car the won best of show at the Pebble Beach Concours d'Elegance in 1953. (Photo by Sicnag, [125])

Also on this day: **1897** – The first production car from Daimler was delivered to Ernest Estcourt. **1908** – Brooklands hosted the first British Motorcycle Club race.

Danica Patrick at Infineon, the same vehicle used at the 2008 Indy Japan 300. (Photo by dodge challenger1 [126])

Danica Patrick in 2011. (Photo by Bryce Womeldurf. [127])

April 21, 1967
GM hits 100,000,000 vehicles

Introduced in 1965 as a luxury trim package for the Impala, journalists were quick to compare the Chevrolet Caprice to the Cadillac DeVille in style and comfort. In 1967, the Caprice received a complete restyling, including an updated dashboard and a more rounded body. It was on this day in 1967 that a Nantucket Blue Chevrolet Caprice Custom Coupé rolled out of the Janesville, Wisconsin General Motors assembly plant. The vehicle, which retailed for $3078, marked two major milestones for the auto industry. Not only was it the 100,000,000th automobile produced by GM, it was also the first time any automaker reached such a production feat.

Also on this day: 1983 – The 1984 Chevrolet Corvette was introduced. It featured a complete restyle, the first time the Corvette had received such dramatic changes since 1968. 2011 – Fiat announced a deal to purchase another 16 per cent share of Chrysler, making it majority shareholder.

1967 Chevrolet Caprice in Nantucket Blue. The 100,000,000th GM vehicle produced.
(Photo by John Lloyd [128])

April 22, 1870
Mitsubishi gets its start

Yataro Iwasaki.
(Public domain)

Yataro Iwasaki purchased three aging steamships in order to start a shipping company, which he officially founded as Mitsubishi Group on this day in 1870. It became the first Japanese steamship business to offer mail delivery to China, but, as competition in the shipping industry grew, the company diversified its interests, making stakes in coal and copper mining, as well as shipbuilding. In 1917 the company made its automotive debut with the Mitsubishi Model A. The car was the first mass-produced personal automobile from Japan.

Also on this day: 1956 – Carroll Shelby won the Del Monte Trophy 100 mile race on a Pebble Beach public road circuit, driving a Ferrari. 1970 – Citing environmental concerns, many attributed to automobile pollution, the first Earth Day is held in the United States, as created by Senator Gaylord Nelson.

A 1917 Mitsubishi Model A. (Public domain)

April 23, 1987
Chrysler buys a bull

Chrysler Corporation turned heads on this day in 1987, when it purchased Lamborghini for $25.2 million. Chrysler bought the supercar company from the Mimram brothers, Swiss entrepreneurs who made their fortune in banking and sugar production, and were the only people to make money as the owners of Lamborghini to date. Under Chrysler ownership, Lamborghini launched the iconic Diablo, bringing a million-dollar profit to the company in 1991. Only three years later Chrysler sold Lamborghini to MegaTech, who then sold it to VW in 1998, while the German automaker was on a luxury buying spree that included Bentley and Bugatti. The $110 million transaction left the reins in the hands of VW subsidiary Audi, which aimed to benefit from Lamborghini's sporty profile.

Also on this day: 1947 – The one millionth Packard was manufactured. 2000 – David Coulthard won the 55th British Grand Prix in front of his hometown crowd at Silverstone.

Lamborghini Huracan Spyder. (Photo by Devin Noh [129])

Lamborghini Diablo.
(Photo by Ben [130])

April 24, 1918
Tank-to-tank-combat

In a different kind of automobile first, a tank-versus-tank fight occurred in war for the first time on this day in 1918, when the Second Battle of Villers-Bretonneux began near Amiens, in northern France, during World War I. The fight occurred when a group of three German A7V tanks advanced on three British Mark IV tanks. Two of the British tanks were armed only with machine guns, while one had a 6-pound gun. The lead Mark IV fired on the lead German tank and hit it, disabling it. The British tanks continued to fire on the remaining German tanks, which eventually withdrew.

Also on this day: **1937** – The first race meetings were held at Crystal Palace circuit. **1969** – British Leyland unveiled the 1500 Austin. **1975** – The last Citroën DS was manufactured.

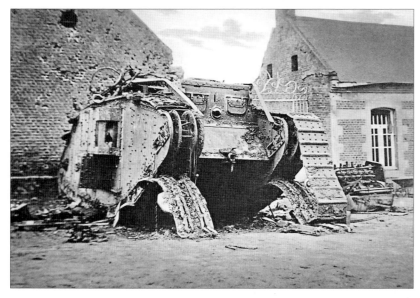

"From the Western Front: Destroyed English tank in Rumilly, France."
(Photo courtesy of The Library of Congress)

German AV7 Tank captured at Brimont, Champagne, 1918.
(Photo courtesy of The Library of Congress)

April 25, 2001
A deadly test drive

Italian race car driver Michele Alboreto was killed on this day in 2001 when the Audi R8 he was test-driving blew a tire during straight line speed tests, resulting in a fatal crash. Alboreto competed in Formula One from 1981 until 1994, racing for a number of different teams, including five seasons with Ferrari. In 1985 he placed second in the Formula One World Championship, behind Alain Prost – a personal best, but he would go on to capture numerous victories throughout his racing career. Notable first place trophies were earned at the 1997 24 Hours of Le Mans, and the 2001 12 Hours of Sebring sports car races.

Also on this day: **1940** – The final Duesenberg Model J was completed. It was delivered to artist Rudolf Bauer. **1959** – Mario Andretti made his racing debut, driving his 1948 Hudson to victory at Nazareth Speedway in Pennsylvania.

Michele Alboreto Minardi M194 at the 1994 British Grand Prix.
(Photo by Martin Lee [131])

Michele Alboreto driving an Audi R8, similar to the one in which he died. (Photo by lecates [132])

April 26, 1945
Dick Johnson is born

Richard "Dick" Johnson of Dick Johnson Racing was born on this day in 1945 in Queensland, Australia. He would become a part-owner of the V8 Supercar team DJR Team Penske, and was a racing driver himself. As a driver he was a five-time Australian Touring Car Champion, and three-time winner of the Bathurst 1000. As of 2008, Johnson had claimed more than 20 awards and honors including a 2001 induction into the V8 Supercars Hall of Fame.

1990 Ford Sierra RS500 DJR06. Six Dick Johnson Racing Sierras were built, with Johnson and John Bowe winning the Bathurst 1000 in chassis DJR05 in 1989. This car is car DJR06, used by Johnson and Bowe in the 1990 and 1991 Bathurst 1000s. (Photo by Sicnag [133])

Dick Johnson Racing's Ford Falcon at the V8 Supercar test day at Sydney Motorsports Park in 2013. (Photo by Jason Goulding [134])

Also on this day: **1921** – Police officers in London used motorcycles for patrol for the first time. **1983** – Honda dedicated its new manufacturing facility in the US state of Ohio.

April 27, 2009
Goodbye, Pontiac

General Motors made a fateful announcement on this day in 2009 when it declared plans to phase out Pontiac, maker of the GTO, Trans Am and other iconic models. Oakland Motorcars, the predecessor of Pontiac, was founded in 1909 in Pontiac, Michigan; just two years later General Motors bought it. Oakland was an upscale automobile, and GM wanted to capitalize on its longstanding success by putting out a companion make, which debuted in 1926 under the name Pontiac. Sales of the new make soared, leading to it absorbing Oakland in 1932. The economic downturn of the 2000s struck GM with massive financial problems, forcing it to drop several brands, including Oldsmobile, Saturn and Hummer. The last Pontiac, a G6, was built at the Orion Township Assembly Line in January of 2010, leaving GM with Chevrolet, GMC, Buick and Cadillac.

Also on this day: **1971** – The Morris Marina was publicly launched. **2011** – Tony Fernandes, owner of Team Lotus, announced that he had purchased Caterham Cars.

A 1926 Oakland, the year that Pontiac was introduced as a companion make. (Photo by David Berry [135])

1964 Pontiac GTO. The Pontiac GTO is often given credit for starting the muscle car craze of the 1960s and early 1970s.
(Photo by iowagto [136])

April 28, 1916
Ferruccio Lamborghini

Ferruccio Lamborghini was born in a small Italian town to grape farmers on this day in 1916. He would learn to work on airplanes and other machines after being drafted into WWII by the Royal Italian Air Force in 1940. With his newfound skill set he founded Lamborghini Trattori after the war, to manufacture tractors and other agricultural equipment. The business soon made Lamborghini a rich man, and this success funded his love of auto racing. He purchased a collection of high-end vehicles including Alfa Romeos, Lancias, a Mercedes 300S, a Jaguar E-type, two Maseratis and, in 1958, he purchased his first Ferrari, a 250GT. Following mechanical complications with the Ferrari, Lamborghini tried to schedule a meeting with the founder of the sports car company, Enzo Ferrari, to talk about improvements that could be made to the car, but he was refused. Lamborghini then decided to build his own grand touring cars, as he believed high performance shouldn't negate ride quality and comfort. Automobili Lamborghini was founded in 1963, with the first production model launching the following year.

Ferruccio Lamborghini with a 1965 Lamborghini 350 GT (top), the first production Lamborghini, and the 1963 GTV prototype (below).
(Illustration by Brian Corey [137])

Also on this day: **1921** – Douglas Davidson became the first person to ride a motorcycle faster than 100mph in Brooklands when he hit 100.76mph on his Harley-Davidson at Brooklands. **1974** – Niki Lauda earned his first F1 victory, and the 50th win for Ferrari, at the Spanish Grand Prix.

April 29, 2004
The last Oldsmobile

At 107 years old, Oldsmobile was the oldest existing American automaker when it closed its doors for the final time on this day in 2004. Founded in 1897 by Ransom E Olds, Oldsmobile, which started its life as Olds Motor Works, produced more than 35 million cars in its lifetime. It was the top selling American brand for 1903 and 1904 after becoming the first company to mass-produce a gas-powered vehicle, the Curved Dash, on an automotive assembly line. After remaining a viable brand for nearly a century, Oldsmobile slumped in the 1990s, forcing GM to announce its shutdown in 2000. The final Oldsmobile was an Alero GLS four-door sedan, which was signed by all of the assembly line employees who worked on the car.

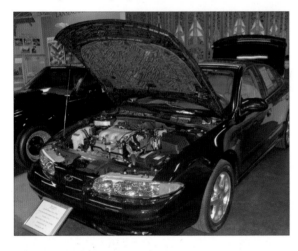

The last Oldsmobile, an Alero. Assembly line workers signed their names on the underside of the hood.
(Photo by Joe Ross [138])

Advertisement for the Oldsmobile, from a 1903 copy of The Automobile Review.

Also on this day: 1915 – Chevrolet introduced the Model 490 at a cost of $490. **1951** – NASCAR superstar Dale Earnhardt was born in North Carolina. **1969** – The Porsche 917 made its public debut at the Le Mans test weekend.

1915 Dodge Brothers Touring Car photographed at the Walter P Chrysler Car Museum in Auburn Hills, Michigan. *(Photo by Douglas Wilkinson [404a])*

April 30, 1925
A charitable sale

Dillon, Read & Company was a prominent American investment bank from the 1920s that had a strong track record for making daring deals, including one that saved Goodyear Tires from failure. On this day in 1925 it closed a record-setting transaction that secured the purchase of Dodge Brothers, Inc. When brothers Horace and John died unrelated and untimely deaths in 1920, their wives were left in control of the family business. When they decided to sell the company, the investment bank approached them and a deal was inked. It was the largest sale of an automaker to date, at $146 million, plus an additional $50 million to be given to various charities. Adjusted for inflation, the sale totaled more than $2.7 billion. Three years later Dillon, Read & Company sold Dodge Brothers to Chrysler.

Also on this day: 1948 – The Land Rover was launched at the Amsterdam Motor Show. **1978** – The Mazda RX-7 made its US debut.

1915 Dodge Brothers Touring Car photographed at the Walter P Chrysler Car Museum in Auburn Hills, Michigan. (Photo by Douglas Wilkinson [404a])

May 1, 1994
A brazen Brazilian

Tragedy struck on this day in 1994 at the San Marino Grand Prix when Brazilian Formula One driver Ayrton Senna da Silva was killed in a crash while leading the race. He held a record six victories at the Monaco Grand Prix, and was the fifth-most successful F1 driver of all time in terms of race wins. Senna attracted controversy throughout his career, particularly during his turbulent rivalry with Alain Prost. The drivers competed hard for the top spot at the Japanese Grand Prix of both 1989 and 1990, the race that would determine each season's champion. At both events Senna and Prost collided, resulting in Prost taking home the championships thanks to current point positions.

Ayrton Senna at the 1991 Formula One United States Grand Prix.
(Photo by Stuart Seeger [140])

Senna's win at the 1993 European Grand Prix is considered by to be one of the best races of his career. (Photo by Martin Lee [141])

Senna's death was considered by many of his Brazilian fans to be a national tragedy, and the Brazilian government declared three days of national mourning.

Also on this day: 1917 – The first Nelson Motor Car Company automobile was manufactured in Detroit. **1924** – The MG octagon logo was registered as a trademark.

May 2, 1918
General Motors acquires Chevrolet

On this day in 1918 General Motors (GM) purchased the Chevrolet Motor Company. In a bit of irony, William C Durant, founder of Chevrolet, had also founded GM several years earlier. When profits began to fall at GM, stockholders blamed the issue on Durant and forced him out of the company in 1910, but just a year later he had Chevrolet up and running. After regaining control of GM in the sale of Chevrolet, he was quickly pushed out by Pierre S du Pont. Durant had acquired quite a bit of debt,

William C Durant, circa 1915-1920. (Photo by Bain News Service)

1918 Chevrolet, inscription reads: Broughton & Howard families, 1919.

and du Pont offered to pay it off as long as he left the General Motors Corporation. He did, and he went on to found Durant Motors in 1921, which failed with the onset of the Great Depression, effectively ending Durant's career in the auto industry.

Also on this day: 1923 – The first Triumph automobile was manufactured. **1972** – Buddy Baker became the first stock car driver to finish a 500 mile race in less than three hours when he won the Winston Select 500 at Talladega.

May 3, 1924

The founder of Tyrrell Racing

Robert Kenneth 'Ken' Tyrrell, the founder of the Tyrrell Formula One constructor and a British Formula Two racing driver, was born on this day in 1924, in East Horsley, Surrey, England. Tyrrell began his career racing a Norton-powered Cooper in 500cc Formula Three, advancing to Formula Two by 1958. While racing brought him the occasional podium appearance, he decided to focus on team management, and in 1959 he gave up driving to begin his management career with John Cooper. In 1970 Tyrrell Racing began building its own cars, and in the early 1970s the team won three Drivers' Championships and one Constructors' Championship with driver Jackie Stewart. The team continued to reach the podium in races through the later 1970s and into the early 1980s, but never reached such spectacular heights again. The team was bought by British American Tobacco in 1997 and completed its final season as Tyrrell in 1998.

Also on this day: **1980** – Cari Lightner, aged 13, is struck and killed by a drunk driver while walking down a street. Her mother, Candy, would go on to found Mothers Against Drunk Driving (MADD), a nonprofit dedicated to keeping intoxicated drivers off the road.

May 4, 1904

Lunch leads to Rolls-Royce

Henry Royce was born poor and was working by age nine. Charles Rolls was born to an affluent family, and had a formal education at Trinity College in Cambridge. The two made an unlikely pair of business partners, but by the time they met they shared two things in common, a background in engineering, and a desire to build the world's greatest automobile. On this day in 1904, their partnership began during a lunch meeting in Manchester organized by a mutual acquaintance. Prior to the meeting Rolls ran a car dealership selling imports, but desired to build and sell top of the line English cars. Royce was already building 10hp cars; his first was completed in early 1904. After Rolls took Royce's automobile for a drive he agreed to sell as many as Royce could build, so long as the name was Rolls-Royce.

The company would be officially founded on March 15, 1906.

Also on this day: **1984** – Bruce Springsteen's rock song *Pink Cadillac* is released. **2006** – Aston Martin debuts the DBS, soon to be James Bond's new ride.

The Tyrell 003 F1 car in which Jackie Stewart won the 1971 World Drivers' Championship. *(Photo by dun_deagh [142])*

Jody Scheckter driving the Elf Tyrell 007 during practice for the Race of Champions at Brands Hatch in 1976. (Photo by John Pease [143])

1909 Rolls-Royce Silver Ghost. *(Photo by Karen Roe [145])*

1905 Rolls-Royce 15hp. *(Photo by Michel Curi [144])*

May 5, 1914
Cannonball run

Erwin 'Cannonball' Baker, the winner of the first race ever held at the Indianapolis Motor Speedway – a motorcycle race in which he rode an Indian – took off from San Diego, on this day in 1914, in his first of many runs across America. He reached New York City riding an Indian motorcycle in just 11 days, smashing the previous timed record by nine days. After the run, a journalist stated that Baker was faster than the Cannonball express train. The name stuck. Cross country races, usually unsanctioned and outlawed, are known as cannonball runs all across the world to this day.

Also on this day: **1938** – The five millionth Ford V8 is manufactured. **2006** – Fiat announced the reintroduction of the 500.

May 6, 1889
Motorcar in Paris

On this day in 1889, Gottlieb Daimler exhibited his first car to be shown in Paris, France, at the opening of the Paris World Exhibition. While this event is well known for the debut of a much larger attraction, the Eiffel Tower, Gottlieb did his best not to be outshone – literally! He lined his booth with 30 light bulbs connected to a home-built generator, in order to attract people to his stand, as both electric lighting and the automobile were still new to the world. The vehicle was known as the wire wheel car, and featured several engineering feats, including a twin cylinder V-engine, reminiscent of engines used in modern vehicles, attached to a four-speed transmission and a ground-breaking cooling system.

Also on this day: **1906** – The first Targa Florio endurance road race took place. **1935** – Louis Fontas drove an Alfa Romeo 2.3 to victory at Brooklands, winning the JCC International Trophy.

Erwin "Cannonball" Baker.
(Public domain)

Vincenzo Trucco, winner of the 1908 Targa Florio, an event that first took place two years earlier on this day. (Public domain)

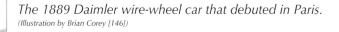

The 1889 Daimler wire-wheel car that debuted in Paris.
(Illustration by Brian Corey [146])

May 7, 1998

Daimler-Benz buys Chrysler

On this day in 1998 Daimler-Benz announced it had purchased Chrysler Corporation for $36 billion. This deal was the largest acquisition of a US company by a foreign buyer to date. After the official merger took place the following November, the sale proved to be quite beneficial in the short term. Stock prices rose quickly when trading of the company began on the New York Stock Exchange, but the flowers soon wilted. In 2006, following a $1.5 billion loss on the year, Daimler sold Chrysler to Cerberus Capital Management for a measly $7.4 billion.

Also on this day: **1927** – The first DKW automobile was built. **1990** – Production of the Lamborghini Countach ceased.

1998 Dodge Viper GTSR4, a Chrysler product from the year of the merger. (Photo by Jack Snell/Erick [147])

Lamborghini ended production of the Countach on this day in 1990.
(Photo by Mark van Seeters [148])

May 8, 1956

Ford Foundation loses its chairman

The Ford Foundation was founded in 1936 with a mission statement that claimed it was created "for scientific, educational and charitable purposes, all for the public welfare," and until the founding of the Bill and Melinda Gates Foundation in 2000 it continually ranked as the highest giving US non-profit. But the foundation did a lot for the Ford family directly. When the FDR administration introduced 'soak the rich' taxes that were forced on estates worth at least $50 million, the Ford family started the Ford Foundation, passing a bulk of Henry Ford's estate and an endowment from Edsel Ford to the organization, resulting in a 95 per cent non-voting stake in Ford that saved the family hundreds of millions, including more than $321 million in inheritance taxes. Henry Ford II resigned as the chairman of the foundation on this day in 1956.

Gilles Villeneuve, sitting on his car at Imola in 1979, was killed on this day in 1982 during qualifying for the Belgian Grand Prix. (Photo by ideogibs [149])

Also on this day: **1879** – George Selden filed for a US patent for his automobile design, but it wouldn't be granted for nearly two decades. **1974** – Britain lifts the temporary 50mph speed limit it set in response to the 1973 oil crisis. **1982** – Canadian F1 driver Gilles Villeneuve was killed during qualifying for the Belgian Grand Prix.

May 9, 1950
SEAT gets seeded

Sociedad Española de Automóviles de Turismo, better known as SEAT, was founded on this day in 1950 by the Instituto Nacional de Industria, with the modern equivalent of about 3.6 million Euros in capital. The idea for SEAT began as early as 1940 following the Spanish Civil War, when many international automakers showed little interest in the poor buying power of the war-torn country. A domestic automaker was sought to get Spaniards on the road, but World War II delayed the project. SEAT was officially organized, and a partnership with Fiat was formed to assist in the development of the new car brand, building a path to the SEAT 1400 in 1953, the company's first production model.

Also on this day: **1896** – Lawson's Motor Car Club held Britain's first horseless carriage show in South Kensington, London at the Imperial Institute; it featured ten models. **1908** – The first motor race for women was held at Brooklands. **1980** – A span of Skyway Bridge in Tampa, Florida collapsed after a freight ship hit a support column.

The SEAT 1400 A launched in 1955, two years after the original 1400.
(Photo by M Peinado [151])

May 10, 2012
Carroll Shelby passes away

A racer, team owner and car builder, Carroll Shelby's career is highly revered in many arenas, but his accomplishments crafting American racecars in the 1960s is what solidified him as an automotive legend. Influenced by the English AC Ace after seeing its performance during his winning run at the 1959 24 Hours of Le Mans, Shelby requested a specially designed Ace that could be fitted with a V8 instead of the six-cylinder it normally came with. Shelby secured two newly developed Windsor 221 cu in (3.6-liter) engines from Ford to begin the project. After testing he began to import the bodies from AC and installed the drivetrain of most of the vehicles at his Los Angeles workshop, creating the Shelby Cobra, beginning in 1962. Shelby would continue working with Ford, leading to the development of the Ford GT40, followed by the Mustang-based Shelby GT350 and GT500. After a career dedicated to building high-performance vehicles Shelby passed away on this day in 2012.

SEAT León Mk1 Cupra R.
(Photo by Geoff Jones [152])

Also on this day: **1923** – Alfred P Sloan was elected President and Chairman of General Motors. **1960** – Motorcycle racer and endurance rider Erwin 'Cannonball' Baker died at age 78.

Shelby beside his 1957 Maserati 450S at Virginia International Raceway in 2007.
(Photo by Sherry Lambert Stapleton [150])

1962 Shelby Cobra Mk 1 260, chassis CSX2000 – the first Shelby Cobra built. (Photo by Sicnag [153])

May 11, 1965

Head of the bull

Imola, Italy is home to the racing circuit Autodromo Internazionale Enzo e Dino Ferrari. The sights, smells and sounds of growing up in the vicinity of such an impressive, power-packed venue is sure to influence a young mind. As was the case of Stefano Domenicali, born in the city on this day in 1965. He spent his youth working weekends at the track, before earning a degree in business administration. Following graduation he landed a job in Ferrari's fiscal administration division, launching his professional automotive career. After spending more than two decades in numerous positions at Ferrari, including as racing team manager for nearly a decade, Domenicali handed in his resignation. Only six months later he accepted a job with Audi where he flourished, leading to his appointment as CEO of Automobili Lamborghini S.p.A.

Also on this day: **1978** – The two millionth Chevrolet Camaro was built. **1986** – Alain Prost won the Monaco Grand Prix.

Stefano Domenicali mingling with Ferrari fans in 2010.
(Photo by Paul Williams [154])

May 12, 1973

Deadly 500

May of 1973 is an infamous month at Indianapolis Motor Speedway, earning it the nickname Bloody May. It all started on this day when Art Lee Pollard, Jr was killed in an accident while running practice laps for the Indianapolis 500. Just after the green flag dropped for the actual race, Salt Walther suffered disfiguring burns in a fiery first lap crash that injured 13 spectators. A rain delay would halt the race for a week, but the blood wasn't washed away. Driver Swede Savage would sustain fatal injuries during the restart of the race. As Armando Teran, a mechanic for Patrick Racing, sprinted towards the Savage accident he was hit and killed by a fire truck in the pits, making him the final victim of Bloody May.

1978 Chevrolet Camaro. The two millionth Chevrolet Camaro left the assembly line on this day in 1978. (Photo by lix [155])

Indianapolis Motor Speedway. (Photo by Josh Hallett [156])

Aerial view of Indianapolis Motor Speedway in Speedway, Indiana, near the state capital of Indianapolis.
(Photo by Carol M Highsmith, Library of Congress, reproduction number: LC-DIG-highsm-40835)

Also on this day: **1934** – Buick introduced the Series 40. **1988** – The Ford Probe debuted. **2000** – Adam Petty, aged 19, a fourth generation NASCAR racer of the sports famous family, was killed during practice for the Busch 200 at New Hampshire International Speedway.

May 13, 1975
Death of the drive-in inventor

In the early 1930s Richard Hollingshead's mother complained to her son about how uncomfortable it was for her to go to the movie theater, as the seats were not made for her large frame. To ease his mother's movie going experience Hollingshead nailed bed sheets between two trees on their family property in Camden, New Jersey and aimed a Kodak movie projector at it. He then drove the family car in front of it, giving his mother a spot to sit where she would be less confined, effectively inventing the drive-in theater. Hollingshead received a patent for his idea, and in June 1933 he opened his first commercial drive-in movie theater in Camden. It could accommodate 400 cars and featured a 40 x 50ft screen. The first movie played was *Wives Beware*. The original price was $0.25 per automobile plus a quarter per person inside with a max rate of $1. Hollingshead passed away on this day in 1975.

Also on this day: **1938** – Pierce-Arrow Motor Car Company was liquidated.

May 14, 1966
Mille Subaru

By 1966 Subaru had been selling its tiny, rear-engine 360 for nearly a decade, and executives knew it was high time the Japanese automaker stepped up its competition in the compact car market. In order to compete with the likes of the Toyota Corolla, Nissan Sunny, Mazda Familia and others, Subaru introduced the 1000, which went on sale on this day in 1966. The 1000 was the first front-wheel drive car produced by Subaru and featured a 977cc engine that put out 54 horsepower. The new production model was the successor of the Subaru 1500 prototype from a dozen years earlier, the car that marked the beginning of Subaru automobiles.

Also on this day: **1968** – British Leyland Motor Corporation was formed, following the merger of Leyland Motor Corp and British Motor Holdings.

The first drive-in movie theater in Camden, New Jersey. (Public domain)

Center picture: Subaru 1000 coupé. (Photo by TTTNIS [158])
Lower picture: 1967 Subaru 1000. (Photo by Iwao [159])

May 15, 1922
Building Monza

Only Brooklands in the UK and Indianapolis Motor Speedway in the US preceded the Autodromo Nazionale Monza as purpose built racetracks, when construction of the venue began in Monza, Italy, on this day in 1922. The official grand opening took place the following September with the second annual running of the Italian Grand Prix, which has been held at the course every year since with the exception of 1980. Featuring three different courses, the Autodromo hosts multiple racing series, including Formula One, World Touring Car Championship and Superbike World Championship.

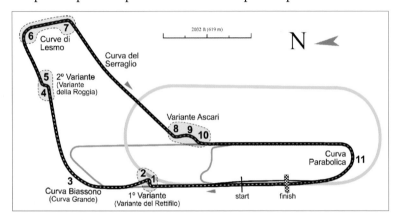

Track map of the Grand Prix circuit at Autodromo Nazionale Monza. The hi-speed track is shown in light blue. (Will Pittenger [161])

Also on this day: 1903 – London's first electric tram service opened, serving a route between Tooting and Westminster Bridge. **1962** – The Chrysler Turbine Car was introduced at the Waldorf-Astoria in New York. **1981** – The 20 millionth Volkswagen Beetle was manufactured.

May 16, 2013
Rest in peace, Dick Trickle

With more than 2200 races and one million laps under his belt, Richard 'Dick' Trickle left a deep groove in short tracks around the USA, especially in his home state of Wisconsin. Considered to be the most successful driver in short track history, he collected more than a few first place trophies, including 67 in 1972 alone. Trickle won seven ARTGO Championships, multiple ASA AC-Delco Challenge Championships, and even earned the title of NASCAR Rookie of the Year in 1989. After a lengthy career in the driver's seat Trickle was left battling chronic pain that no doctor was able to relieve. His family cites this as a reason why Trickle took his own life on this day in 2013.

Also on this day: 1952 – Porsche and Studebaker signed a contract for Porsche to design a car for Studebaker. A prototype codenamed the 542 emerged but was never built. **1956** – MG produced its 100,000th car – an MGA 1500.

Racing at Monza in 2014. (Photo by marek.boeckmann [160])

Dick Trickle, center, facing away, before a race in 1998.
(Photo by Spikerogan [162])

Below: The 1968 Ford Torino raced by Dick Trickle.
(Photo by Royal Broil [163])

May 17, 1994
A champion retires

Al Unser Sr raced his way into the record books with four Indianapolis 500 wins, as well as being the oldest to win the race when he did so in 1987 at age 48. His incredible career started in 1957 at age 18, when he began racing modifieds. In 1965 he drove in his first Indy 500, a race he would first win five years later. His mountain of accomplishments include winning the 1970 USAC National Championship, a 1978 Triple Crown of Ovals – IndyCar Championship, and he was crowned PPG IndyCar World Series Champion in 1983 and 1985. After being unable to qualify for his 28th Indy 500, he announced his retirement from racing on this day in 1994, just prior to his 55th birthday.

Al Unser Sr waving to the crowd while attending the 2015 Indy 500. *(Photo by SarahStierch [164])*

Al Unser's 1987 Indy 500 winning car. *(Photo by Doctorindy [165])*

Also on this day: **1922** – English race car driver Dorothy Levitt died at age 40. **1934** – Gordon M Buehrig filed for a patent for a vehicle design that would become the Cord 810.

May 18, 1958
Lotus enters F1

Team Lotus made its Formula One debut on this day in 1958 at the Monaco Grand Prix. Lotus entered two Type 12s driven by Cliff Allison and Graham Hill. While Ferrari was the favored team in the race, it was the Brits who took home the checkered flag that day, thanks to the driving of Maurice Trintignant behind the wheel of his Cooper. Allison and Hill finished in 6th and 26th, respectively. Anthony Chapman, founder of Lotus Engineering Company, took notes at the race and redesigned his cars based on the successes of competitors. Just two years later he entered a Type 18 Lotus into the Monaco Grand Prix with Stirling Moss behind the wheel, leading to the first of many Grand Prix wins for Lotus. In 1963, driver Jim Clark won Lotus' first World Driver's Championship, ushering in the golden age of racing for the team.

Lotus 12, chassis 353. This car was entered in Lotus' first F1 appearance, the 1958 Monaco Grand Prix. *(Photos by GTHO [166], [167])*

Also on this day: **1958** – Italian Maria Teresa de Filippis drove a Maserati in the Monaco Grand Prix, becoming the first woman to participate in a Formula One event. **1971** – Georg von Opel drove an electric powered Opel GT to a new standing-start kilometre record of 31.07 seconds.

May 19, 1903
Buick begins business

On this day in 1903 the Buick Motor Company was founded as a subdivision of Buick Auto-Vim and Power Company. The Buick Model B would go on sale in 1904, with production hitting 37 units for the year. After William C Durant joined the company as General Manager he quickly made it the best selling automobile in America. He would use the profits generated from Buick to found General Motors in 1908, which then acquired Buick. As of 2017, Buick is the oldest operating American passenger automobile brand.

Also on this day: **1935** – Adolf Hitler hosted a grand opening ceremony for the Frankfurt-Darmstadt Autobahn. **1976** – Triumph launched the TR7 in the UK. **1991** – Willy T Ribbs became the first African-American driver to qualify for the Indianapolis 500.

1905 Buick Model C. (Photo by Greg Gjerdingen [168])

1915 Buick Model C-55 Touring. (Photo by Jack Snell [169])

Underfunded Playboy Automobile Company tried to sell 20 million shares of stock, starting on this day in 1948. Only 97 cars were produced between 1947 and 1951, when the company went bankrupt. Pictured is a 1948 Playboy retractable hardtop. (Photo by Zombieite [170])

May 20, 1899
A need for speed

On this day in 1899, New York City taxicab driver Jacob German left his mark in history by becoming the first person in the United States to be cited for speeding while driving an automobile. German was a driver for the Electric Vehicle Company, which leased its cars to be used as taxis in the bustling city. At the time New York had speed limits for horses and cars of 8mph when traveling straight, and 4mph when going around a corner. German was traveling a breakneck 12 miles per hour! The bicycle officer who pulled him over arrested him and imprisoned him on speeding charges, but it is unclear if German was given a written speeding ticket. The first known paper citation in the US was given to Harry Myers in Dayton, Ohio in 1904.

Also on this day: **1948** – The Playboy Motor Car Corporation offers 20 million shares of stock at $1 per share. **1987** – American Motors Corporation approved a deal allowing Chrysler to acquire it.

May 21, 1901
First US speed limits

On this day in 1901 Connecticut became the first state in the US to pass a speed limit law strictly for motor carriages, officially separating animal-drawn and powered vehicles in the law. The law stated that on city streets automobiles could travel no faster than 12 miles per hour, and on country roads the speed limit was set at 15 miles per hour. Speed limits in the United States had been in effect as early as 1652 for animal-drawn wagons. The colony of New Amsterdam, now New York, had a regimen that stated, "[N]o wagons, carts or sleighs shall be run, rode or driven at a gallop." Drivers who disobeyed this law could be fined "two pounds Flemish" (the equivalent of about $150 USD in 2017).

Also on this day: **1933** – Top German auto racer Otto Merz was killed during a practice run for the Avusrennen. **1988** – Bobby Ore drove a double decker bus on two of its side wheels for 246 meters.

Otto Merz's wife and daughter in his racing car. Merz was killed on May 21 in 1933 during race practice. (Public domain)

May 22, 1897
Blackwall Tunnel officially opens

The original Blackwall Tunnel, connecting the London Borough of Tower Hamlets with the Royal Borough of Greenwich, was first proposed in the 1880s to improve traffic for the heavily commercial district in East London. For construction to commence, more than 600 people had to be rehoused, with many homes being demolished, including one reportedly once owned by Sir Walter Raleigh. It took five years, 800 men, including seven who died, and a cost of £1.4 million to complete the tunnel. Then Prince of Wales, Edward VII, opened the tunnel on this day in 1897. It has since been expanded to multiple bores to accommodate increased traffic.

Also on this day: **1913** – Guido Bigio, racecar driver and co-founder of car manufacturer Itala, died while testing a new model prior to the French Grand Prix. **1935** – Luigi Fagioli led the race flag to flag at the Monaco Grand Prix, the first driver to do so.

Opening ceremonies of the Blackwall Tunnel. (Public domain)

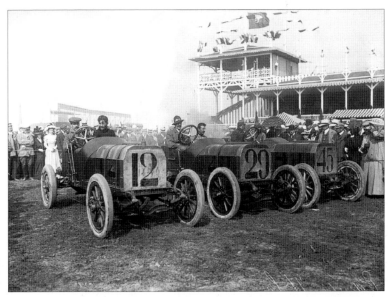

Team Itala at the 1908 French Grand Prix, consisting of Alessandro Cagno, Henri Fournier and Giovanni Piacenza. Co-founder of Itala, Guido Bigio, died on this day in 1913 while testing a car for upcoming French Grand Prix. (Photo courtesy Bibliothèque Nationale de France [171])

May 23, 1934

Bonnie & Clyde meet their end in a Ford

In true outlaw fashion, Bonnie Elizabeth Parker and Clyde Champion Barrow were shot to death during a police ambush while driving a stolen 1934 Ford V8 in Bienville Parish, Louisiana on this day in 1934. The two had met in January 1930 at a mutual friend's house, and Bonnie was quickly smitten with Clyde. Over the next few years the Barrow Gang would become suspects in at least 13 murders, including those of nine lawmen. While it was a violent gang, the members were often sought for crimes relating to automobile theft. This was in part because Clyde fancied the new Ford V8s, as they were extremely quick compared to most other vehicles on the road. Clyde went so far as to write Henry Ford a letter the month before he died, exclaiming, "While I still have got breath in my lungs I will tell you what a dandy car you make."

Also on this day: **1896** – The Riley Cycle Co was founded in West Midlands. **1989** – Citroën launched the XM.

Bonnie and Clyde posing in front of a 1932 Ford.
(Courtesy of US Library of Congress, digital id cph.3c34474, public domain)

Below: A real 1934 Ford that has been dressed as the Bonnie and Clyde car.
(Photo by CreepShot [172])

May 24, 2010

Lights out on Hummer

While filming for a movie, actor Arnold Schwarzenegger got a peek of a convoy of Army issued Humvees, AM General's military transport vehicles. He made it known he wanted one and his persistence played a role in AM General first offering a civilian model in 1992 under the name Hummer. General Motors acquired the brand in 1999, placing GM in charge of marketing and sales, while AM General continued to manufacture the vehicle. GM soon introduced the smaller Hummer H2 and H3, and then renamed the original Hummer the H1, which remained in production through 2006. Financial woes during the mid 2000s sent GM scrambling to unload less profitable makes. Multiple deals to sell Hummer fell through, and GM shut the door on the factory for the last time on this day in 2010.

The Hummer H1 was based off the military version of the Humvee.
(Photo by R-E-AL [174])

Hummer H3T, similar to the last Hummer to leave the assembly line.
(Photo by RL GNZLZ [173])

Also on this day: **1883** – The Brooklyn Bridge opened in New York City. **2002** – Debut of the Volkswagen Golf R32, the most powerful version of the Golf to date.

May 25, 1950
Green Hornet disaster

On the night of May 24, 1950, heavy rains flooded an underpass used by Chicago's electric streetcars, known as Green Hornets. The following day a flagman was positioned on 63rd street to inform Green Hornet drivers of a diversion. Paul Manning was at the controls of one of the newest Green Hornets, on this day in 1950, when he blew by the flagman at a breakneck 35mph (56km/h), thus sending his trolley onto a diversion track and straight into the path of a tanker truck carrying 8000 gallons of fuel. The collision sent a fireball three storeys high into the sky, and claimed the lives of 33 people, including the drivers of the tanker and the trolley, 30 others were gravely injured. The Green Hornet tragedy remains one of the worst public transportation disasters in US history.

"Concentration" – the driver of a Green Hornet streetcar in Chicago. (Photo by H Michael Miley [176])

A restored Green Hornet streetcar in Chicago. (Photo by H Michael Miley [175])

Also on this day: 1950 – The Brooklyn-Battery Tunnel officially opened. **2004** – TVR unveiled the Sagaris and Tuscan 2.

May 26, 1927
15 million Ts

Henry Ford and his son Edsel drove the 15 millionth Model T out of the Ford Highland Park, Michigan factory on this day in 1927, marking the last day of production for the T. The Model T, or 'Tin Lizzie' as it was affectionately known, was first introduced in October 1908 and was the car that introduced the automobile to the American masses. It initially sold for approximately $850 (equivalent to about $20,000 in 2017). Later, basic, no-frills models would be priced at just $260,

1908 Ford Model T, the first year of production. (Photo by How I See Life [177])

The 15 millionth Model T. (Photo by F D Richards [178])

(about $6000 in 2017) making them attainable for just about anyone with a steady job.

Also on this day: 1923 – The first 24 Hours of Le Mans begun. **1962** – The founder of Rapp Motorwerke GmbH, Karl Friedrich Rapp, died at age 80. His company would eventually become BMW.

May 27, 1923

The first 24 Hours at Le Mans

The inaugural 24 Hours of Le Mans ended on this day in 1923. This automobile endurance race held in Le Mans, France began the day before, with 33 cars on the track. All but three would still be driving when the race came to an end. The winners of the race were Frenchmen André Lagache and René Léonard, who were driving a Chenard et Walcker Sport. They completed 128 laps, while second place finished at 124. The winner of the race was originally to be determined after three years of competition, combining the distance traveled at the race each year. This idea was abandoned after the first three year period. The race has been held every year since 1932, except 1936, and between the years 1940 to 1948 due to WWII.

Also on this day: **1930** – The Chrysler Building opened in New York City. **1992** – Louis Schweitzer was elected Chairman of Renault.

The start of the the 1923 24 Hours of Le Mans. (Public domain)

May 28, 1937

Volkswagen is founded

The German Labor Front, under Nazi rule, founded Volkswagen on this day in 1937 at the command of Adolf Hitler. In an effort to mobilize his countrymen, Hitler aimed to produce an extremely affordable, highly reliable automobile; Volkswagen translates to 'people's car.' Austrian automotive engineer Ferdinand Porsche was hired to head the endeavor in 1934, after he showed a keen interest in small cars with air-cooled engines, which is what Hitler desired. Prototypes began to appear in 1938, and a small handful of production vehicles were manufactured before war broke out the next year. The Volkswagen Type 1 would begin mass production following the end of WWII and the vehicle would remain relatively unchanged until the last one rolled off the assembly line in 2003.

Also on this day: **1902** – *Car Illustrated* magazine first appeared in Britain. **1962** – Volvo co-founder Assar Gabrielsson died at age 70. **2014** – Google announced plans for a driverless car that has no steering wheel or pedals.

The Porsche Type 32 prototype designed in 1933 for NSU Motorenwerke AG. A precursor to the Volkswagen Type 1. (Photo by Luc106 [179]

A split window Volkswagen Type 1, characteristic of early models. (Photo by Shelby Bell [180])

VW logo during the 1930s, initials surrounded by a stylized cogwheel and swastika wings.

May 29, 1946
Frazer begins production

Frazer Automobiles from Kaiser-Frazer Corporation started production on this day in 1946, aimed at the upper-medium price point for luxury vehicles. The new Frazer was the first car to feature brand new postwar styling, going on to win the Fashion Academy of New York Gold Medal for design achievement. The company experienced minor success in its early years of competing with established luxury brands like Lincoln and Cadillac, taking 1.5 per cent of the US automobile market in 1948. Although more than 50,000 orders were placed for 1951 Frazers following a dramatic restyle, Kaiser-Frazer abruptly decided to focus on the less expensive Kaiser brand after just over 10,000 of the 1951 models came off the assembly line, effectively ending Frazer's life.

Also on this day: **1960** – Stirling Moss won his first race for Lotus at the Monaco Grand Prix. **2005** – Dan Wheldon became the first Englishman to win the Indianapolis 500 since Graham Hill in 1966. Danica Patrick finished fourth in the race, the highest finish for a woman in the Indy 500.

May 30, 1911
The Indy 500

With 80,000 fans looking on from the grandstands of Indianapolis Motor Speedway, and a $25,000 prize purse up for grabs, the inaugural Indianapolis 500 got under way on this day in 1911. The race hosted 40 drivers, and when the checkered flag flew, it was Ray Harroun in his Marmon Model 32-based Wasp racer at the finish line. Harroun had outfitted his car with a rear-view mirror, an invention of his own, and was the only racer to compete without a riding mechanic. He was cited as a hazard on the racetrack due to this, as it was the mechanic's job to keep tabs on the oil pressure, and inform the driver of approaching racers. The following year the purse was raised to $50,000 and a riding mechanic was made mandatory.

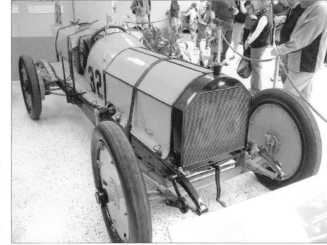

Ray Horroun's Marmon Wasp Racer.
(Photo by The359 [183])

1947 Frazer Manhattan.
(Photos by John Lloyd [181], [182])

Bob Burman, Louis Disbrow, Jack Tower and Joe Grennon at the 1911 Indianapolis 500. *(Public domain)*

Also on this day: **1967** –Mazda launched the Cosmo, the first two-rotor rotary engine production car.

May 31, 1929

Ford heads to the Soviet Union

An historic agreement between Ford Motor Company and the Soviet Union was signed on this day in 1929, stating that Ford would begin to produce cars in the USSR, which was eager to create jobs in the automotive industry. Henry Ford thought the best way to undermine communism was to introduce capitalism, which is why he had no qualms about doing business in the USSR, a country not formally recognized by the US government during diplomatic negotiations. A May 1929 *New York Times* article quoted Ford as saying, "No matter where industry prospers, whether in India or China, or Russia, all the world is bound to catch some good from it." The first Fords wouldn't be assembled in the USSR until 1932.

Also on this day: **1973** – Audi introduced the Fox. **1982** – Bobby Rahal averaged more than 170mph in the Indianapolis 500, becoming the first person to do so. **1995** – The one millionth Saturn was manufactured.

A 1937 Ford in Moscow. (Photo by Artem Svetlov [184])

Main entrance to Gorky Automobile Plant, where Ford vehicles were assembled starting in 1932.

(Photo by Vitaly Kuzmin [185])

June 1, 1909
Ocean to Ocean

To raise interest in the 1909 Alaska-Yukon-Pacific Exposition being held in Seattle, Washington, a transcontinental race from New York to Seattle was organized, which started on this day. Dubbed the Ocean to Ocean Automobile Endurance Contest, the event was sponsored, in part, by Henry Ford and Robert Guggenheim, who put up the trophy and prize money. The race was run in two segments. The first part was an endurance race from New York City to St Louis, where drivers had to drive in daylight and obey speed limits. The second half, from St Louis to Seattle, was a speed race, as there were fewer laws regarding automobiles west of the Mississippi River. Bert Scott in his stripped down Model T was declared the winner, after arriving in Seattle at 12:55pm on June 23rd, covering the 4106 miles in 23 days. It was later discovered he cheated by switching engines halfway through the race and the trophy was passed on to the driver of a Shawmut.

The 1909 Ford Model T driven by Bert Scott that was declared winner of the Ocean to Ocean race. It was later disqualified. (Photo by Cullen328 [186])

The Thomas Flyer pace car that established the Ocean to Ocean race route was also the winner of the 1908 New York to Paris race. (Public domain)

Also on this day: **1905** – Emile Delahaye, founder of Delahaye Automobiles, died at age 62. **1934** – Tokyo's Jidosha-Seizo Kabushiki-Kaisha (Automobile Manufacturing Co) changed its name to Nissan Motor Company. **1981** – Corvette production began at Chevrolet's Bowling Green, Kentucky plant.

June 2, 1970
Bruce McLaren dies in a crash

The namesake of English Formula One racing team McLaren Racing, Bruce Leslie McLaren, died on this day in 1970 when he crashed during a test run at the Greenwood Circuit in England. McLaren was a race car designer, driver, engineer and inventor. The racing team, founded by Bruce in 1963, has been largely successful. McLaren cars and drivers have won a total of 20 F1 World Championships to date, with eight Constructors' Championships and 12 Drivers' Championships, the first of each coming in 1974.

Also on this day: **1954** – Volvo unveiled its first sports car, the P1900. **1990** – Construction of the National Corvette Museum commenced.

Bruce McLaren racing at the 1969 German Grand Prix.
(Photo by Lothar Spurzem [187])

Sergio Pérez driving for McLaren at the 2013 Malaysian Grand Prix.
(Photo by Morio [188])

June 3, 1864

Ransom E Olds is born

The founder of Oldsmobile, Ransom Eli Olds, was born on this day in 1864 in Geneva, Ohio. When Oldsmobile was closed 140 years after his birth, it was the oldest functioning American car brand. By 1901, Olds had produced 11 prototype automobiles, at least one was gasoline, one was electric, and one was steam. A March 1901 fire burned the factory to the ground and, according to folklore, a single Curved Dash Runabout was saved from the flames. Olds claimed that because this car survived he decided to put it into production. Although, he already had orders for 300 of the cars before the fire broke out.

Ransom E Olds, circa 1901.
(Public domain)

1902 Oldsmobile Model R Curved Dash Runabout. (Photo by Sicnag [189])

Also on this day: 1925 – The 100,000th Chevrolet was built. **2011** – The US Treasury finalized an agreement to sell the rest of its holdings in Chrysler Corporation to Fiat.

June 4, 1896

The Ford Quadricycle goes for a spin

On this day in 1896, Henry Ford test-drove his first automobile, the Quadricycle. It was named for its use of four bicycle tires. He rolled the two-cylinder, four horsepower buggy out of his workshop after more than two years of experimentation, and was able to achieve speeds of more than 20 miles per hour during his initial tests. It featured a two-

The Lotus 49 driven by Jim Clark to victory at the car's debut at the 1967 Dutch Grand Prix.
(Photo by Mikaël Restoux [190])

Henry Ford with his first car, the Quadricycle, and the ten millionth Model T, in 1924.

(Photo courtesy of the Library of Congress Prints & Photographs Division, call number LC-D420-2659).

speed transmission, without reverse, a chain driven, ethanol powered engine, and no brakes. Ford sold his first Quadricycle for $200 to Charles Ainsley. He later built two more, one in 1899, and another in 1901. He bought his first one back for $60, and it now resides at the Henry Ford Museum in Dearborn, Michigan.

Also on this day: 1959 – American Honda Motor Company was organized in Los Angeles, California. **1967** – Jim Clark debuted the Lotus 49 at the Dutch Grand Prix, winning the race.

June 5, 1909
The Brickyard's first race is up in the air

It is easy to assume that the first competition at the Indianapolis Motor Speedway in Indianapolis, Indiana, would be a race involving automobiles, or at least motorcycles. It was not. On this day in 1909, the first competitive event at the raceway began, a manned gas balloon race, in which the winner was determined by most distance covered from the take off point. Track founder Carl Fisher was anxious to generate revenue for himself and his investors, so he held the balloon race before the automobile track was finished. In order to participate in the race himself, Fisher acquired a balloon pilot's license, just the 21st person to do so in America. The start of the 1909 event took place in turbulent winds, providing 40,000 spectators with a great race. Nine balloons floated up from the Speedway infield, and more than 24 hours later a balloon named Universal City, which landed 382 miles away in Alabama, was declared winner.

Also on this day: **1948** – Stirling Moss won his first major race in a cross between a hillclimb and a speed trial at Stanmer Park while driving a Cooper in the 500cc class. **2014** – The founder of the International Motor Sports Association, John Bishop, died at age 87.

Indianapolis balloon race, 1909. Balloons: Chicago, Indiana, and Hoosier netted down to ground.
(Photo courtesy of Library of Congress Prints and Photographs Division LOT 10960-2)

June 6, 1925
The Chrysler Corporation

Walter Chrysler took a controlling interest in Maxwell-Chalmers automobiles in 1921 while the company was suffering from operational ailments that were causing the company to flounder. He had intended to revitalize the company, but his efforts led to the founding of Chrysler on this day in 1925 when Maxwell was reorganized into the Chrysler Corporation. It was the success of the first Chrysler automobile, the six cylinder B-70, which launched in January 1924 under Maxwell, that ultimately secured the demise of the Maxwell name. The highly engineered Chrysler featured many innovations, including a carburetor air filter, full pressure lubrication and a replaceable oil filter. The mechanical advancements that went into the new Chryslers lifted the young automaker to the second best selling automobile brand in America by the mid 1930s.

Also on this day: **1948** – Charles Nash, co-founder of Buick and founder of Nash Motors, died at age 84.

A 1928 Chrysler 70. Chrysler's innovations helped push the car brand to the second highest sales in the US by 1936. (Photo by Tony Hisgett [191])

The front end of a 1918 Maxwell truck. Walter Chrysler would take over the company in 1921. (Public domain)

June 7, 1907
Russian Grand Prix

The second official Grand Prix season featured eight races, the second of which was the Moscow to St Petersburg race held on public roads on this day in 1907. Arthur Duray was the winning driver, crossing the finish line in his 60hp Lorraine-Dietrich. Duray was an accomplished driver and an early pioneer in aviation, holding just the third Belgian pilot license. Prior to Grand Prix racing, Duray set the land speed record three separate times in 1903 and 1904. He would continue driving competitively through 1930 in Hispano-Suiza, Ariès, Amilcar, Excelsior and other automobiles.

Arthur Duray at the 1914 French Grand Prix. (Public domain)

Arthur Duray behind the wheel of a Lorraine-Dietrich in 1908.
(Public domain)

Also on this day: 1928 – Full scale production of the Plymouth began, and the first one came off the line on June 11. **1992** – NASCAR co-founder Bill France Sr died at age 82. **2002** – The revamped Mini Cooper S went on sale in the UK.

June 8, 1948
The original Porsche

On this day in 1948 the 356 prototype was completed, making it the first car badged as a Porsche. The vehicle was hand built, primarily by Ferdinand Porsche's son, Ferry. Ferdinand was jailed on war crimes following WWII, leaving Ferry to navigate the postwar period in Germany at the head of his father's automobile engineering and consulting company. What Ferry and his team built was an aluminum bodied, mid-engine sports car with a modified Volkswagen drivetrain. The car, designated 356/1, was designed by Erwin Komenda, and it laid the groundwork for the production 356, which saw the engine moved behind the rear axle. Once Ferdinand was released he was hired as a consultant at Volkswagen. He used his salary to build a Porsche production facility to build up to 500 of the cars per year. In the next two decades more than 75,000 Porsches left the assembly line.

The 1948 Porsche 356 prototype. (Photo by califlier001 [192])

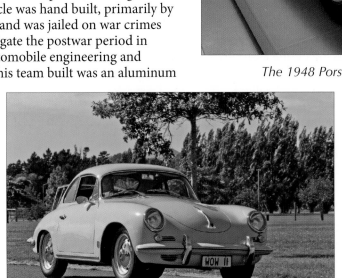

Also on this day: 1938 – Franklin D Roosevelt signed the Federal-Aid Highway Act of 1938, which requested a report on the usefulness of a national, tolled, highway system.

1961 Porsche 356.
(Photo by Staffan Andersson, public domain)

June 9, 1898
An old racer is born

Formula One driver Luigi Fagioli was born on this day in 1898 in Osimo, Italy, where he developed a passion for the relatively new invention of the automobile. Early success in hillclimb and sports car racing led Fagioli to enter his first Grand Prix race in 1926. He caught the eyes of Maserati, and was invited to race the Grand Prix Circuit for it in 1930. His Grand Prix wins included the Italian Grand Prix, Coppa Ciano, Monaco Grand Prix and

Luigi Fagioli at the 1932 Targa Florio. (Public domain)

Coppa Acerbo. Health issues forced him to stop racing prior to WWII but he couldn't stay out of the driver's seat. He rejoined the Alfa Romeo team in 1950 and made six podium appearances that season. The next year he entered only one Grand Prix, the French Grand Prix, which he won at the age of 53 years and 22 days, making him the oldest F1 Grand Prix winner to date.

Also on this day: **1922** – General Motors founder William C Durant purchased the former Duesenberg factory in Elizabeth New Jersey to produce Flint automobiles.

Luigi Fagioli at the 1928 Targa Florio. (Photo courtesy Agence de presse Meurisse - Bibliothèque nationale de France, public domain)

Despite losing the intended racing cars in the fire, Camille Jenatzy was still able to win the 1903 Gordon Bennett race in a different Mercedes.

June 10, 1903
Fire destroys Mercedes factory

When fire broke out at the original Mercedes Seelberg-Cannstatt automobile plant on this day in 1903, a quarter of the company's annual production, 93 cars, were destroyed, along with all of the manufacturing machinery. Several historical items, including the first Daimler-Maybach motorcycle, were also caught in the fire and lost, along with three 90hp race cars intended for the Gordon Bennett Trophy race. While workers received displacement salaries and increased bread rations, neighboring workshops offered space so that production could continue. The following year a new facility was opened in Untertürkheim.

Also on this day: **2013** – Brazil's government announced plans to build an auto crash test facility in order to improve the safety of car's built in the fourth largest auto market in the world.

Daimler Konzernzentrale Mercedes-Benz werk Untertürkheim. Entrance to Daimler headquarters Mercedes-Benz factory Untertürkheim (a city district in Stuttgart). (Photo by Ben Garrett [193])

June 11, 1986
A Ferrari steals the show

American cult classic film *Ferris Bueller's Day Off* premiered on this day in 1986, featuring a 1961 Ferrari. Written and directed by John Hughes, the comedy follows high school senior Ferris Bueller (Matthew Broderick) as he pretends to be sick in order to get out of going to school, so he can hangout in downtown Chicago for a day. He spends the afternoon with his girlfriend Sloane Peterson (Mia Sara) and best friend Cameron Frye (Alan Ruck). A high point of the film came when Ferris convinces Cameron to borrow his father's 1961 Ferrari 250 GT California. While the film featured three replicas, tight shots of the car were of a real California, of which only 100 were made.

A Ferrari 250 GT California Spider, similar to the vehicle featured in Ferris Bueller's Day Off. (Photo by Mike Roberts [194])

Of the three replicas, one is at Planet Hollywood in Cancún, Mexico and the other two are unaccounted for.

The new Hammersmith Bridge in London officially opened on this day in 1887. (Photo by Paul Hudson [195])

Also on this day: 1887 – London's current Hammersmith Bridge was officially opened. **1964** – Jack Sears' AC Cobra GT was clocked on the M1 motorway going 185mph at 4:30am, in preparation for Le Mans. **1968** – The Daimler DS420 limo was officially launched.

June 12, 1971
Mark III moves on

When Ford executive Lee Iacocca told Design Vice President Gene Bordinat to "put a Rolls-Royce grille on a Thunderbird" for Lincoln's next top luxury model, the Continental Mark III, was born. It took three years to get the Cadillac Eldorado competition into the market, but it landed with great success. Introduced in April 1968 as a 1969 model, the Mark III outsold the Eldorado that year, and in multiple years after. The car was developed for only $30 million, and sold high volumes, making it one of the greatest successes of Iacocca's career at Ford. The last Mark III left the factory on this day in 1971, succeeded by the Mark IV, which continued the same successful sales pattern.

1971 Lincoln Continental Mark III. (Photo by Michel Curi [196])

Magazine advertisement for the 1910 Peerless, an automobile brand that was founded on this day in 1901.

Also on this day: 1901 – The Peerless automobile was introduced. **2003** – The Audi A3 went on sale in the UK.

June 13, 1996
Designer is lost

German automobile designer Friedrich Geiger, responsible for some of Mercedes' most memorable cars, passed away on this day in 1996 at the age of 88. Geiger joined Daimler-Benz's special vehicles manufacturing department in 1933. Within the decade he would head development of the Mercedes 500K and 540K. After designing the iconic 300SL gullwing coupé he was promoted to the head of styling for Mercedes. Before retiring in 1973, he would oversee the creation of the many inspiring models, including late 1950s and early 1960s iconic 'Fintails' and the Mercedes SL coupés and convertibles.

Mercedes-Benz 230 S.
(Photo by nakhon100 [198])

Also on this day: **1911** – The first long distance race in London, totaling 277 miles, took place in Brooklands. **1978** – Lee Iacocca was relieved of his position at Ford Motor Company by Chairman Henry Ford II.

June 14, 1959
Take a ride on the Disneyland monorail

On this day in 1959, the Disneyland Monorail System opened at Disneyland Resort in Anaheim, California, becoming the first daily operating monorail in the Western Hemisphere. Walt Disney had envisioned the monorail as a futuristic and efficient means of public transport, but the automobile's popularity was on the rise during this time, thanks to affordable fuel and increasing options when it came to cars and trucks. America's love of the automobile all but erased the potential for the monorail as a means of mass transit.

Also on this day: **1916** – The International Model F truck reached the summit of Pikes Peak, Colorado, US, the first commercial truck to do so. **1924** – The ten millionth Ford is manufactured. **1964** – Jim Clark won the Belgian Grand Prix driving a Lotus-Climax 25.

Center photo: The Disneyland Monorail stopped at the Disneyland Hotel in August 1963. (*Photo by EditorASC [199]*)
Below: A modern image of Monorail Orange in Disneyland.
(*Photo by Carterhawk [200]*)

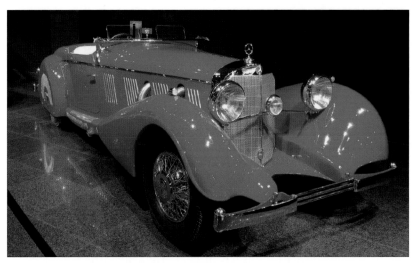

1936 Mercedes-Benz 500K. (*Photo by AmateurArtGuy [174]*)

June 15, 1911

Starting just got a lot easier

Many early automobiles required a hand crank to get the engine started, which could result in serious injuries, including broken bones, if it malfunctioned. In one instance, Cartercar founder Byron Carter stopped to help a stranded motorist get back on the road. He went to crank the car, but it kicked back and broke his jaw. Carter would later die from complications of his injury. When Cadillac founder Henry Leland heard his close friend was killed by the crank mechanism he vowed to make a safer starting system. He put his team of engineers to work to develop a practical self-starter. Charles Kettering was hired by Leland to improve upon the design his crew developed. Kettering succeeded, and originally filed for a patent in April of 1911, but additional improvements led to a final patent filing for his electric engine starting device on this day in 1911. The self-starter would be introduced on Cadillacs the following model year.

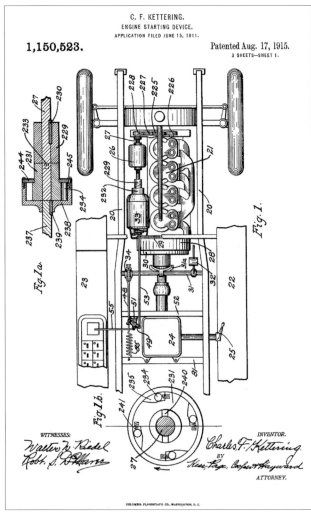

Original illustration filed with Charles Kettering's patent application.

Also on this day: 1909 – The first motorized hearse in the US was introduced by Crane & Breed of Cincinnati, Ohio. **1952** – Mercedes-Benz 300SLs finished in first and second at the 24 Hours of Le Mans. **1986** – Richard Petty made his 1000th start in a NASCAR race at the Miller American 400 in Michigan.

1912 Cadillac, the year Cadillac introduced the electric self starter. (Photo by Greg Gjerdingen [2011])

June 16, 1903

Ford Motor Company is incorporated

Original logo for Ford Motor Company.

At approximately 9:30 am on this day in 1903, in Detroit, Michigan, Henry Ford and 12 stockholders met to sign the paperwork necessary to form a new corporation to be called Ford Motor Company. The documents were notarized and sent to the office of the Michigan Secretary of State. The papers were dated June 16, 1903, however they were not received until the next day, which is when the company was legally incorporated.

Also on this day: 1917 – The Golden Submarine, a fully enclosed race car, was completed at a cost of $35,000. **2003** – In celebration of Ford's 100th anniversary, the company released the GT, reminiscent of the GT40s from the 1960s.

1903 Ford Model A. (Photo by Arvin Govindaraj [2012])

June 17, 1994
Chasing a white Bronco

It was this day in 1994 that a certain white 1993 Ford Bronco went stampeding, rather slowly, down Interstate 405 in Los Angeles carrying O J Simpson with Al Cowlings at the reins. More than 90 million people watched live as police gave chase. Simpson, wanted in connection with the June 13, 1994, murders of his wife Nicole Brown-Simpson and her friend Ronald Goldman, sent a suspected suicide note to his defense lawyers, the day he was to turn himself in. This resulted in an all points bulletin being put out in order to bring Simpson in.

During the chase, Simpson was said to have a gun pointed at his head, and later surrendered to police. Simpson would be found not guilty of criminal charges. The Bronco was parked in an LA parking garage from 1995 until 2012, barely moving 20 miles and is destined for a life in museums.

A fifth generation Ford Bronco, similar to the one used in the Simpson pursuit, aside from the color. (Public domain)

Enzo Ferrari in the 1920s, who won his first race on this day in 1923. (Public domain)

Also on this day: **1923** – Enzo Ferrari won his first race, a 166 mile event in Ravenna, Italy. **1928** – The Cord Corporation, headed by EL Cord, was founded. **1946** – The first car-phone call was placed.

June 18, 1923
Checker cab of Kalamazoo

Chicago clothier Morris Markin became owner of an auto body manufacturing business, after the previous owner defaulted on a personal loan from Markin. The business, now called Markin Automobile Body, received an order from Commonwealth Motors requesting bodies to build Checker Taxis. Commonwealth Motors was on the verge of bankruptcy, so in order to honor the contract Markin organized a merger between Markin Automobile Body and Commonwealth Motors in 1922, forming Checker Motors Corporation. The new business found success, and Markin moved the production facility from Joliet, Illinois to Kalamazoo, Michigan. It was on this day in 1923 the first Checker was assembled at the Kalamazoo factory. Checkers would be built here for six decades before the factory closed.

Also on this day: **1927** – The Nürburgring circuit in Germany held its first race meeting. **1966** – Bruce McLaren and Chris Amon became the first to exceed 3000 miles during 24 Hours of Le Mans.

Check Marathon taxi.
(Photo by Artem Svetlov [203])

A run down Checker Motors Corporation car.
(Photo by Robert Couse-Baker [204])

June 19, 1966

Ford goes 1,2,3 at Le Mans

When the 1966 24 Hours of Le Mans came to an end on this day in 1966, there was a Ford GT40 Mk II in first, second and third place, marking the first time an American automobile won the race. With the three Mk II Fords so far out in front of the rest of the field during a final pit stop, Ford decided to stage a publicity photo at the finish line, having all three cross nearly simultaneously. The leading #1 car driven by Ken Miles and Denny Hulme crossed the finish line next to the #2 car driven by Bruce McLaren and Chris Amon, with the #5 GT40 trailing shortly behind. The #1 and #2 cars had both completed 360 laps, but the #2 car started further back, meaning that since they essentially tied, the first place trophy would go to that team. Miles, who was going for the endurance racing triple crown after winning the 24 Hours of Daytona and 12 Hours of Sebring and Le Mans, was disheartened when he learned he lost the race due to the publicity stunt, saying, "I'm disappointed, of course, but what are you going to do about it."

Ford GT 40, #2, winner of the 1966 24 Hour of Le Mans.
(Photo by David Merrett [205])

Also on this day: 1947 – The Tucker Torpedo made its public debut. **1969** – The two millionth Mini was manufactured.

A 1969 Mini. The 2,000,000th Mini left the assembly line on this day in 1969.
(Photo by Sicnag [206])

June 20, 1942

Escape from Auschwitz

On this day in 1942, four prisoners of Auschwitz staged a daring escape utilizing a stolen SS member's personal vehicle, a Steyr 220 sedan, to drive right out the front gate. The escapees, three Polish men named Kazimierz Piechowski, Stanisław Gustaw Jaster and Józef Lempart along with an auto mechanic from Czortków, now Ukraine, named Eugeniusz Bendera, stole Nazi SS uniforms, weapons and the car in order to drive safely out of the concentration camp. When the four men reached the main gate, each armed with a machine gun and grenades, the gate did not go up. Piechowski leaned out of the vehicle so the gate attendant could see his rank on his uniform and in crude German ordered the soldier to open it. He did so and the men drove off to freedom.

Also on this day: 1903 – Barney Oldfield reached 60mph driving the Henry Ford built 999 and the Indianapolis Fairgrounds. **1982** – Porsche 956s finished first, second and third at the 24 Hours of Le Mans.

1938 Steyr 200, similar to the car used in the escape. *(Photo by René CC [207])*

Porsche 956s finished 1, 2, 3 today at the finish of the 1982 24 Hours of Le Mans. *(Photo by Andrew Basterfield [208])*

June 21, 1947
Mille Miglia rides again

The Mille Miglia was an open road endurance race that took place in Italy 24 times between 1927 and 1957. The races began after Aymo Maggi and Franco Mazzotti became upset about the Italian Grand Prix being moved from their hometown of Brescia. They designed a figure-of-eight type course, that ran approximately one thousand miles, – which translates in Italian to 'mille miglia.' The inaugural race started with 77 racers, of which 51 made it to the end. Ferdinando Minoia and Giuseppe Morando won the first race, driving an OM 665 S. The race was put on pause for WWII, with the first postwar Mille Miglia taking place on this day in 1947. Italians Clemente Biondetti and Emilio Romano won the event driving an Alfa Romeo 8C 2900 B Berlinetta Touring.

Also on this day: **1945** – Ford announced the start of post WWII production in Great Britain.

The Alfa Romeo 8C 2900B MM that Clemente Biondetti drove to victory at the 1938 Mille Miglia. Biondetti and Emilio Romano won the 1947 race in a similar car. (Photo by Hurstad [209])

June 22, 1933
The passing of a Bentley Boy

On this day in 1933 English race car driver Tim Birkin passed away in an English care facility. Birkin began motor racing in 1921 and following a short absence from the track, he re-entered the race scene in 1927 with a 3 litre Bentley. He achieved success at Brooklands and Le Mans, later becoming one of the 'Bentley Boys,' a group of wealthy British motoring enthusiasts who drove Bentleys to numerous wins throughout the 1920s. They're often given credit for helping to keep the marque's reputation for high-performance cars alive during financial troubles of the 1920s. Birkin's death was suspected to be a combination of malaria and a septic wound caused by a burn he received after touching a hot exhaust pipe weeks prior to his death.

Tim Birkin in 1931. (Public domain)

An OM 665, similar to the car Ferdinando Minoia and Giuseppe Morandi drove to victory at the first Mille Miglia in 1927. (Photo by Stahlkocher [210])

Also on this day: **1972** – Volvo manufactured its last 1800E sports coupé. **2001** – *The Fast and the Furious* debuted in theaters, launching the film franchise.

Birkin single seater Bentley, raced at Brooklands. (Photo by Adam Singer [211])

June 23, 2007
Ferrari tours the world

To celebrate its 60th anniversary, Ferrari conducted a global relay that lasted nearly five months, and passed through more than 50 countries before coming to an end on this day in 2007, at Ferrari headquarters in Maranello, Italy. The event began in January of that year in Abu Dhabi and traveled through Saudi Arabia, China, Australia, Mexico, United States, Canada, Russia and many more nations. Thousands of Ferrari owners and their cars took part in the relay, each carrying a baton featuring 60 badges that represented important milestones in Ferrari's history.

Also on this day: **1902** – Daimler registered 'Mercedes' as a trademark. **1963** – Jim Clark scored Team Lotus' 10th win in the World Championship when he won the Belgian Grand Prix.

Ferrari 430 Scuderia, a model introduced in 2007, Ferrari's 60th anniversary. (Photo by Alexandre Prévot [212])

Jim Clark in the 1962 German Grand Prix. The next year, on this day, he would score team Lotus' 10th win in the World Championship. He would go on to win his first World Championship the same season. (Photo by Lothar Spurzem [213])

June 24, 1910
Alfa Romeo opens for business

Anonima Lombarda Fabbrica Automobili (ALFA) got its start after Italian designer Giuseppe Merosi was hired by French Darracq to design more appealing cars for the Italian market. Upon finding success in Italy ALFA broke away from Darracq on this day in 1910, officially becoming its own entity. The next year ALFA made its racing debut at the Targa Florio with two 24hp models, leading to more than a century of racing success. The company name was officially changed to ALFA Romeo after Nicola Romeo acquired the company in 1918. Just seven years later Alfa Romeo would win the inaugural world championship for Grand Prix cars.

A Darracq 8/10 hp built at the Portello factory in Milan and kept at the Alfa Romeo museum in Arese. It is an immediate predecessor to ALFA. (Photo by James Temple [214])

Also on this day: 1951 – Jaguar earned its first victory at Le Mans, with Peter Walker and Peter Whitehead behind the wheel. **2001** – Michael Schumacher won the European Grand Prix at Nürburgring, driving a Ferrari F2001.

1922 Alfa Romeo. (Photo by Doug Letterman [215])

June 25, 2002
VW outdoes itself

When the 21,517,415th Volkswagen Golf left the Wolfsburg assembly factory on this day in 2002, Volkswagen beat its own production record for a single model. The original Volkswagen Type 1, often referred to as the Beetle, was VW's most manufactured model, until that silver Golf left the assembly line. In celebration, VW held an event that was attended by board members, political figures, production workers and the press. A lucky motorist in Hamburg, Germany was able to purchase the monumental hatchback.

Also on this day: **1939** – Hans Stuck drove an Auto Union Type D to victory at the Bucharest Grand Prix. **1980** – Rolls-Royce Motors and Vickers, Sons & Company announced plans for a merger.

2002 Volkswagen Golf, similar in style to the 21,517,415th Golf that beat the Beetle production number. (Photo by RL GNZLZ [216])

June 26, 1906
The French Grand Prix

The Grand Prix de l'Automobile Club de France, the first Grand Prix event in France, started on this day in 1906, and would come to an end the following evening. Each day of the race had the drivers completing six laps of a 103.18km (64.11 mile) circuit, composed of closed public roads outside the city of Le Mans, with the driver's daily times being combined for their total time. The Grand Prix was won by Ferenc Szisz driving a Renault, followed by Felice Nazzaro in a FIAT, and Albert Clément with his Clément-Bayard in third.

Also on this day: **1930** – Frederick Henry Royce was knighted by King George V. **1953** – The last Henry J was built by the Kaiser-Frazer Corporation.

A 1939 Auto Union Type D. This car is similar to or is the car Hans Struck drove to victory on this day in 1939 at the Bucharest Grand Prix. (Photo by Morten Brunbjerg Bech [217])

Ferenc Szisz, winner of the first French Grand Prix, in 1906, is seen here at the same event in 1914. (Public domain)

A sculpture by Ferenc Sziss at the main entrance to the Hungaroring. (Photo by Fekist [218])

June 27, 1985
Main Street of America is decertified

The 'Main Street of America,' US Route 66, was officially decertified on this day in 1985, when the American Association of State Highway and Transportation Officials voted to remove all of its highway signs. The road, which was completed and given a highway designation in 1926, stretched from Chicago, Illinois to Santa Monica, California, roughly 2200 miles. The road was constructed along a path forged in 1857 by US Navy Lieutenant Edward Beale and his pack of camels. Before it was a highway the path was a popular route for people heading west in the growing country, and, over the years, horses and wagons gave way to cars and trucks. In the 1950s new multi-lane highways were being built all across the country as part of a government program, many of which bypassed the old two lane Route 66, eventually leading to its decertification.

Also on this day: **1909** – The three point Mercedes logo was introduced, as designed by Gottlieb Daimler. **1964** – The Sunbeam Tiger went into production.

Old Route 66 near Amboy, CA. (Photo by Dietmar Rabich [219])

Route 66 between Oatman, Arizona and Kingman, Arizona. (Photo by Dietmar Rabich [220])

June 28, 2001
End of the line for Plymouth

Plymouth was introduced in July 1928 as Chrysler Corporation's entry into the low cost auto market. The Plymouth brand carried Chrysler, Dodge and DeSoto through the Great Depression, rising to number three in overall sales in the US by 1931. By the late 1960s, sales started to slip as Plymouths became less and less unique, as they shared features with other Chrysler products. By the mid 1990s, when only four models were being branded as Plymouth – the Voyager minivan, Neon, Breeze and Prowler – sales rarely exceeded 200,000 units per year. At the end of 1999, Chrysler announced it would discontinue the Plymouth brand, leading to the final

Plymouth, a silver Neon, rolling off the assembly line on this day in 2001.

Also on this day:
1914 – Archduke Franz Ferdinand was assassinated while riding in an Austro-Daimler, resulting in the outbreak of World War I. **1931** – NASCAR all star Junior Johnson was born in Wilkes County, North Carolina.

A second generation Plymouth Neon, nearly identical to the last one that left the assembly line. (Public domain)

The first page of the July 5-12, 1914, edition of the Domenica del Corriere, a weekly Italian paper, featuring a drawing by Achille Beltrame depicting Gavrilo Princip killing Archduke Franz Ferdinand of Austria in Sarajevo on this day in 1914, launching Europe into WWI.

June 29, 1956
Roadbuilder

President Dwight D Eisenhower signed the Federal-Aid Highway Act on this day in 1956. The bill allowed for the creation of a 41,000 mile highway system that Eisenhower stated would eliminate inefficient routes and traffic jams, as well as all other things that stood in the way of 'speedy, safe, transcontinental travel.' The 'National System of Interstate and Defense Highways' was largely approved in part because of the argument that the express roadways would allow for quick evacuation of major cities in the event of a nuclear attack. The highways were deemed essential to national interest, and the system was soon under construction.

Dwight D Eisenhower in 1959. (Public domain)

Also on this day: **1932** – Audi, DKW, Horch and Wanderer merged to create Auto Union AG. **1985** – John Lennon's psychedelic painted 1966 Rolls-Royce Phantom V limousine sold at auction for $2,229,000.

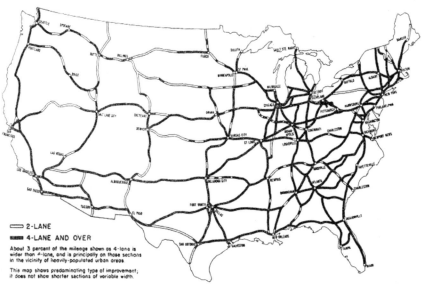

A 1955 map of proposed US highways to be built by 1965 as a result of developing the Interstate Highway System. (Public domain)

The standard road sign for the Dwight D Eisenhower National System of Interstate and Defense Highways. The five stars represent Eisenhower's rank as General of the Army during WWII.

June 30, 1953
Corvette number one

The automotive industry changed forever when the first production Corvette rolled out of General Motors' Flint, Michigan assembly facility on this day in 1953. The Chevrolet Corvette started out as a dream car of famed auto designer Harley J Earl, but it became reality when the fiberglass-bodied two-seater was introduced to the public in January 1953 at the Waldorf Astoria Hotel in New York City. Every production 1953 Corvette built was a white convertible with red interior and a black canvas top. The flashy exterior hid the mild drivetrain made up of a Blue Flame six-cylinder and a two-speed Powerglide transmission, all

A 1953 Corvette, one of only 300 built. (Photo by Brian Corey)

halted by drum brakes. Sales were initially disappointing, largely due to the car's underperformance. The introduction of a V8 option in 1955 saw sales skyrocket in the following years, allowing for the Corvette to earn the title of America's sports car.

Also on this day: **1956** – Engineer Alfredo Ferrari, son of Ferrari's founder Enzo, died at the age of 24. **2000** – Ford took ownership of Land Rover from BMW Group.

In 1955 the Corvette was available with a V8, paving the way for Corvette to become America's sports car. (Photo by Rex Gray [221])

July 1, 2005
The final Thunderbird

On this day in 2005 the last Ford Thunderbird rolled off the assembly line at Ford's Wixom, Michigan plant. The Thunderbird was developed in the years following World War II as a competitor to the Chevrolet Corvette. When it was released in 1955 it outsold the Corvette nearly 15 to 1. In the decades the followed the Thunderbird would undergo numerous alterations, including going from a two-seater to four in 1958. In an attempt to capitalize on buyers' nostalgia, Ford released a retro Thunderbird in 2002, which got a great reception. Despite excellent initial sales of the retro T-Bird, the success eventually waned and the car was discontinued.

Also on this day: **1860** – Charles Goodyear, inventor of vulcanized rubber, died at age 59. **1927** – Protos cars ended production after 27 years.

1955 Ford Thunderbird, the first year of production.
(Photo by Greg Gjerdingen, [223])

2005 Ford Thunderbird.
(Photo by Greg Gjerdingen [222])

July 2, 1992
One million Corvettes

On this day in 1992, just two days after the Corvette's 39th production birthday, the 1,000,000th Corvette rolled out of the Bowling Green, Kentucky assembly plant. It was a convertible with a red interior, white exterior, and a black top, the same color scheme as all of the original 1953 Corvettes. The one millionth Corvette was severely damaged on February 12, 2014 when a sinkhole opened up inside the National Corvette Museum in Bowling Green, Kentucky. Several other important Corvettes were also damaged, some much worse. A painstaking restoration took place to save this car; it was returned to factory condition, and still contains all the signatures from the workers who helped assemble it.

Also on this day: **1909** – Hudson Motor Car Company finished its first production car. **1962** – Packard was officially dropped from the Studebaker-Packard Corporation name. **2006** – Michael Schumacher won his fifth United States Grand Prix, becoming the first driver to win a major event at Indianapolis Motor Speedway five times.

The one millionth Corvette was white, with a black convertible top and a red interior to match the original 1953 Corvettes. (Photo by Nick Ares [224])

1909 Hudson. Hudson Motor Car Company completed its first production automobile on this day in 1909.
(Photo by Joe Ross [225])

July 3, 1945
America gets back on the road

Ford got a jump on postwar production by, well, not waiting until the war was actually over. On this day in 1945 Ford began manufacturing 1946 model cars, more than a month before the second World War come to an end on the Pacific front. Ford was the first major American automaker to begin producing personal vehicles after the government freeze on automobile production that was instituted in January 1942. Henry Ford II sent the first new Ford, a white Super DeLuxe Tudor sedan, to President Harry S Truman. In 1945, Ford produced 34,440 vehicles for the 1946 model year, more than any other carmaker. The 1946 models, like most major models of that year from major automakers, were more or less the same cars and trucks produced in 1942. Many manufacturers would not come out with a brand new body style until 1949.

1946 Ford Coupé. (Photo by Riley [226])

Interior of an unrestored 1946 Ford. (Photo by Mark Spearman [227])

Also on this day: **1916** – The first Jordan automobile was manufactured in Cleveland, Ohio. **1952** – The final Crosley was manufactured in Marion, Indiana. **1962** – Dan Gurney won the French Grand Prix driving a Porsche 804, the only time the car won an F1 race. **1985** – Feature film *Back to the Future* is released in the USA, starring a time-travelling DeLorean DMC-12.

July 4, 1903
The first female racer

On this day in 1903 Dorothy Levitt became the first woman reported in the press to compete in an automobile motor race, and she won. She earned first place at the Southport Speed Trials driving a 12hp Gladiator for her class, but there is more to her initiation to auto racing than meets the eye. While working as a secretary at Napier Car Company, Levitt's boss taught her to drive and race as part of a

Dorothy Levitt. (Public domain)

publicity stunt to boost sales of his cars. Her natural ability behind the wheel led to her becoming a fearless automobile driver, a record-setting speed-boater and an airplane pilot. Levitt even taught Queen Alexandra and the Royal Princesses how to drive.

Also on this day: **1914** – Mercedes finished 1-2-3 at the French Grand Prix, the last major Grand Prix held before the breakout of World War I. **1984** – Richard Petty earned his 200th career win at the Firecracker 400 in Daytona, Florida.

July 5, 1933
The Autobahn constructor

Fritz Todt was appointed as Inspector General for German Roadways on this day in 1933. Todt received a degree in construction engineering from Technische Hochschule Karlsruhe, and later, in 1931, his doctorate from Technische Hochschule München, after writing his thesis, "Sources of failure in building state roads from tar and asphalt." That same year he was made a senior colonel in the Nazi party, which he had joined almost a decade prior. Hitler himself named Todt to his new position as the General for German Roadways. It was to be his responsibility to develop a series of comprehensive roadways. The controlled-access highways that crisscross Germany today are Todt's legacy, and are known collectively as the Autobahn.

Fritz Todt in March 1940.
(Photo by Bundesarchiv [228])

Also on this day: **2013** – BMW manufactured the last M3 coupé.

July 6, 1851
Death of an electric motor inventor

The inventor of the battery-powered electric motor, Thomas Davenport, passed away on this day in 1851, at the age of 48. Davenport completed his motor in 1834, and received a patent for his invention in 1837. He demonstrated his motor by powering a small car on a short section of track, leading to the electrification of street cars. In 1840 he used his invention to print *The Electro-Magnet and Mechanics Intelligencer*, the first newspaper printed using electricity. Further development of Davenport's invention was key in the production of early electric automobiles.

Thomas Davenport.
(Public domain)

Also on this day: **1895** – Hon Evelyn Ellis purchased a French Panhard-Levassor to become Britain's first motorist. **1903** – George Wyman finished his transcontinental ride across the US riding a motorcycle, traveling from San Francisco, California to New York City. **1961** – The final Renault 4CV, the first French car to sell one million units, was built.

Map of the Autobahn in Germany.
(Photo by fremantleboy [229])

Production of the Renault 4CV ended today in 1961.
(Photo by Pedro Ribeiro Simões [230])

July 7, 1953
Subaru – It was all in the stars

On this day in 1953 Fuji Heavy Industries Co, Ltd (FHI) established the Subaru brand. Subaru is the Japanese name for the Pleiades star cluster shown on the company logo – the six stars represent the six companies that merged together to create FHI. The first Subaru car, the 1500, debuted the following year, but only 20 were manufactured. The first mass produced Subaru, the tiny 360, boasted a 16hp engine that achieved 66 miles per gallon. The car, affectionately nicknamed ladybug, also earned the title of "people's car," as it is acknowledged as the first affordable personal vehicle offered in Japan. The 360 was later upgraded to a 36hp engine that could hit 50 miles per hour, in 37 seconds that is.

Subaru 360. (Photo by ilikewaffles11 [231])

Dashboard of a Subaru 360.
(Photo by ocean yamaha, [232])

Also on this day: **1958** – Joseph Merkel, designer of Merkel automobiles and motorcycles in the early 20th century, died. **2003** – The 10,000th Aston Martin V12 Vanquish was manufactured at the Newport Pagnell factory.

July 8, 1968
A wildcat strike rocks Detroit

On this day in 1968 the Dodge Revolutionary Union Movement (DRUM), which consisted primarily of black autoworkers, went on a wildcat strike to protest working conditions at Dodge's Hamtramck assembly plant. A wildcat strike is one that is supported or endorsed by the leadership of the Union of which the workers are members of, in this case the United Auto Workers. At the time of the strike it was estimated that 70 per cent of the workers at the plant were black, yet it was exceedingly rare for black men or women to rise to any sort of management position or higher within the auto industry. The strike, which was observed by some 4000 workers, lasted two and half days and prevented the production of 3000 cars, was largely viewed as a civil rights movement.

Also on this day: **1901** – France set its speed limit for automobiles at 10km/h (6mph). **1962** – Driving a Porsche 804 Dan Gurney won the French Grand Prix, the only time the car won an F1 race.

The Dodge plant in Hamtramck, as seen here in 1914, was the site of the DRUM wildcat strike. (Library of Congress, call number, HAER MICH,82-HAMT,1—8, public domain)

Joakim Bonnier driving a Porsche 804, the same type of car in which Dan Gurney won the French Grand Prix on this day in 1962.
(Photo by Lothar Spurzem [233])

July 9, 1985
Malaysian moves

The Malaysian auto industry became tangible on this day in 1985 when the Proton Saga was launched. Proton, the first Malaysian automaker, built the Saga in collaboration with Mitsubishi. It was based off of the 1983 Lancer Fiore, which was powered by a 1.3-litre Orian engine. The very first Proton Saga is preserved at the Muzium Negara in Kuala Lumpur, Malaysia, which recognizes it as the beginning of the auto industry in the country. Proton originally struggled to keep up with demand for the new car, but, within one year of the vehicle's debut, the company captured a domestic market share of 64 per cent, in the under 1600cc category.

Also on this day: **1908** – Rolls-Royce opened its new manufacturing facility in Derby, England. **1933** – Work crews broke ground on the San Francisco-Oakland Bay Bridge. **1979** – A car bomb destroyed a Renault owned by Nazi hunters Serge and Beate Klarsfeld at their home in France. ODESSA claimed responsibility for the attack, in which nobody was injured.

A first generation Proton Saga. (Photos by Manoj Prasad [234], 235])

July 10, 1962
Three-point safety

Nils Bohlin received a US patent for his three-point automobile safety belt "for use in vehicles, especially road vehicles" on this day in 1962. Volvo had hired the Swedish engineer four years earlier, making him the company's first chief safety engineer. At the time seatbelts were rarely used outside of auto racing, in part because the lap belt style often resulted in internal injuries in the event of an accident. To remedy the problem Bohlin designed the three-point system used today, which holds both the upper and lower parts of the body in place during an accident. The design would become standard in all production automobiles by the end of the 1970s.

Also on this day: **1950** – Max Hoffman received the first official import shipment of Volkswagens to the US, when 20 Type 1s arrived by boat in New York City.

The work of Nils Bohlin led Volvo to introduce seatbelts as standard equipment on 1959 models, such as this Volvo 544. (Photo by Bob Adams [236])

1950 Volkswagen Type 1, similar to the vehicles imported by Max Hoffman when he received the first official shipment of VWs to the United States. (Photo by H Michael Miley [237])

July 11, 1899
Fabbrica Italiana di Automobili Torino

Giovanni Agnelli. (Public domain)

Count Emanuele Cacherano of Bricherasio was seeking investors in a horseless carriage project and Giovanni Agnelli wanted in. Agnelli paid $400 to buy into the founding of Fabbrica Italiana di Automobili Torino, which occurred on this day in 1899. Translated to English, Italian Automobiles Factory, Turin, or FIAT, as it was known, opened its first factory in 1900, with Agnelli appointed as managing director. He oversaw a staff of 35 who produced 24 cars that year. Production grew to 135 cars in 1904, and 1149 cars in 1906, by which time Fiat had opened a dealership in New York City.

Also on this day: 1847 – German inventor Georg Lankensperger, who developed the modern steering mechanism known as the Ackermann steering geometry, died at age 67. **1984** – The US government announced a mandate, stating all passenger cars produced after April 1, 1989 must be fitted with driver-side airbags or automatic seat belts.

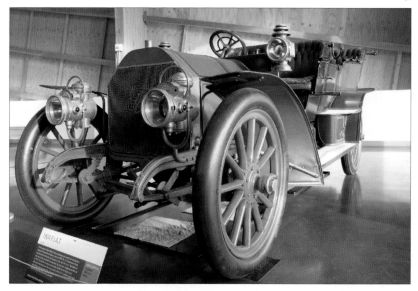

1904 FIAT that was formerly owned by Augustus Busch of Anheuser Busch Brewery fame. The chassis alone cost $13,500 in 1904, the body another $4000. (Photo by Brian Corey, all rights reserved)

July 12, 1933
The Dymaxion

Buckminster Fuller completed his first Dymaxion prototype automobile on this day in 1933, the inventor's 33rd birthday. The Dymaxion, a make up of the words dynamic, maximum, and tension, was not designed to be just an automobile per se, but a vehicle that may, one day, jump from the roads and land again. Fuller described the Dymaxion to his daughter as a "zoom-mobile," that, similar to a bird, could take off, fly about and settle back into ground traffic as necessary. With engineering assistance from naval architects and Rolls-Royce mechanics, three prototypes would be built, each carried by two wheels in front and a centered, third wheel that turned the vehicle in the back. The cars were powered by Ford V8s, which gave them an unofficial top speed of 128mph (205km/h). Of the three prototypes only one survives.

Also on this day: 1916 – Mr and Mrs William Warwick, along with their 4 year old daughter Daisy, left Seattle in a GMC truck on the first long distance truck haul, with a load of 2000 pounds of milk. They reached New York City 70 days later. **2009** – Mark Webber scored his first F1 win, taking the checkers at the German Grand Prix.

Above, a 1934 Dymaxion, the last surviving original of three built.
(Photo by brewbooks [238])

Dymaxion replica.
(Photo by Supermac1961 [239])

July 13, 1805
The first amphibian

Oliver Evans was an American inventor who focused on the development of steam locomotion. He wished to build steam carriages, and after demonstrating his capabilities by creating a high-pressure steam engine that could power a saw through marble in the early 1800s, he set about to find a financier for a carriage. When the Philadelphia Board of Health announced its concerns about the problem of dredging and cleaning the city's dockyard and removing sandbars, Evans convinced the board to let him build an amphibious, steam-powered dredging machine. What resulted was the first self-propelled vehicle in the US, and the first known self-powered amphibious vehicle

Engraved portrait of Oliver Evans by W G Jackman. (Public domain)

Artist rendition of Evan's amphibious steam carriage. (Public domain)

in the world, which he tested for the first time on this day in 1805. He built the floating dredger, and attached the engine to wheels so that he could drive it to, and into, the river. By Evan's accounts it worked perfectly, but he was known to exaggerate his successes.

Also on this day: **1940** – Henry Ford II was married to Ann McDonnell. **1968** – The world's first high production Wankel rotary-engined automobile, the Mazda R100, was introduced.

1955 Volkswagen Karmann Ghia (T14), the first year of production.
(Photo by Karen Roe [240])

July 14, 1955
Oh, Karmann Ghia

In the early 1950s automakers all over the world were looking to build small sports cars; for Chevrolet it was the Corvette, at Ford, the Thunderbird, and at Volkswagen it was the Karmann Ghia, which launched on this day in 1955. Coachbuilder Wilhelm Karmann hired Luigi Segre of Italian design house Carrozzeria Ghia to develop a new body that would fit the VW Type 1 pan, before even consulting Volkswagen about his plan. The result was a smash with VW executives and the sleek and sexy Karmann Ghia was born, making its public debut at the Kasino Hotel in Westfalia, Germany. Between its launch and its demise in 1974 more than 450,000 coupés and convertibles were built.

Also on this day: **1915** – Chevrolet purchased Mason Motor Company. **1996** – American race car driver Jeff Krosnoff is killed during the Molson Indy Toronto.

1974 VW Karmann Ghia (T14), the last year of German production.
(Photo by Brian Corey, all rights reserved.)

July 15, 1956
Racing from South Africa

South African sports car driver Wayne Taylor was born on this day in 1956. Taylor's racing career took off after winning the 1986 South African National Drivers' Championship. The next year he finished fourth in the 24 Hours of Le Mans. Highlights of his racing career included wins at the 1996 and 2005 24 Hours of Daytona, and the 2005 Grand-Am Rolex Sports Car Series Daytona Prototype Drivers' Championship. In 2007, Taylor and car builder Bob Riley formed Wayne Taylor Racing; later adding Taylor's sons Jordan and Ricky as drivers for the team.

Also on this day: 1959 – The Jaguar Mark II went into production.

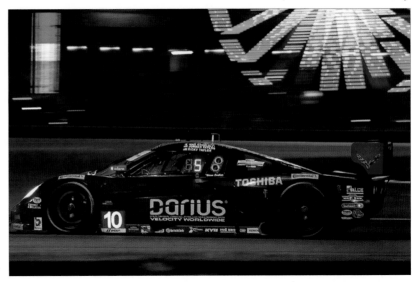

Wayne Taylor Racing at the 2014 Rolex 24. *(Photo by Scott Daniels [241])*

1963 Jaguar Mk II 3.4. The Mark II went into production on this day in 1959. (Photo by Sicnag [242])

July 16, 2006
Another F1 record

Michael Schumacher made Formula One history on this day in 2006 when he became the first F1 driver to win the same Grand Prix eight times, when he snagged the checkered flag at the 2006 French Grand Prix. He previously won the race in 1994, 1995, 1997, 1998, 2001, 2002 and 2004. Schumacher also set a record for most career hat tricks during this Grand Prix, earning his 22nd pole position, win and fastest lap all in the same race.

Also on this day: 1899 – The first Tour de France Automobile race was held. **1935** – The first parking meter in the world was installed in Oklahoma City, Oklahoma.

Michael Schumacher at Indianapolis in 2004.
(Photo by Rick Dikeman [243])

René de Knyff in 1912, winner of the first Tour de France Automobile race on July 16, 1899. (Photo by Agence de Presse Meurisse, Bibliothèque Nationale de France, public domain)

July 17, 2007
One fast Mercedes

Just as McLaren was becoming the favorite to win the driver and constructor F1 titles in 2007, Mercedes-Benz announced the release of its SLR McLaren Roadster on this day that year. It would go on sale the following September for £200,000, four years after the coupé version debuted. The roadster, which was built in the same factory as F1 racers, offered astonishing performance for a road-going car. It mixed F1 technology with the comfort features of a true touring vehicle. The body was primarily constructed of carbon fiber, and it featured carbon fiber enforced disk brakes and suspension components. Under the hood an AMG V8 compressor engine produced 626hp, powering the car to a top speed of 332km/h (206mph). At the end of the season it was Ferrari who claimed both F1 titles, but Mercedes-McLaren drivers finished in second and third.

Also on this day: **1951** – General Motors offered a preview of the Le Sabre concept car, an aircraft-inspired, two seat roadster capable of 180mph. **1981** – The Humber Bridge at Kingston-upon-Hull was opened by Queen Elizabeth II. **1995** – Argentinian race car driver Juan Manuel Fangio died at age 84.

July 18, 1936
The Weinermobile

The first Oscar Mayer Weinermobile left the General Body Assembly plant in Chicago, Illinois on this day in 1936. Designed by Oscar Mayer's nephew Carl Mayer, the Wienermobile is a marketing and advertising device in the form of a hot dog shaped automobile. Since its inception there have been ten more versions built, all driven by 'Hotdoggers.' While the cars tended to get bigger over the years, Oscar Mayer built a small version in 2008, based on a Mini Cooper S hardtop.

Mercedes-Benz SLR McLaren Roadster. (Photo by Marco Pagni [244])

Interior of a Mercedes Benz SLR McLaren. (Photo by Robin Corps [245])

Also on this day: **1883** – Francis Macerone and John Squire of Paddington Wharf received a patent for their 'Steam carriage for common roads.' **1930** – Rudolf Caracciola drove an SSK to victory at the Grand Prix of Ireland. **1954** – The builder of the first internal combustion powered vehicle in Great Britain, Sir Ernest W Petter, died at age 81.

Left: A 1953 Oscar Mayer Wienermobile. (Photo by Joanna Poe [246])

A modern version of the Wienermobile. (Photo by rg-fotos [247])

July 19, 2006
An electric prototype

On this day in 2006, Tesla Motors unveiled its Roadster prototype to 350 special guests at Barker Hangar in Santa Monica, California. The high-performance, fully electric vehicle produced zero emissions, which in turn produced massive enthusiasm. Less than two years later Tesla Motors began production, selling out the 2008 model year cars before the first one even left the factory. The Roadster offers a 0-60mph (100km/h) time of just 3.7 seconds and a range of 244 miles (393km) on a single charge, making it the first production electric car to break the 200 miles per charge mark.

Also on this day: **1902** – The Jackson Automobile Company was founded with Byron J Carter at the helm. **1934** – Harold T Ames filed a patent for retractable headlamps, which would be featured on the Cord 810 that he had designed.

A 2008 Tesla Roadster next to a 1911 Detroit Electric.
(Photo by Jack Snell [248])

A Tesla Roadster charging its batteries.
(Photo by theregeneration [249])

July 20, 1954
A Thame little Ford

The 5cwt Ford Thames 300E first left the factory on this day in 1954. The small van was based on the Ford Anglia/Prefect 100E, and had a starting price of just £358. Featuring 66cu ft (1.9m³) of load space, and a carrying capacity of 560lb (254kg), the Thames was an ideal delivery and service vehicle for many different types of business. Ford would later introduce a 7cwt model, offering a load capacity of 784lb (356kg) in the same area. By the time the 300E was replaced by the 307E in 1961, nearly 200,000 had been produced.

Also on this day: **1872** – Bertha Ringer and Karl Benz were married. **1931** – English race car driver Tony Marsh was born. **1940** – The UK government banned the buying and selling of personal automobiles due to the outbreak of World War II. **1940** – The Arroyo Seco Parkway, California's first freeway, opened.

A Ford Thames 300E panel van. *(Photo by Geni ([250])*

A 1956 Ford Thames 300E. *(Photo by Andrew Bone [251])*

July 21, 1987
Enzo's last approval

When the Ferrari F40 made its public debut on this day in 1987, an 89 year old Enzo Ferrari offered an impassioned speech, proclaiming, "A little more than a year ago, I expressed my wish to the engineers: build a car to be the best in the world. And now the car is here." Built for the company's 40th anniversary, the F40 was the last Ferrari model approved for production by Enzo himself. The F40 was built to be driven. It had no radio, no electric windows, no power seats, and certainly no cup holder, but what the no-frills Ferrari did have was thrills. Topping out at an unofficial 201mph (321km/h), it was the first production car to break the 200mph mark. Between 1987 and 1992, when production of non-racing models was halted, a total of 1,311 of the turbocharged V8s had hit the streets.

Also on this day: **1932** – Hudson Motor Car Company launched Terraplane, its new companion brand. **1943** – Austrian race car driver Fritz Glatz was born. **1974** – The final VW Karmann Ghia was built in Osnabruck, West Germany.

Ferrari F40s. (Photo by Paul Williams [252])

July 22, 1908
Body by Fisher

Brothers Fred and Charles Fisher founded automobile coachbuilder Fisher Body, on this day in 1908, in Detroit, Michigan. Prior to forming the business the brothers built horse-drawn carriages for C R Wilson Company. During his time there, Fred participated in the building of the Cadillac Osceola, the first fully enclosed automobile. Starting in 1910 Fisher Body became the sole supplier of all closed bodies for Cadillac, and three years later it was manufacturing more than 100,000 bodies

Mid-20th century photograph showing an aerial view of the Fisher Body factory in Cleveland, Ohio. (Photo courtesy Cleveland Public Library, Library of Congress, reproduction number HAER OHIO,18-CLEV,25H--1)

A mid-20th century photograph showing the interior of the Fisher Body press building in Cleveland, Ohio. (Photo courtesy The Plain Dealer, Library of Congress, reproduction number HAER OHIO,18-CLEV,25H--3)

per year for Ford, Krit, Chalmers, Studebaker, Cadillac and Buick. The company nearly quadrupled its capacity within three more years, leading to a buyout offer from General Motors. The brothers accepted, and in 1926 Fisher Body became an in-house division of GM.

Also on this day: **1894** – The first motor race in France was run between Paris and Rouen. The official victor was Albert Lemaitre in a Peugeot. **1942** – The US government began civilian gas rationing to meet the demands of fighting in WWII. **1961** – English race car driver and TV commentator Calvin Fish was born.

July 23, 2006
Cougar Ace and the Mazda mishap

On the night of July 23, 2006, the Singapore flagged cargo ship Cougar Ace was south of the Aleutian Islands heading from Japan to Vancouver, British Columbia. It was carrying a cargo of 4812 vehicles, including 4703 Mazdas, at a total value of $117 million. During an exchange of ballast water, the ship developed a 60-degree list to port, which may have been caused by a large wave striking the ship during the process. The next morning the crew of 22 had to be saved by the US Coast Guard and the Alaska Air National Guard. The ship was righted and pulled to Portland, Oregon for inspection and repair. Mazda initially reported minimal damage to "some" of the cars but by December Mazda announced it would scrap all of the vehicles. Each of the cars' airbags were deployed before being crushed on-site at the Port of Portland.

The Cougar Ace listing on July 24, 2006. *(Public domain)*

Also on this day:
1901 – Ransom E Olds received a patent for the Curved Dash body design. **1988** – The 1,000,000th Vauxhall Cavalier was sold. **1941** – American racing driver Richie Evans was born.

Vauxhall Cavalier, similar to the one millionth sold today in 1988. (Photo by Rob [253])

July 24, 1998
KIA goes to auction

After falling into bankruptcy with more than $10 billion in debt, KIA Motors was placed up for auction by the South Korean government on this day in 1998. Originally founded in 1944 as a producer of bicycle parts and steel tubing, KIA soon expanded and began manufacturing Korea's first domestic bike. It would move into licensed productions of numerous motorized vehicles, starting with Honda motorcycles in 1957. A few years later KIA was building Mazda licensed cars and light trucks, followed by Fiat and Peugeot models, and, in 1986, KIA formed a partnership with Ford. Following a massive economical crisis in Asia in 1997 the company floundered and was put up for the highest bid. Hyundai Motor Company outbid Daewoo and Ford to take ownership.

Also on this day: **1902** – A German patent was issued to Robert Schwenke for a front-wheel-drive system. **1980** – Ford opened the Batavia Transmission factory in Ohio, USA.

1998 Kia Besta 2.7d. (Photo by RL GNZLZ [254])

1998 Kia Clarus.
(Photo by RL GNZLZ [255])

July 25, 1959

Hovering over the English Channel

On this day in 1959, the 50th anniversary of Louis Bleriot's cross channel flight, the first practical hovercraft crossed the English Channel in just more than two hours. The vehicle was built by British aero- and marine-engineering company Saunders-Roe Limited, on the Isle of Man, and was dubbed SR-N1 (Saunders-Roe Nautical 1). Its first public viewing took place the previous month at a press showing, demonstrating its ability to cross land and water. The crew for the channel crossing consisted of Captain Peter Lamb, navigator John Chaplin and Christopher Cockerell, the inventor of the momentum curtain as applied to the hovercraft principle. The SR-N1 resides at the Science Museum at Wroughton.

Experimental Hovercraft SRN-1 during trials by the Royal Navy. circa 1963. (Photo courtesy of The National Archives, UK)

Also on this day: 1915 – Barney Oldfield set a 5 mile time record of 3:0162 minutes driving a Fiat. **1921** – Rickenbacker Motor Company was incorporated. **2004** – British racing driver Fiona Leggate completed five races in a 24 hour period at Silverstone, setting a record for most auto races driven in a single day by a driver.

1924 Rickenbacker Model C.
(Photo by Anackire [256])

July 26, 1998

Disaster strikes at Michigan Speedway

On lap 175 of 250 at the CART series US 500, on this day in 1998, Adrián Fernández hit the wall at Michigan International Speedway, causing a tire and suspension parts to break loose and fly into the crowd, resulting in the deaths of three fans. Two were killed instantly and another passed away moments after being severely injured. There were six other people who suffered minor injuries. The car driven by Fernández was traveling at upwards of 200mph (321km/h) when he impacted the wall. The race was placed

Adrián Fernández.
(Photo by Christian Madden [257])

The front stretch at Michigan International Speedway. (Photo by N8huckins [258])

under caution but was not stopped, much to the dismay of reporters covering the event. In an effort to prevent further tragedies the fencing was extended to 17 feet high around any grandstand areas.

Also on this day: 1916 – Studebaker introduced the Series 18. **1926** – Six months after sending a memo to Henry Ford recommending replacing the Ford Model T, Ford executive Ernest Kanzler resigned. **1932** – Frederick S Duesenberg died at age 56. **2003** – Ford produced its last car in the UK.

July 27, 1948
'Bentley Boy' Woolf Barnato passes away

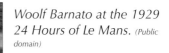

Woolf Barnato at the 1929 24 Hours of Le Mans. *(Public domain)*

On this day in 1948 British auto racer 'Bentley Boy' Woolf Barnato passed away at the age of 52. Barnato had a massive impact on the racing industry, and the continued success of Bentley. Using a large inheritance, he purchased a controlling share of the struggling Bentley Motors in the mid 1920s after falling in love with its racecars. Barnato began his racing career in 1921 when he imported a Locomobile from the US to race at the Brooklands Easter meeting. He would eventually find himself behind the wheel of a prototype Bentley 3-liter, a car that he fell in love with and led to his keen interest in the brand. Driving a Bentley, he entered and won 24 Hours of Le Mans three times, in 1928, 1929 and 1930, and he also participated in The Blue Train Races in France.

Also on this day: **1904** – The first Buick was sold to Dr. Hilbert Hills of Flint, Michigan. **1950** – The 5 millionth Oldsmobile was produced. **1990** – The final Citroën 2CV, which went into production in 1948, was produced.

1926 Speed Six Bentley. *(Public domain)*

July 28, 1973
Summer Jam at Watkins Glen

The scenic Watkins Glen Grand Prix Raceway hosted a record-setting crowd on this day in 1973. It wasn't a race that brought an estimated 600,000 people together, but a concert known as 'Summer Jam at Watkins Glen.' The size of the crowd meant that approximately one out of every 350 people in the US attended the concert, which hosted The Grateful Dead, The Band and the Allman Brothers Band. The secluded setting of the racetrack resulted in a scene similar to that at Woodstock four years earlier, including fans abandoning their cars on the long and windy country roads as far as

The Band, who played at Summer Jam at Watkins Glen, seen here in 1974 with Bob Dylan.
(Photo by Jim Summaria [259])

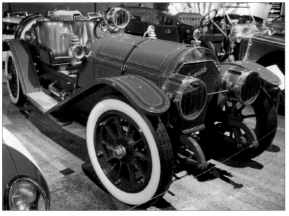

1916 Locomobile Speedster. *(Photo by Tony Hisgett [260])*

eight miles from the event. The US Grand Prix would take place at the track the following October, after an extensive cleanup.

Also on this day: **1922** – William C Durant took a controlling interest in Locomobile. **1924** – Italian race car driver Luigi Musso was born. **1973** – Gangsters Bonnie and Clyde's death car, a 1934 Ford V8, was sold at auction for $175,000.

July 29, 1909
General Motors buys Cadillac

When General Motors (GM) purchased Cadillac on this day in 1909 for $4.5 million in GM stock, Cadillac was already the top seller of luxury automobiles in the United States. Cadillac, born out of the ashes of Henry Ford's second attempt at starting a car company, was fueled by competition between Detroit machinist Henry Leland and Henry Ford. Leland participated in the founding of Cadillac in August 1902, and introduced the first model at the 1903 New York Auto Show. To build the debut Cadillac, a Ford chassis and an Oldsmobile engine were used. Leland took full control of the company in 1904, after Cadillac produced an astounding 2500 vehicles in its first year of production. GM founder William C Durant persuaded Leland to sell him Cadillac, promising to keep him and Leland's son in their management positions, leaving them in full control of production.

Also on this day: **1916** – The Nash Motor Company was founded in Kenosha, Wisconsin. **1973** – Roger Williamson was killed at the Dutch Grand Prix after his car careened into the wall at high speeds.

1910 Cadillac Touring. (Photo by FD Richards [261])

1920 Nash Touring 631. (Photo by Jack Snell [262])

The 1898 Winton advertisement, as seen in Scientific America.

July 30, 1898
The first auto ad

Scientific America released a new edition on this day in 1898; contained within its pages was the very first magazine advertisement for an automobile. Winton Motor Carriage Company, based in Cleveland, Ohio, ran the ad asking readers to "Dispense with a horse, and save the expense, care and anxiety of keeping it. To run a motor carriage costs about ½ cent a mile."

Within two years, Winton would be operating the largest automotive manufacturing facility in the US to produce its expensive cars. The company remained successful until the early 1920s, when sales began to fall. The decline is often attributed to the company's lack of development in style and engineering, which led to the company shutting its doors in 1924.

Also on this day: **1928** – The Chrysler Corporation purchased Dodge Brothers for $170 million from Dillon Reed & Company. **1954** – Lister Cars was founded in Cambridge, England by George Lister.

Lister cars was founded on this day in 1954. The Lister Jaguar seen here was built for the 1958 Race of the Two Worlds, held at Monza.
(Photo by Jason Goulding [263])

The Lunar Roving Vehicle in action on the moon during the Apollo 15 mission. (Public domain)

July 31, 1971
A lunar buggy

In a truly out of this world event, astronauts David Scott and James Irwin became the first people to drive an automobile on a martian surface on this day in 1971, during the Apollo 15 NASA mission to the moon. The Lunar Roving Vehicles (LRV) were used during the final three Apollo missions to the moon, 15, 16 and 17, allowing astronauts to cover greater distances in order to survey and collect surface samples. However, the astronauts were restricted to distances that they could walk back, should the LRV break down. The electric powered LRVs had an approximate top speed of 8mph (13km/h), but during the Apollo 17 mission astronaut Eugene Cernan recorded a top speed of 11.2mph (18.0km/h), giving him the unofficial land-speed record for the moon. All three of the LRVs remain on the lunar surface.

Also on this day: **1911** – Mason Motor Company was founded in Flint, Michigan. **1960** – Atlanta Motor Speedway opened. **1981** – The final Corvette was produced in St Louis, before production moved to Bowling Green, Kentucky.

Eugene Cernan drives the LRV during the Apollo 17 mission. (Public domain)

August 1, 2007

I-35 bridge collapses during rush hour

At 6:05pm on this day in 2007, traffic was moving exceptionally slow during the evening rush across the eight-lane I-35 bridge in Minneapolis, Minnesota. The excessive load caused by the bumper-to-bumper gridlock was cited as one cause of the sudden collapse of the central span of the bridge into the Mississippi River. This triggered adjoining segments of the bridge to fall as well. Following an investigation into the crumbling of the 40-year-old structure, the National Transportation Safety Board also blamed too-thin gusset plates, which ripped along a line of rivets. Nearly 150 people were injured and 13 were killed as cars fell as far as 115 feet. It was Minnesota's third busiest bridge, carrying more than 140,000 cars per day.

Cars that were on the bridge when it collapsed remained in the wreckage for some days. They were numbered as part of the investigation. (Photo by Kevin Rofidal)

Minneapolis Mayor R T Rybak surveys the damage.
(Photo by Kevin Rofidal)

Also on this day: **1922** – Hungarian inventor Donat Banki, 63, died. He developed the carburettor for the stationary engine. **1947** – Ferdinand Porsche was released from a French prison after serving jail time for war crimes. **1997** – The Ford Puma was introduced in the UK.

August 2, 1987

A new speed record at Marlboro 500

Michael Andretti in 1991.
(Photo by Stuart Seeger [264])

On this day in 1987 Michael Andretti set the average speed record for an entire Indy race, coming to a first place finish at the Marlboro 500 at the Michigan International Speedway with an average speed of 171.490mph (275.986km/h). Michael Andretti made his debut on the Indy circuit three years earlier, quickly becoming a top competitor. In racing to his quick win at the 1987 Marlboro 500, Andretti benefited from his legend of a father Mario Andretti's bad luck. When Mario's engine failed after building a two-lap lead, Michael was able to overtake him. Michael then held off Al Unser Sr and Bobby Rahal over the final

Michael Andretti at the 1993 European GP at Donington.
(Photo by Martin Lee [265])

94 laps to win. Unser finished 9.11 seconds after the winner, edging out Rahal for the number two spot. Rahal held the previous speed record for an Indy race, winning the 1986 Indianapolis 500 with an average speed of 170.722mph (274.750km/h).

Also on this day: **1937** – Raymond Mays won the JCC International Trophy at Brooklands driving an ERA. **1964** – The Saab V4 was introduced. **1985** – The 100,000th Rolls-Royce was manufactured, a Silver Spur saloon in royal blue.

August 3, 1900
Firestone Tire & Rubber

On this day in 1900 Harvey Firestone organized Firestone Tire and Rubber Company in Akron, Ohio. The company's mission was to manufacture pneumatic tires for wagons and buggies, but Firestone soon saw the immense possibilities surrounding the emerging automobile market. Leveraging a friendship with Henry Ford, Firestone became the Ford Motor Company's original equipment supplier of tires in 1906, sealing the rubber company's early success. In 1979 Firestone found itself more than a billion dollars in debt. A new president, John Nevin, the ex-head of Zenith Electronics, was brought in to try and save the company. He closed nine of Firestone's 17 manufacturing plants, and in 1988 he negotiated a sale to Bridgestone Tires.

Also on this day: **1958** – English race car driver Peter Collins died. **1960** – Lee Petty and his sons Richard and Maurice competed against each other for the first and only time. The race took place at Dixie Speedway in Birmingham, Alabama. Richard finished second, Lee placed third and Maurice took eighth.

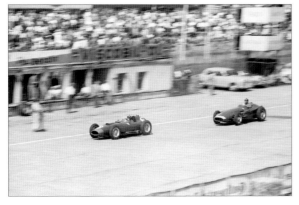

Harvey Firestone, far left, with Christian, Thomas Edison and Henry Ford, who is fishing. Library of Congress reproduction number LC-USZ62-104977 (public domain)

Peter Collins leads Juan Manuel Fangio during the 1957 German Grand Prix in a Ferrari 801. He would die at the same event on this day the following year. (Photo by Willy Pragher [266])

August 4, 1928
DeSoto gets moving

Walter Chrysler aimed to secure a slice of competition in the mid-priced automarket, when he founded DeSoto on this day in 1928. The brand debuted for the next model year, selling more than 81,000 units – a record for first year sales that stood until 1960. Chrysler also added Dodge and Plymouth to its line-up in 1928, and originally priced Dodge slightly higher than DeSoto. In an attempt to boost Dodge sales in 1933, the two flip-flopped, proving

1929 DeSoto Series K dashboard. (Photo by David Berry [268])

1929 DeSoto Series K. (Photo by David Berry [267])

almost catastrophic for DeSoto in the following years, as it received Chrysler Airflow bodies on its shorter wheelbase. The design was not popular with consumers, and DeSoto struggled until the introduction of the Airstream in 1935. Desoto flourished in postwar America but an economic downturn in 1958 sent Chrysler executives scrambling when sales plummeted. The company's answer was to kill the marque, an announcement it made less than two months after the introduction of the 1961 models.

Also on this day: **1956** – Wilhelm Herz became the first person to drive a motorcycle at speeds faster than 200mph, when he was clocked at 210mph in Wendover, Utah. **1963** – John Surtees drove a Ferrari to his first Formula One victory, the German Grand Prix.

August 5, 1914

The first electric traffic signal

On this day in 1914, the American Traffic Signal Co held a lighting ceremony for the first electric traffic light system in the world to control multiple traffic streams. Installed at East 105th Street and Euclid Avenue in Cleveland, Ohio, USA, the Municipal Traffic Control System utilized four sets of red and green lights with a buzzer that warned when the color was going to change, and was based on a design by James Hoge. The lights were mounted on corner posts and wired to a central control room, operated by a sole individual. It was configured in a way that made conflicting signals impossible and allowed for police and fire stations to control the signals during emergency situations.

Also on this day: **1899** – The Detroit Automobile Company was organized. **1923** – Ford began offering tours of its River Rouge plant. **1955** – The one millionth Volkswagen Beetle was manufactured, painted gold for the special occasion.

A manned electric traffic signal in Detroit, circa 1920. (Photo courtesy Library of Congress, Detroit Publishing Company Collection, reproduction number: LC-DIG-det-4a27913, public domain)

Ford's River Rouge Plant, seen here in 1927. (Photo courtesy Library of Congress, Detroit Publishing Company Collection, reproduction number: LC-DIG-det-4a25915, public domain)

August 6, 1991

Peugeot leaves North America

As sales of Peugeot automobiles, as well as many other European automakers, slumped in the US and Canada in the late 1980s and early 1990s, the company tried to remain competitive by introducing the 405. It proved unsuccessful, selling less than 1000 units. When total Peugeot sales only hit 4261 in 1990, and 2240 between January and July of the following year, the company decided to pull out of the US and Canadian markets after 33 years, an announcement it made on this day in 1991.

1991 Peugeot 405 SR. (Photo by RL GNZLZ [269])

1991 Peugeot 205 XS. (Photo by Riley [270])

Also on this day: **1907** – The Imperial Motor Car Company was founded in Jackson, Michigan. **1959** – Chevrolet registered the Corvair name. **1965** – The first Ford Transit was manufactured in Berkshire, England.

August 7, 1926
The British GP

The inaugural British Grand Prix took place at Brooklands on this day in 1926. Organized by racer Henry Segrave, the event played host to teams from around the world. When the checkered flag dropped, it was a Delage 155B driven by Frenchmen Louis Wagner and Robert Sénéchal at the finish line. Brooklands, the first purpose built automobile racetrack in the world, would host the event again the following year, before the British Grand Prix was halted for more than two decades. It returned three years after the end of WWII at Silverstone, and was hosted at two other racetracks before Silverstone became the lone venue for the race in 1987.

Also on this day: **1935** – The one millionth General Motors vehicle was manufactured. **1937** – The last Cord left the factory, marking the end of Auburn Automobile Company. **2001** – Ford and Navistar formed the Diamond Truck Company.

The winning car of the inaugural British Grand Prix was a Delage 155B, seen here at the 1926 San Sebastian Grand Prix with driver Robert Benoist. (Public domain)

August 8, 1934
Record setting production

In a record setting time of just six years, Plymouth was able to hit the one million vehicle production mark, with number one million leaving the factory on this day in 1934. The woman who purchased the very first Plymouth in 1928, Ethel Miller of Turlock, California, was invited to exchange her current Plymouth for the new landmark car. She drove her 'first' Plymouth to the Century of Progress Exposition in Chicago, where she traded it for the new four-door Deluxe. Miller would also own the two millionth Plymouth.

Jackie Ickx at practice for the 1974 British Grand Prix. (Photo by John Pease [271])

Also on this day: **1938** – Ford registered Mercury as a trademark. **1975** – The final Fiat 500 was manufactured. **1986** – The last episode of the TV show *Knight Rider*, featuring a talking Pontiac Firebird named KITT, was aired. **2004** – Jeff Gordon became the first four-time winner of NASCAR's Allstate 400 at the Brickyard.

1934 Plymouth, similar to the one millionth produced.
(Photo by Bernard Spragg [272])

Production of the original Fiat 500 lasted from 1957 until this day in 1975. (Photo by Surreal Name Given [273])

August 9, 1918

Halt order for US automakers issued

The US government issued an announcement to automakers on this day in 1918, stating all civilian auto production must be halted by January 1, 1919, in order to shift to military manufacturing for World War I. When the new year rolled around the car companies began to produce shells, ambulances and staff vehicles. Many race car engine manufacturers were contracted to build light and powerful motors for aircraft. The cohesion of the US auto industry, as well as those in Europe, greatly assisted in the allied victory of the war.

Also on this day: 1944 – French race car driver Patrick Depailler was born. **1990** – Al Unser Jr set a world record for a 500 mile race when he finished the Michigan 500 with an average speed of 189.727mph.

French racecar driver Patrick Depailler was born on this day in 1944. He is seen here driving at Nürburgring in 1970.
(Photo by Lothar Spurzem [274])

August 10, 1907

Peking to Paris

On January 31, 1907 the Paris newspaper *Le Matin* put out a challenge to prove to the world that the automobile was indeed a great machine. The paper read, "What needs to be proved today is that as long as a man has a car, he can do anything and go anywhere. Is there anyone who will undertake to travel this summer from Peking to Paris by automobile?" On June 10, 1907, an Itala, Spyker, Contral and two DeDions, each manned by a driver and a journalist, left Peking (now Beijing) to embark on a 9317 mile race across untamed lands.

In 2010 an Itala recreated the winning run of 1907. (Photo by Adam Singer [275])

When this Dearborn, Michigan Ford plant was originally built in 1918 it built Eagle Boats for WWI. It would eventually manufacture Model As and Mustangs. (Photo courtesy Library of Congress, reproduction number HAER MI-356-1, public domain)

Kirov, Russia is home to this sculpture of the Itala driven by Prince Scipione Borghese in the original Peking to Paris race.
(Photo by Ylitvinenko [276])

On this day in 1907 the first team crossed the finish line in Paris. It was the Itala, driven by Prince Scipione Borghese, accompanied by journalist Luigi Barzini, Sr. The grand prize was a magnum of Mumm champagne.

Also on this day: 1872 – The British Government passed legislation against being drunk and in charge of carriages, horses, cattle or steam engines. Penalties ranged from a fine not exceeding 50 shillings to one month imprisonment. **1938** – Vaclav Klement, co-founder of what is now Skoda Auto, died at age 70.

Peking to Paris Auto Race, Peking, China, 1907. (Photo restored by Ralph Repo)

August 11, 1966
Hello, Camaro

It is possible that a typo in an English-French translation dictionary is responsible for the name Camaro. The first production model of Chevrolet's new Ford Mustang competition left the factory on this day in 1966, officially going on sale the following month. The car was announced at a live press conference hosted by Chevrolet General Manager, Pete Estes, who revealed Chevrolet chose to keep with its current trend of naming cars with C words, such as the Corvair, Chevelle, Chevy II and Corvette. After unveiling the Camaro name Estes was asked, "What is a Camaro?" He quaintly responded that it was a small, vicious animal that eats Mustangs. However, two other Chevrolet executives found the name in a translation book from the 1930s, which gave the definition of the non-existent French word as friend, pal or comrade.

Also on this day: **1914** – The first automobile speed trials were held at Bonneville Salt Flats in Utah. **1956** – Artist Jackson Pollock died at age 44 after crashing his vehicle while under the influence of alcohol. **1975** – British Leyland was nationalized.

1967 Chevrolet Camaro RS-SS.
(Photo by Jack Snell [277])

Interior of 1967 Chevrolet Camaro convertible.
(Photo by Greg Gjerdingen [278])

August 12, 1916
Climbing Pikes Peak

In the early 20th century, Spencer Penrose took it upon himself to redevelop a narrow carriage road that climbed Pikes Peak in Colorado, into a wider highway acceptable for automobile travel. In order to promote the new roadway he sponsored the Pikes Peak Hillclimb automobile race, which began August 10, and ended two days later on this day in 1916. At the end of the event Rea Lentz, in his Romano Eight, received the first Penrose Trophy. The annual race is 12.42 miles

A Porsche GT2 RS at the 2011 Pikes Peak Hill Climb.
(Photo by Jasen Miller, [279])

(19.99km) long and puts drivers through 156 turns while climbing 4720ft (1440m). Parts of the track remained gravel, until it was fully paved in 2012. As of 2017, the course record stands at 8:13.878 minutes, set by Sébastien Loeb driving a Peugeot 208 during the 2013 competition.

Also on this day: **1933** – US Formula One driver and team owner Rufus 'Parnelli' Jones was born. **1947** – The Renault 4CV went into production. **1988** – *Tucker: The Man & His Dream*, a feature film about car designer Preston Tucker, premiered in US theaters.

One of two Lexington racecars that placed first and second in the 1920 race, circa 1921. (Photo courtesy National Photo Company glass negative)

August 13, 1898

No car like your own car

James Packard was likely quite excited when he purchased a Winton Automobile on this day in 1898, as it was just the 12th one produced. Unfortunately, he found himself dissatisfied with the purchase, and went directly to Alexander Winton with suggestions for improvement. His complaints went unanswered, and Winton in fact challenged Packard to do better. Packard took him up on the dare and rolled out his first automobile on November 6, 1899, in Warren, Ohio. Originally branded as the Ohio Automobile Company, with the models called Packards, the company name was officially changed to Packard Motor Car Company in 1902.

Also on this day: **1907** – New York City's first metered taxicab went into business. **1971** – Bentley founder Walter Owen Bentley died at age 82.

Willistead Concours 1903 Packard. (Photos by jodelli [280], [281])

"Indianapolis Motor Speedway, greatest race course in the world." 1909 advertisement for Indianapolis Motor Speedway.
(Photo © Otis Lithograph Co, NY, 1909).

August 14, 1909

Wheels at Indy

On this day in 1909 the first motorized race at Indianapolis Motor Speedway was held. The day at the track consisted of seven motorcycle races organized by the Federation of American Motorcyclists. It was originally supposed to be a two-day, 15 race event but the second day was canceled after concerns about the track surface, as many of the bikes had their tires popped due to the gritty finish that covered the track. At the end of the first race it was Erwin 'Cannonball' Baker at the top of the podium.

Also on this day: **1921** – The first race was held at Cotati Speedway in Santa Rosa, California; it was won by Eddie Hearne driving a Duesenberg. **1977** – Alan Jones won his first Grand Prix, the Austrian Grand Prix, driving a Shadow DN8.

Alan Jones during practice for the 1985 European Grand Prix. He won his first GP on this day in 1977. (Photo by Jerry Lewis-Evans [282])

August 15, 1938
Nicola Romeo departs

In 1911, Italian Nicola Romeo started a company that manufactured mining machines and equipment. Ing Nicola Romeo e Co was soon quite successful, leading to further entrepreneurial adventures for Romeo. He purchased a majority share of Milan based A.L.F.A. (Anonima Lombarda Fabbrica Automobili) in 1915, and three years later owned it outright, changing the name to Anonima Lombarda Fabbrica Automobili Romeo. The first car badged as an Alfa Romeo to come off the assembly line was the Torpedo 20/30 HP. Romeo would depart from the car company in 1928, and from the world on this day a decade later.

Also on this day: **1927** – Eddie Rickenbacker purchased the Indianapolis Speedway for $700,000. **1973** – British motorcycle designer Edward Turner died at age 72. **1982** – Jock Taylor, Scottish motorcycle sidecar racer, was killed during the Finnish Grand Prix.

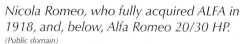

Nicola Romeo, who fully acquired ALFA in 1918, and, below, Alfa Romeo 20/30 HP. (Public domain)

August 16, 1906
Mason Motor Cars

The first Mason Motor Car rolled off the assembly line on this day in 1906. Financed by Edward Mason, and designed by brothers Fred and August Duesenberg, the Mason was advertised for its strength and fuel efficiency, claiming the Duesenberg engineered two-cylinder engine could carry the car 475 miles on 18 gallons of gasoline. In 1910, washing machine magnate Frederick Maytag purchased the company, and the cars were badged as Maytags. Mr Maytag's adventures in the auto industry ended two years later when he sold his interest in the company, and the autos were then reverted back to being called Masons. By 1917, the business was bankrupt and shuttered.

A 1910 Maytag C. Mason Motor Cars became Maytag-Mason Motor Company that year. (Photo by Greg Gjerdingen [283])

HARVARD UNIVERSITY

Also on this day: **1937** – Harvard University in Cambridge, Massachusetts became the first US university to offer courses in traffic engineering and administration. **1984** – Automotive executive John DeLorean was acquitted of drug trafficking. **2004** – General Motors began producing Cadillacs in China.

Harvard University, as seen here in Richard Rummell's 1906 watercolor, became the first US university to offer courses in traffic engineering and administration, stating on this day in 1937. (Courtesy of Arader Galleries, public domain)

123

August 17, 1896
First pedestrian killed by a car

On this day in 1896, Bridget Driscoll unfortunately made her way into the history books by becoming the first pedestrian to be hit and killed by a car in the United Kingdom. As Driscoll and her teenage daughter May, and her friend Elizabeth Murphy, crossed Dolphin Terrace in the grounds of the Crystal Palace in London, an automobile belonging to the Anglo-French Motor Carriage Company struck her. One witness described the car as travelling at "a reckless pace, in fact, like a fire engine." The driver, Arthur James Edsall of Upper Norwood, was brought to trial for the death of Driscoll. The jury returned a verdict of 'accidental death,' after an inquest lasting some six hours, and no prosecution was made. The coroner, Percy Morrison said he hoped "such a thing would never happen again."

Also on this day: 1904 – The Ford Motor Company of Canada was established. **1968** – Clessie Cummins, founder of Cummins Engines Co, died in California. **1985** – Three time F1 World Champion Niki Lauda announced his retirement.

Anglo-French vehicles were based on the Benz, such as this 1896 model. (Photo by the 216 [284])

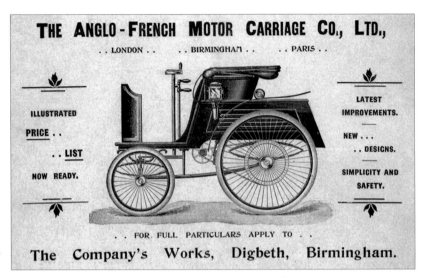

Advertisement for Anglo-French Motor Carriage Co, the company that owned the vehicle which killed Bridget Driscoll. (Public domain)

A 1957 Vanwall, as driven by Stirling Moss. (Photo by Supermac1961 [286])

August 18, 1957
A British win for Moss

Formula One driver Stirling Moss placed first at the Pescara Grand Prix in a Vanwall 57 on this day in 1957. This Grand Prix was the only Formula One World Championship held at the track, and it was the first of two consecutive Italian races, as the next race was at Monza, marking the first time that two F1 World Champion races took place in the same country in the same year. The 25km (16 mile) course is now part of a highway along the coast of Pescara.

Also on this day: 1955 – The Saab 93 was introduced. **1962** – Brothers Ahmad and Mahmoud Khayami founded Iran National to produce automobiles.

Stirling Moss exiting an airplane in Copenhagen in 1958. (Photo by SAS Scandinavian Airlines [285])

August 19, 1958
The last car to bear the Packard name

The 1956 merger between Studebaker and Packard left the latter struggling to maintain the exclusivity it once held in the American auto market. A recession in the 1950s, along with heavy competition from Ford, General Motors and Chrysler, resulted in a massive decline in sales. The last true Packard came off the assembly line in June 1956, but the name was carried over onto rebadged Studebakers for more than two years. Packard, once the favorite of movie stars and millionaires, had become another cheap car with an even cheaper face-lift. It was on this day in 1958, the once prominent Packard name was finally let go as the last car to wear the badge left the factory.

1958 Packard Hawk. (Photo by Greg Gjerdingen [287])

1958 Packard. (Photo by Greg Gjerdingen [288])

Also on this day: 1934 – The first All-American Soap Box Derby was held in Dayton, Ohio; it was won by Robert Turner. **1959** – Radar was used for the first time to convict someone of speeding. **2001** – Michael Schumacher won his fourth World Championship. **2003** – The Shmuel HaNavi bus bombing, a suicide attack, killed 23 people in Jerusalem.

August 20, 1970
A step up for Triumph

Triumph launched its small economy car, the 1500, on this day in 1970. The front-wheel drive auto was a replacement to the 1300 model, and featured an updated interior, larger engine and restyled body. The 1493cc motor made the 1500 capable of reaching a top speed of 87mph (140km/h), and gave it a 0–60mph time of a whopping 16.5 seconds.

It entered the market at £2441, and remained in production until October 1973, when it was replaced by the 1500TC, a similar car that was reworked to a rear-wheel drive configuration.

Immaculate Triumph 1500. (Photo by Sludge G [289])

Also on this day: 1939 – Bremgarten in Switzerland hosted the last major Grand Prix before the outbreak of WWII. **1941** – The last personal Ford was manufactured in Britain before production was shut down due to the war effort. **2000** – The Saleen S7, an American supercar, debuted.

The Saleen S7, which made its debut on August 20, 2000. (Photo by Simon Davison [290])

August 21, 1903
'Thank God, it's over'

On this day in 1903, the first United States transcontinental automobile race came to an end when Tom Fetch concluded the drive to San Francisco, 63 days after he had left New York City. He drove a 1903 Packard Model F, which became just the second car to make the cross-country trip. Horatio Jackson and Sewall Crocker had completed a similar journey less than a month earlier. Fetch had been hired by Packard investor Henry Joy to participate in the journey, to prove that American-made cars could "negotiate the all but impassible mountain and desert roads and trails of the Far West." The Packard was stripped of its fenders, outfitted with extra gas tanks, and had an additional low gear installed for crawling up mountains. The car, nicknamed Old Pacific, also carried a pick, shovel, canvas and chains to get the car through the rough terrain. When addressing the crowd in San Francisco after his arrival, the first thing Fetch had to say was "Thank God, it's over."

Also on this day: 1947 – Ettore Bugatti, founder of the company that bears his name, died at age 65. **1991** – Al Teague set a wheel driven speed record at the Bonneville Salt Flats when he hit 432.692mph (696.331km/h).

Top: The 1903 Packard Model F, nicknamed 'Old Pacific,' and below: rear view of the same car. (Photos by Rain0975 [291] and Joe Ross [292])

August 22, 1902
A presidential journey

Theodore Roosevelt became the first sitting President of the United States to ride in an automobile, when he rode in a Columbia electric car during a parade in Hartford, Connecticut, on this day in 1902. Roosevelt made it known that he strongly preferred horse and carriage, but would occasionally travel by car throughout his presidency.

Also on this day: **1910** – The first official trials of the Elgin Automobile road course began, just outside of Chicago. **1937** – Mercedes finished 1-2-3 at the Swiss Grand Prix at Bremgarten. **1967** – The AMC Javelin debuted, going on sale the next month as a 1968 model.

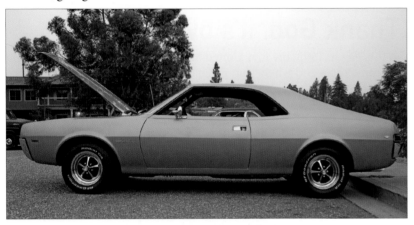

1968 AMC Javelin. (Photo by Nick Ares [293])

August 23, 1922
Chitty Bang Bang takes first place

On this day in 1922, Chitty Bang Bang won the Southsea Speed Carnival in England. The vehicle was built and driven by Count Louis Zborowski, with help from his engineer, Clive Gallop. Zborowski reached 73.1mph (117km/h) during the race in his chain-driven, customized Mercedes that featured a 23-liter, six-cylinder Maybach aero-engine. This was the first car known as Chitty Bang Bang, but

Count Zborowski with Chitty Bang Bang 1 at Brooklands, circa 1921.
(Illustration by Brian Corey, based on original photo in public domain)

While this isn't the first car he rode in, President Theodore Roosevelt did make use of automobiles throughout his presidency, such as during this 1910 parade. (Photo by HG Moon, public domain)

The original Chitty Chitty Bang Bang car built for the movies based on Ian Fleming's novel of the same name. (Photo by Martin Pettitt [294])

three more would be built by Zborowski and Gallop at Zborowski's home near Canterbury, Kent. These cars would later inspire a book, movie, and musical all by the name of *Chitty Chitty Bang Bang.* The Chitty 1 debuted at Brooklands in 1921, where it took second place and hit a top speed of 100.75mph (162.5km/h) with a four-seater body. It was refitted with a two-seat configuration, and received an upgraded exhaust system, propelling it to a top speed of more than 120 mph (193km/h).

Also on this day: **1913** – Personal motor vehicles were for the first time officially allowed inside Yosemite National Park in California. **1953** – Alberto Ascari won the Swiss Grand Prix, locking in his second consecutive World Drivers' Championship.

August 24, 1944
Birth of a hot rodder

American hot rod designer and constructor Boyd Coddington was born on this day in 1944, in Idaho, USA. In his early 20s, he moved to Southern California, where he built hot rods by day and worked as a machinist at Disneyland at night. His custom cars quickly gained popularity, and in 1977 he opened his own shop, Hot Rods by Boyd, in Cypress, California. In 1989 Boyd was commissioned by ZZ Tops's Billy Gibbons to build CadZZilla, a custom 1949 Cadillac, which is often referred to as one of his most immaculate builds, and is acclaimed as one of the greatest expressions of automotive customization. The auto editors of *Consumer Guide* praised it as "The first really new type of custom since the heyday of the 1950s." After a lifetime of awards for his numerous creations, Boyd passed away in 2008 following complications from a recent surgery.

Also on this day: 1945 – The last M-24 tank built by Cadillac left the factory. **1967** – Automobile executive Henry J Kaiser died at age 85. **2015** – English Indy racer Justin Wilson died of injuries received in a crash during the ABC Supply 500 at Pocono Raceway the day before.

August 25, 1921
6 cylinder Love

Starring Ernest Truex, June Walker, Donald Meek and Ralph Sipperly, *6 Cylinder Love* opened at the Sam H Harris Theatre in New York City on this day in 1921, becoming the first play that centered completely around the automobile. The comedy focused on one family's purchase of an expensive automobile, and the adventures, and misadventures, which followed. The play stayed on Broadway through July 1922, before becoming a silent movie in 1923, and a talking picture in 1931.

Also on this day: 1927 – Lucy O'Reilly became the first American woman to participate in a Grand Prix race, when she drove her Bugatti to a 12th place finish at the Baule Grand Prix in France. **1991** – Michael Schumacher made his Formula One debut at Spa.

Boyd Coddington, right, signs autographs for fans in 2005, alongside his wife, Jo, on board the USS Nimitz. (Public domain)

One of hot rodding's greatest treasures, Cadzilla, built by Boyd Coddington. (Photo by Brian Corey)

Michael Schumacher at Eau Rouge 2011. Schumacher made his F1 debut at the Belgian Grand Prix on this day in 1991.
(Photo by Paul Williams [295])

LOVE WORKS FAST WHEN CUPID STEPS ON THE GAS
WILLIAM FOX *Presents*
ELMER CLIFTON PRODUCTION
6 CYLINDER LOVE
with ERNEST TRUEX
From the biggest stage success in twenty years by William Anthony McGuire

Poster for the 1923 film 6 Cylinder Love.

August 26, 1959
Introducing the Mini

Due to Egypt's communist ties and its nationalization of the Suez Canal in 1956, much of Europe was facing massive fuel shortages. In response, Sir Leonard Lord, head of British Motor Corporation (BMC), set out to build a small, fuel efficient car to compete with the German cars that currently controlled the market. His efforts led to BMC launching the Mark I Mini on this day in 1959. When development began in 1957 it took place under a veil of secrecy. Code named ADO 15, for Austin Drawing Office, the car was ready for approval in just two and half years. Lord signed off on the car and it soon began to roll off production lines with a price tag equivalent to just $800. Originally badged as the Austin Seven and the Morris Mini-Minor, by 1962 it was known simply as the Mini. Production of the original Mini continued through to 2000, putting more than 5.3 million of them on the road.

Also on this day: **1935** – John North Willys, founder of Willys-Overland Motor Company, died at age 61. **1940** – The final LaSalle was built. **1985** – The Yugoslavian Yugo was introduced in the USA.

A 1959 Morris Mini-Minor. This particular car was the first Mini off the production line to be badged Morris. It was never sold, and is now kept at the British Motor Museum, Gaydon, UK. Photographed at the Gaydon Mini Festival 2007. (Photo by DeFacto [296])

1959 Morris Mini-Minor interior. (Photo by DeFacto [297])

August 27, 1859
Black gold in Pennsylvania

Edwin Drake discovered the first successful oil well in the United States, initiating the original oil boom in the country. While oil had been found previously while digging water wells, Drake Well, located in Cherry Township, Pennsylvania, was dug specifically for oil, and led directly to massive investment in oil drilling, refining and marketing. To reach the black gold, Drake dug three feet per day, and hit the 69.5ft mark on this day in 1859. Initially there were no promising signs of oil, but when he returned the next day he found the hole was full of crude oil. The well began producing 12 to 20 barrels of oil per day, but due to the resulting boom, and the massive drop in the price of oil, this well was never particularly profitable.

Portrait of Edwin Drake.
(Public domain)

Also on this day: **1912** – Thomas Willby began the first trans-Canada automobile journey. **1987** – AJ Foyt set a new closed-course speed record when he hit 257mph in an Oldsmobile Aerotech. **2006** – Felipe Massa won the Turkish Grand Prix, marking his first Grand Prix win.

Replica of original engine house and derrick at the Drake Well Museum in Titusville, Pennsylvania. (Photo by Niagara [298])

August 28, 2008
An American champion

Phil Hill, the only American-born racecar driver to win the Formula One World Drivers' Championship, died on this day in 2008 at the age of 81. Hill made his F1 debut at the 1958 French Grand Prix behind the wheel of a Maserati. That same year he would win his first of three 24 Hours of Le Mans. The next season Hill joined Ferrari, landing on the podium three times. In 1960 he earned his first win at the Italian Grand Prix, the first American to win a Grand Prix race in almost four decades. His success continued in 1961, when he won the World Drivers' Championship. During his career he would also win three 12 Hours of Sebring races, before retiring from the driver's seat in 1967. After leaving the track he and a partner started a classic car restoration business, and he also became a TV personality and automotive journalist.

Phil Hill driving a Ferrari 250 at the 1958 12 Hours of Sebring.
(Photo by C5813 [299])

Hill driving a Ferrari at the 1962 German Grand Prix.
(Photo by Lothar Spurzem [300])

Also on this day: **1898** – Goodyear Tire and Rubber Company was founded. **1951** – The 1000th Porsche was completed. **2008** – The first American to win the Formula One World Championship, Phil Hill, died at age 81.

August 29, 1885
The first motorcycle?

The development of technology builds on existing success, not failure. With that idea in mind, on this day in 1885, Gottlieb Daimler and

Replica of the Daimler Reitwagen. (Photo by Brian Corey)

Wilhelm Maybach received a patent for the Daimler Reitwagen, often regarded as the first motorcycle. There is some controversy over whether or not it is actually the first motorcycle, as there were creations built prior that featured motorcycle-like characteristics. For example, the Montrice Pia, a child's tricycle fitted with an internal combustion engine in 1882 by Enrico Bernardi. Other prospects include the Michaux-Perreaux steam velocipede, and Roper steam velocipede. The Daimler Reitwagen had auxiliary stabilizers, a wood beam frame, rear drum brakes and a 264cc four stroke, single cylinder engine. The original bike was destroyed in a fire in 1903.

Also on this day: **2004** – Michael Schumacher secured his 5th consecutive, and 7th overall F1 Drivers' Championship following a second place finish at the Belgian Grand Prix.

Close up of the engine and rear wheel of the Daimler Reitwagen replica. (Photo by Brian Corey)

August 30, 1980
On the Road Again

American driving anthem *On the Road Again* entered the Billboard 100 music charts on this day in 1980, coming in at number 78. Willie Nelson wrote the Grammy-winning song on a barf bag on an airplane, after movie director Jerry Schatzberg and executive producer Sydney Pollack requested him to come up with a tune for an upcoming film Nelson was to star in. The movie, *Honeysuckle Rose*, was about an aging country music star that had yet to achieve the fame he dreamed of. The character spent much of his time on the highway, playing show after show. After being asked to write a song, Nelson asked what it was to be about, to which the producer responded, "Can it be something about being on the road."

Also on this day: **1926** – General Motors, New Zealand began operations in Petone. **1945** – Hudson produced its first post-WWII vehicle, a green Super Six coupé. **2002** – The final Rolls-Royce was built at the Crewe Factory in Cheshire.

Willie Nelson in 2009. (Photo by Bob Tilden [301])

August 31, 1869
First automobile related death

Mary Ward, first person to die in an automobile related accident.
(Public domain)

On this day in 1869, Mary Ward sadly made her way into the history books as the first person killed in an automobile accident. Mary, her husband Henry, Richard Biggs, and her cousins Richard and Charles Parsons, who built the experimental automobile they were travelling in, were riding through the Irish countryside near present day Birr. During the drive Mary was tossed from the car and run over as the vehicle went around a bend, killing her almost instantly. A doctor near the scene found her cut and bleeding from the ears. Further observation discovered she had also suffered a broken neck.

Also on this day: **1937** – The final Ford Model Y is produced in Great Britain. **1956** – The Oldsmobile Golden Rocket show car debuted.

1946 Hudson coupé, similar to the first post-WWII vehicle produced by Hudson on this day in 1945.
(Photo by Alberto from Spain [302])

The Oldsmobile Golden Rocket show car debuted on this day in 1956. (Public domain)

September 1, 1903
License plate #1

New York State was the first state in the Union to require automobile license plates, beginning in 1901. However, the law required that the automobile owner fashion their own license plate, which was to include their initials to indicate ownership. Massachusetts became the first state to issue pre-made license plates, starting on this day in 1903 when Frederick Tudor received a blue license plate with white lettering, that read "1." Other states soon followed suit, and by 1918 all US states were distributing mandatory automobile license plates.

1909 Massachusetts license plate.
(Photo by Jerry 'Woody' [303])

Also on this day: **1941** – The 1942 DeSotos were introduced, which featured Airfoil headlights that were hidden when not in use. **1956** – The Volvo Amazon was introduced.

September 2, 1959
Ford Falcon flies high

For much of the first half of the 20th century, the Big Three of General Motors, Ford and Chrysler focused on building large, elaborate vehicles. The late 1950s witnessed a styling shift when small imports

A 1960 Ford Falcon. (Photo by Greg Gjerdingen [304])

A Kissel Kar with Massachusetts license plate.
(Photo courtesy Library of Congress, LC-USZ62-40544)

from Volkswagen, Toyota, and others began to see increasing sales in the USA. In order to adapt, American automakers put focus on building small cars that consumers would likely buy as a second vehicle, such as the Ford Falcon. The driving force behind the Falcon was Ford General Manager Robert McNamara, who quickly pushed the project from concept to production to ensure that Ford could compete with imports and new American models, such as the Plymouth Valiant and Chevrolet Corvair. Introduced on this day in 1959, and sold in America from 1960 to 1970, the Falcon carried Ford into the age of the second car in the driveway. The Falcon was manufactured in Argentina until 1991 and the last Ford Falcon was produced in Australia in 2016.

Also on this day: **1994** – The National Corvette Museum opened in Bowling Green, Kentucky, where the Corvette is manufactured.

The dashboard of a 1960 Ford Falcon. (Photo by Brian Corey)

September 3, 1875
The very beginning of Porsche

International Motorsports Hall of Fame member, and 'Car Engineer of the 20th Century,' Ferdinand Porsche, was born on this day in 1875 in current day Czech Republic. Porsche's automotive career started long before the sports car company that bears his name was founded. By age 25 he co-created the Lohner-Porsche Mixte, an electric-gas hybrid manufactured between 1900 and 1905. During military service in his late 20s he served as a chauffeur to Archduke Franz Ferdinand of Austria, whose assassination would ignite WWI a decade later. Following his service, he worked for Austro-Daimler and Mercedes as a designer. He would later be recruited by the Nazi party to put Germany on wheels, giving birth to the Volkswagen Type 1. In 1939 Porsche built his Type 64, considered by many to be the first car of the yet-to-be Porsche Company. The first car badged as a Porsche, the 356, was developed in postwar Germany, becoming the first car of present day Porsche.

The Lohner-Porsche Semper Vivus was the first hybrid vehicle ever built, and one of Ferdinand Porsche's earliest automotive creations. This is a replica of that vehicle. (Photo by Autoviva [305])

The Lohner-Porsche hybrid with Ferdinand Porsche at the controls in 1900. (Public domain)

Also on this day: 1895 – Duryea Motor Wagon Co was incorporated. **1976** – The Ford Fiesta was officially launched. **2012** – Hong Kong-owned National Electric Vehicle Sweden acquired bankrupt Saab in order to sell electric vehicles under the brand.

Porsche quickly gained a following with the introduction of the 356. This 1963 model is a 356 B; the 356, 356 Pre A, 356 A, 356 B and 356 C, were all produced during between 1948-1965. (Photo by Brian Corey)

1936 SS Jaguar 100. (Photo by David Merrett [306])

September 4, 1922
A cat is born

When motorcycle enthusiasts William Lyons and William Walmsley founded Swallow Sidecar Company on this day in 1922, they hadn't mentioned any intentions of getting into the automobile business. As the sidecar company expanded, they purchased a large building that provided them with ample space to offer auto repair, painting and upholstery work, and would later add coach building to their services. The first car they designed that sold in high quantities was the Austin 7, introduced in May 1927. In 1934, Walmsley bought his way out of the business, and with the money Lyons founded SS Cars Limited. The next year, the name SS Jaguar appeared on one of the company's new cars. On March 23, 1945, shareholders agreed to change the company's name to Jaguar Cars Limited.

Also on this day: 1906 – Terry Stafford received a US patent for his three-speed progressive transmission. **1950** – The first 500 mile NASCAR race, the Southern 500, takes place, hosted by Darlington Raceway. **1980** – The White Motor Company filed for chapter 11 bankruptcy protection.

September 5, 1939
Overcoming disability

Swedish Formula One racer Clay Regazzoni was born on this day in 1939. He launched a successful racing career in 1970 when he landed a spot on the Ferrari team, after spending half a decade in Formula Two and Three. He earned his first F1 win at the 1970 Italian Grand Prix in Monza, Ferrari's home event. He regularly found himself on the podium over the next five years, until a crash at the 1980 United States Grand Prix West left him paralyzed from the waist down. Following his recovery, Regazzoni became well known for his role in helping other disabled people reach their full potential, and for climbing back behind the wheel. After earning back his racing license he participated in rally and sports car racing, paving the way for other disabled drivers.

Also on this day: **1948** – Ferrari made its Grand Prix debut at the Italian Grand Prix in Turin, finishing third. **1991** – Chrysler Chairman Lee Iacocca announced he would retire at the end of the year. **2006** – The BUB Seven hits 350.884mph, becoming the first two-wheeled streamliner to crack the 350mph barrier.

The BUB Seven hit 350.884mph on this day in 2006, becoming the first two-wheeled streamliner to crack the 350mph barrier. (Photo by cole24_ [308])

September 6, 1949
VW is German, again

Following WWII the allies assisted in putting the German people back to work to help them rebuild their country and economy, both ravaged by war. A large part of this effort involved getting manufacturing facilities, such as the British occupied Volkswagen plant at Wolfsburg, back up and running. The factory, which had been almost completely dismantled during the war, was operating again only a few months following the German surrender. Throughout the rest of 1945 about 1785 Type 1s were built, nearly all of which went to occupying forces. On this day in 1949, control of Volkswagen was placed back in the hands of the Germans, placing it under regulation of the West German government.

Also on this day: **1891** – Peugeot introduced its Type 3 quadricycle, the first automobile it marketed for sale to the public. **1951** – BMW introduced its first post WWII car, the 501, at the Frankfurt Motor Show.

Clay Regazzoni in a Ferrari 312B3 approaches Druids Hill Bend at the 1974 Race of Champions, Brands Hatch. (Photo by Martin Lee [307])

A view inside the Volkswagen factory in Wolfsburg, Germany, showing the assembly line in 1960. (Photo by Roger Wollstadt [309])

Old VW power plant at Wolfsburg. (Photo by mroach [310])

September 7, 1896
The American racetrack

The first organized automobile race on a track in the United States started so slow that people began to yell, "Get a horse." When seven vehicles took off from the starting line of the one mile long Narragansett Trotting Park dirt oval horserace track in Cranston, Rhode Island on this day in 1896 nearly 60,000 people looked on. The race was sponsored by automobile manufacturers in an attempt to draw interest to the new form of transportation, and the five mile "Providence Horseless Carriage Race" did just that. Quickly after the race began, Andrew Riker and his Riker Electric took the lead and maintained it throughout the race. He won with an average speed of 20 miles per hour (32 km/h). Second place was snagged by another electric car from Electric Carriage and Wagon Company and a Duryea Motor Wagon took home third.

Also on this day: 1946 – John Cooper drove a 500cc prototype Cooper to victory in the 850cc class at the Brighton Speed Trials, marking the first victory for Cooper vehicles. **1987** – Ford announced it acquired 75 per cent of Aston Martin.

1987 Aston Martin Lagonda. Ford acquired 75 per cent of Aston Martin on this day in 1987. (Photo by Staffan Vilcans [311])

A rare image of the first race at Narragansett Trotting Park. (Public domain)

The Rover Jet 1, the first gas turbine powered vehicle, which was introduced in 1949. (Photo by Oxyman [312])

September 8, 1963
An engineering master

Often regarded as one of the most forward thinking automotive engineers the industry had ever known, Maurice Wilks passed away on this day in 1963. Wilks started his engineering career with Hillman in 1922, spent two years with General Motors in the mid 1920s, then returned to Hillman before accepting a position as chief engineer at Rover Company in 1930. His accomplishments at Rover include the introduction of the first gas turbine automobile, and heading development of Land Rover alongside his brother Spencer. A series of promotions between the end of WWII and 1962 would lead to Wilks being named chairman of Rover, a position he held at the time of his death.

Also on this day: 1895 – Adam Opel, namesake of Opel automobiles, died at age 58. **1957** – Stirling Moss drove a Vanwall to victory at the Italian Grand Prix at Monza.

Land Rover Series 1. (Photo by Firing up the quattro [313])

September 9, 1982
No longer a family affair

On this day in 1982, Henry Ford II announced his retirement from all involvement with the Ford Motor Company, and formally stepped down the next month. Ford II, grandson of Henry Ford, was named president of Ford in 1945, two years after the death of his father Edsel. At the time Edsel passed away, Ford Motor Company was losing millions of dollars per month, and it was Ford II who saved the family business by reorganizing manufacturing processes and staff. He was instrumental in the introduction of the Thunderbird in 1955, and the Mustang in 1964, two of Ford's most successful models of the era. He also had a large role in the development of the Edsel, which turned out to be a major flop. Even still, his ability to serve at the top of the chain ensured Ford would remain as one of the Big 3.

Also on this day: **1901:** The first long distance automobile race in the US takes place between New York City & Buffalo, NY, a distance of 464 miles. **1954:** The first Ford Thunderbird comes off the assembly line. **2005:** Hein Wagner drove a Maserati Grandsport to a speed of 269km/h (167mph) in South Africa, becoming the world's fastest blind driver.

Henry Ford II with a 1957 Ford Thunderbird and a 1965 Ford Mustang, two vehicles for which he authorized production, and helped revive Ford following postwar losses. (Illustration by Brian Corey, based on public domain images)

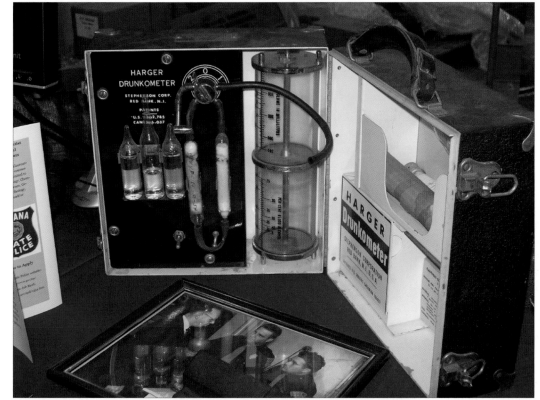

A Harger Drunkometer on display. (Photo by Kat [314])

September 10, 1897
Don't drink and drive

Any unlucky passenger of George Smith's London cab on this day in 1897 may not have received the safe transport they were looking for; instead they may have witnessed the first arrest for drunk driving of an automobile. Smith wasn't pulled over for swerving over the yellow line, no, he smashed his cab into the side of a building prior to being arrested. He pleaded guilty to driving under the influence of alcohol, and was fined 20 shillings. While Smith admitted his guilt, it wasn't until 1931 that police had a reliable, scientific way of testing a person to see if they were in fact drunk at the scene, thanks to the Drunkometer, invented by Rolla Harger. This device would evolve into the modern breathalyzer.

Also on this day: **1900** – The Coppa Florio (or Florio Cup) was an automobile race first held in Italy as the Coppa Brescia on this day. **1910** – William C Durant lost control of General Motors for the first time. **1950** – Jimmy Jackson set a diesel land speed record in the Cummins Special, hitting 165.23mph (265.9km/h)

135

September 11, 1970

It's a Pinto

Ford's answer to the influx of foreign subcompact cars was the Pinto, introduced to the masses on this day in 1970. More than 3 million were produced between model years 1971 and 1980, but it wasn't the revolutionary rack-and-pinion steering that put it in the headlines. The explosive news coverage the car received throughout the 1970s can be attributed to an ill-placed gas tank, allegedly causing the car to burst into flames when rear-ended at speeds above 20mph. An investigation found Ford knew of the problem and failed to fix it, following an internal cost-benefit analysis of a recall versus paying potential lawsuits. That analysis estimated fixing the recalled vehicles would total

1971 Ford Pinto. (Photo by Greg Gjerdingen [315])

$137 million, while it was assumed lawsuits wouldn't top $50 million, making repairs inefficient. When news of the report broke a massive uproar followed, and Ford ended up having to pay $128 million to a single claimant.

1980 Ford Pinto. (Photo by Mike [316])

Also on this day:

1903 – The Milwaukee Mile, a racetrack in Wisconsin, opened, with William Jones winning the first race.

Road Marker on the main road in Genoa, Nevada (Photo by FAHansson [317])

Below: September 1920 photo near the intersection of Broad Street and Northeast Boulevard in Philadelphia, looking down the Lincoln Highway.

(Public domain)

September 12, 1912

An ambitious plan

Carl Fisher and James Allison sought $10 million in funding to build the first transcontinental highway in the United States, a plan they first made public on this day in 1912. They envisioned a gravel roadway, stretching from New York City to San Francisco, a total of 3389 miles (5454km) crossing 13 states. After failing to get backing from Henry Ford, it appeared their dream roadway, may remain just that, a dream. An acquaintance brought forth the idea of naming the road after former President Abraham Lincoln, which would make the project eligible for a government grant. After putting together a proposal they received $1.7 million from the government and construction moved forward. The Lincoln Highway was officially designated on October 31, 1913.

Also on this day: **1918** – Erwin 'Cannonball' Baker finished a 77-day, 17,000-mile motorcycle journey, in which he visited all 48 US state capitals. **1963** – The NSU Wankel Spider, the first production car to be powered by a Wankel rotary engine, debuted at the Frankfurt Motor Show. **1989** – The Land Rover Discovery was introduced to the public at the Frankfurt Motor Show.

September 13, 1899
The death of Bliss

It was on this day in 1899 when Henry Bliss was exiting a streetcar at West 74th Street and Central Park West in New York City, that he was struck by an electric taxicab driven by Arthur Smith. The taxi crushed Bliss' head and chest, causing him to pass away from his injuries the following morning, making him the first person to die in an automobile related accident in the United States. Smith, who was shuttling Dr David Edson, the son of former NYC mayor Franklin Edson, was charged with manslaughter, but he was later acquitted as he was found to have no malice and was not negligent. A century after his death to the day, a plaque was dedicated at the location of the incident, commemorating Bliss and promoting safety on the streets.

Henry Bliss was the first person killed in an automobile related accident in the United States.
(Public domain)

Also on this day: 1969 – Talladega Superspeedway opened in Alabama. **1977** – Oldsmobile introduced the diesel models 88 and 98. **1986** – Japanese racing driver Kamui Kobayashi was born.

Talladega Superspeedway, seen here from above in 2007, first opened on this day in 1969 with the name Alabama International Motor Speedway.
(Public domain)

September 14, 1960
OPEC is formed

Representatives from Iran, Iraq, Kuwait, Saudi Arabia and Venezuela gathered in Baghdad to form the Organization of the Petroleum Exporting Countries (OPEC), on this day in 1960. OPEC's mission includes the stabilization of oil markets and to coordinate petroleum policies of member countries, while providing a regular supply of oil to consumers and a steady income for producers. As of 2017, OPEC is made up of 13 countries from Africa, South America and the Middle East.

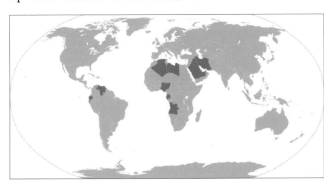

Highlighted areas identify member countries of the Organization of the Petroleum Exporting Countries. (Public domain)

Also on this day: 1914 – FWD sold its first fire truck to the Minneapolis, Minnesota fire department. **1965** – TV comedy *My Mother the Car* premiered on NBC. **1982** – Grace Kelly, AKA Princess Grace of Monaco, died of injuries from a car crash that occurred after she suffered a stroke while driving.

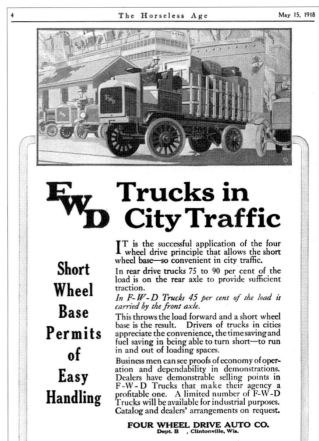

1918 FWD advertisement from The Horseless Age. FWD sold its first truck on this day in 1914.

September 15, 1909

A most important lawsuit

George Selden received an 1895 US patent for the gasoline automobile, making himself eligible to receive royalties from all automakers in the country, without manufacturing any vehicles himself. Selden founded the Association of Licensed Automobile Manufacturers (ALAM) in 1903, to provide a simple way for automakers to pay royalties to himself and his associates. After Henry Ford was denied entry to ALAM, likely due to distressed former business partners who held rank at ALAM, he went forth to build automobiles anyway. He was quickly served with a lawsuit from Selden. Nearly six years later, on this day in 1909, the court ruled in favor of Selden, but Ford immediately filed an appeal. He argued his case on the fact that Selden's patent referenced a Brayton cycle engine, while Ford used an Otto cycle engine. On this evidence Ford won the appeal, effectively ending Selden's monopoly on the auto industry.

Also on this day: 1924 – American racing champion Jimmy Murphy died at age 29 following an accident during a race in Syracuse, New York. **1938** – Brit John Cobb piloted the Napier Lion W-12 Railton Special to 353.30mph, establishing a new land speed record while becoming the first person to break the 350mph barrier. **1965** – The 10 millionth Volkswagen Beetle was manufactured.

1965 Volkswagen convertible. VW produced its 10 millionth Beetle on this day in 1965.
(Photo by Karen Roe [319])

Selden's workshop, which no longer stands, was located behind this house in Rochester, New York's Grove Place Historic district.
(Photo by Daniel Penfield [318])

September 16, 1908

General Motors is established

William C Durant founded General Motors (GM) on this day in 1908 as a holding company. In the beginning GM held only the Buick Motor Company, as Durant was its current owner. Within just a few years GM would acquire more than 20 companies, including Oldsmobile, Cadillac, Cartercar, Reliance Motor Truck Company and Oakland, which later became Pontiac. A deal to purchase Ford in 1910 for about $8 million was approved by the GM board, but Durant was unable to gain

William C Durant, who founded General Motors, circa 1927 with his wife. (Photo courtesy Library of Congress, reproduction number, LC-USZ62-101530, public domain)

GM Renaissance Center, GM World Headquarters, in Detroit, Michigan.
(Public domain)

financing for the purchase, in part due to the massive debt he had already accrued from other acquisitions. This was a decisive factor in Durant's removal from his position at the top of the company. He would later regain control as part of a deal to have GM purchase Chevrolet, a company he co-founded in 1911. As of 2017, General Motors automobiles are built under the brands Vauxhall, Buick, Cadillac, Chevrolet, GMC, Holden, Opel, and Wuling.

Also on this day: 1938 – Less than a day after John Cobb set the landspeed record George Eyston broke it, reaching 357.5mph in his Rolls-Royce powered Thunderbolt. **2007** – Fernando Alonso and Mark Webber both started their 100th Grand Prix at the Belgian Grand Prix. They finished third and seventh, respectively.

September 17, 1909
Ed Cole, automotive giant

Automotive Hall of Fame member and longtime GM executive, Ed Cole, was born on this day in 1909 in Marne, Michigan. Cole got a taste of engineering as a youngster, building and selling homemade radios. He was later accepted to the General Motors Institute where his schooling would earn him a leadership role with GM during development of the 1949 Cadillac V8. His next big project was creating a replacement for the Stovebolt Six engine; his answer was the highly successful small block V8 that would be used for decades to come. He followed this up with a charge in the compact car market, bringing the Corvair to fruition. A series of promotions would land Cole as President of GM in 1967, where he led efforts to wean GM cars off leaded gasoline, before retiring in 1974.

Ed Cole co-led development of the 1949 Cadillac 331 cu in V8, landing in cars such as the Series 62 Convertible. (Photo by Jack Snell [320])

The first Chevrolet small block, built in 1954, a 265 cu in V8.
(Photo by John Lloyd [321])

Also on this day: 1974 – British Motor Corporation debuted the Vanden Plas 1500. **2004** – Jaguar moved production from Coventry to the former Spitfire factory in Castle Bromwich.

September 18, 2004
A compact Bimmer

To replace the 3 Series Compact, BMW forged the new 1 Series, with initial design work attributed to Canadian filmmaker Christopher Chapman. The 1 Series shares as much as 60 per cent of its components with the E90 3 series, as the two were developed at the same time. The 1 series made its public launch in Europe on this day in 2004 as a five-door hatchback, providing a lower cost entry into the BMW market while moving the 3 Series into a higher bracket. By 2008, the 1 Series laid claim to as much as 20 per cent of BMW's sales.

Also on this day: 1948 – The Goodwood racing circuit in West Sussex, England hosted its first race meeting. **1958** – Austin debuted the A40 Farina.

2005 BMW 120i. (Photo by RL GNZLZ [322])

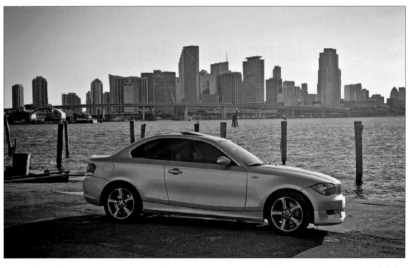

BMW 128i. (Photo by Dan [323])

September 19, 1887

The numbers on the pump

On this day in 1887, Dr Graham Edgar, developer of the octane rating system, was born in Fayetteville, Arkansas. During the pioneering era of the automobile it was impossible to tell if gasoline would cause engine knocking, due to non-standard refining processes and the use of multiple types of fuels within engines. The only real way to find out if a particular fuel would work in a car was to fill it up and turn the crank. In 1926, while working for a division of General Motors, Edgar solved this issue by developing the octane rating system. He found that the chemical isooctane would not knock in any engine, under any operating conditions, while n-heptane would always knock in any engine. By mixing isooctane and n-heptane in different amounts, he was able to create fuels of all qualities. The percentage of isooctane in the mixture is the octane number read on the fuel pump.

Also on this day: **1916** – The final three races held at Indianapolis Motor Speedway until the end of World War I took place on this day, and were all won by Johnny Aitken. **1932** – Ab Jenkins finished the first recorded solo 24-hour drive behind the wheel of a Pierce-Arrow V12 at the Bonneville Salt Flats. He covered 2710 miles.

Gas pump showing octane ratings of 85, 87 and 91.
(Photo by Susan Dussaman [324])

Lee Iacocca seen at Ellis Island (NY/NJ) in September 1990. (Photo by Ron Cogswell [325])

Johnny Aitken, winner of the final three pre WWI races at Indianapolis on this day in 1916, is seen at Sheepshead Bay Speedway the previous May.

September 20, 1979

Iacocca joins Chrysler

In the late 1970s, Chrysler was on the verge of going out of business, losing millions of dollars every month. After automotive executive Lee Iacocca, who was responsible for many iconic vehicles and successful marketing ploys at Ford, including the Mustang, was fired from Ford, Chrysler Corporation strongly courted him. Iacocca accepted the challenge of saving Chrysler on this day in 1979. Shortly after taking the chairman role, Iacocca approached the US government, asking for, and securing, a bailout of $1.5 billion. The loan came with certain stipulations for Chrysler, such as abandoning its turbine engine project, which was nearly production ready after more than 20 years of development. The cash infusion led to the development of the highly successful K-cars like the Dodge Aries and Plymouth Reliant, and later

1963 MGB Roadster. The MGB was introduced on this day in 1962.
(Photo by David Merrett [326])

Iacocca would introduce the Plymouth Voyager and Dodge Caravan, thus saving Chrysler from an almost certain death.

Also on this day: **1952** – John Fitch won the Seneca Cup race at Watkins Glen, New York driving a Jaguar XK120C. **1962** – MG launched the MGB. **2003** – The first production Invicta S1, one piece carbon fiber bodied sports car was sold.

September 21, 1973
The Mustang II

The Mustang II officially launched in showrooms across America on this day in 1973, as a 1974 model. As the first generation Mustang grew larger in the late 1960s, executives at Ford saw it losing its customer base, as a major draw of the original Mustang was its compactness. In order to better compete with small imports, such as the Toyota Celica and Datsun 240Z, as well as domestic subcompacts like the Pontiac Sunbird and Chevrolet Monza, a Mustang based on the small Ford Pinto was developed. Introduced just prior to the 1973 oil crisis, the redesigned, fuel-efficient Mustang was the right car, at the right time, selling more than one million units over four years. It also helped set a precedent for downsizing American muscle throughout the domestic auto industry.

Also on this day: **1873** – Ferenc Szisz, the winner of the first Grand Prix, the 1906 Grand Prix at Le Mans, was born. **1903** – Auto executive Preston Tucker was born. **1935** – Dealers got a first look at the 'coffin-nosed' Cord 810. **1945** – Henry Ford II succeeded his grandfather Henry Ford as president of Ford Motor Company.

1974 Ford Mustang II.
(Photos by RL GNZLZ, [327], [328])

September 22, 1893
Ditching the horse in America

On this day in 1893, brothers Frank and Charles Duryea debuted the first operational personal automobile in the United States on the streets of Springfield, Massachusetts. In the first attempt the car came to a sudden halt after just a few hundred feet, as the belt transmission failed. Frank made a slight adjustment to the design and the car was driven more than half a mile later in the day. Following further trials the brothers launched the Duryea Motor Wagon Company in 1896, producing 13 identical vehicles. This was the first time a US business made multiple copies of an automobile, and placed them for sale.

Also on this day: **1903** – Packard opened its new factory in 1903. **1955** – The BMW 507 was unveiled to the public at the Frankfurt Motor Show. Only 252 would be manufactured. The MGA was introduced at the same show.

The first gas-powered buggy built by Charles E and Frank Duryea.
(Photo courtesy of Library of Congress, reproduction number LC-USZ62-41591)

141

September 23, 1972
End of an era

The Crystal Palace circuit, a motor racing circuit in Crystal Palace Park in south London, England, saw its final professional organized race on this day in 1972. Club events would continue through 1974 before the track closed for good. A motorcycle race opened the circuit in 1927, which featured the use of existing pathways around the lake. The first London Grand Prix was held at the circuit on July 17, 1937 and was won by Prince Bira in his ERA R2B, with an average speed of 56.5mph (90.9km/h). Later that year, the BBC broadcast the International Imperial Trophy meeting here, making it the first televised motor racing event.

Also on this day: **1921** – The Maybach W3 debuted at the Berlin Motor Show. **1968** – The Triumph GT6 MkII went on sale. **1969** – Rally champion Tapio Laukkanen was born.

September 24, 1948
Here comes Honda

In 1937 Soichiro Honda founded a company to produce piston rings, soon winning a contract to manufacture the part for Toyota. During WWII one of Honda's factories was bombed, and the other collapsed in an earthquake in 1945. Honda sold off salvageable parts and machinery to Toyota, and used the funds to start the Honda Technical Research Institute in 1946. This led to the development of a motorized bicycle, which was moved by Honda's first mass-produced engine. These achievements would result in the incorporation of Honda Motor Company on this day in 1948.

Also on this day: **1921** – Fritz Von Opel drove an Opel to victory at the first race at the AVUS circuit in Germany. **1954** – The Routemaster bus was introduced to the public by London Transport at the Commercial Motor Show. **1998** – Jaguar opened its official heritage museum in Coventry.

A section of the former Crystal Palace Circuit, as seen in 2005. (Photo by Christopher Hilton [329])

1969 Triumph GT6 MkII, the MkII went on sale on this day in 1968. (Photo by Andrew Bone [330])

1949 Honda D-Type, the first motorcycle produced by Honda, starting in 1949. (Photo by Rikita [332])

Classic Hondas at the Honda Collection Hall, Twin Ring Motegi. (Photo by Kzaral [331])

September 25, 1913
Ford crosses the Pacific

Ford Motor Company expanded its global reach on this day in 1913 when a contract was signed by Ford to sell Model Ts in China. Ford's sales agency soon shipped its first Model T to China, thus beginning the company's commercial ties to the Eastern land. A decade later Chinese leader Dr Sun Yat-sen wrote a letter to Henry Ford, asking him to help the growing nation build a new industrial system. While Ford didn't make a trip across the Pacific Ocean for that specific reason, his company did establish a sales and service office in Shanghai in 1928, which remained open until the onset of WWII.

Also on this day: **1860** – The supercharger was patented by brothers Francis and Philander Roots. **2005** – Fernando Alonso became the youngest F1 World Drivers' Champion at the age of 24 years and 58 days.

A Ford Model T at the Shanghai Auto Museum. (Photo by emperornie [333])

Fernando Alonso, who became the youngest F1 World Drivers' Champion to date on this day in 2005, is seen here at the 2012 Canadian Grand Prix. (Photo by Nic Redhead [334])

September 26, 1957
A tiny little car

French scooter and automobile manufacturer ACMA was thrilled with its new car and wanted to ensure its debut was not missed. Directors invited three well known racing drivers to the launch of the Vespa 400 microcar on this day in 1957, ensuring many members of the press attended the event, which was held in Monaco. The two seater, with an optional rear cushion for children, had a rear-mounted 393cc two-stroke motorcycle engine, that required drivers to mix oil in with the gas, every time they refueled their car – an issue believed to have hurt sales figures. Following the high-profile launch, more than 12,000 of the vehicles sold in its first year on the market, a number that decreased to just 8717 the following year. Production of the Vespa 400 ended in 1961, as sales continued to slump despite lowering prices.

Also on this day: **1903** – Mercedes was officially registered as a trade name by Emil Jellinek. **1965** – The Mini Marcos was entered in its first race. Driver Geoff Mabbs took the car to victory at Castle Combe. **2002** – Nils Bohlin, Swedish inventor of the three point safety belt, died.

1959 Vespa 400.
(Photo by Phil Kalina [335])

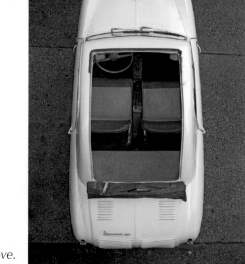

1960 Vespa 400 from above.
(Photo by hell0094 [336])

September 27, 1925
Building Nürburgring

On this day in 1925, construction began on the Nürburgring racing circuit in Nürburg, Rhineland-Palatinate, Germany. The motorsports complex features a Grand Prix track built in 1984, and has a crowd capacity of more than 150,000 people. When completed in 1927, the track could be situated in four configurations for different types of racing. The first races took place on June 18, 1927 for motorcycles with sidecars, and Toni Ulmen won the race on an English 350cc Velocette. Rudolf Caracciola won the first car race in the 5000cc class in a Mercedes Compressor the next day.

Also on this day: **1986** – Clifford Lee Burton, bass player for Metallica, died when the band's tour bus crashed in Sweden.

Jaguar E-Types racing during the 2011 Oldtimer Grand Prix at Nürburgring. (Photo by Marco Verch [337])

September 28, 1949
Small car, big name

Jowett Cars debuted its first and only sports car, the Jupiter, on this day in 1949 at the London Motor Show. The Jupiter was designed in just four months by Austrian engineer Dr. Robert Eberan von Eberhorst, and Jowett's own body stylist Reg Korner. About 900 Jupiters were produced before production ended in 1954, but not before achieving great success in auto racing. The flat-four 1486cc powered Jupiters would take class wins at the 1950 24 Hours of Le Mans, and the 1951 Monte Carlo International Rally, an overall win in the 1951 Lisbon International Rally, and a class one-two win in the public road race at Dundrod in Northern Ireland in September 1951.

Also on this day: **1923** – BMW debuted the 500cc R32 motorcycle to the public. **1926** – Ford opened a sales office in Alexandria, Egypt. **1954** – The Austin Cambridge was introduced. **2002** – The Paris Motor Show hosted the new Mini Cooper.

FIA Masters Historic Formula One at Nürburgring in 2016. (Photo by Stephan Wershoven [338])

Interior of a 1953 Jowett Jupiter. (Photo by Andrew Bone [339])

1951 Jowett Jupiter. (Photo by RL GNZLZ [340])

September 29, 1913
A most mysterious death

Rudolf Diesel earned an engineering degree before beginning work in refrigeration and engine development. During the course of his work he invented a compression-ignition engine, for which he received a patent. Diesel was last seen alive aboard a steamship sailing from Dresden to Antwerp on this day in 1913. When a steward came to alert Diesel for a 6:15 am wake up call the next morning he was nowhere to be found. His bed was not slept in and his room was neatly organized. After his body was found, it was discovered that Diesel had emptied his bank accounts and left the cash with his wife before his trip. Another interesting note was that a cross had been drawn in his diary under September 29. While suicide is thought to be the plausible reason behind his death, some believe bad business dealings could have been motive for murder.

Also on this day: **1965** – The Aston Martin DB6, capable of 150mph, went on sale. **1987** – Henry Ford II died at age 70.

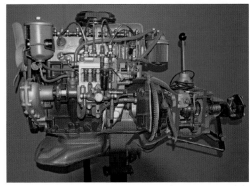

Diesel engine cutaway. (Photo by I, Luc Viatour [341])

Rudolf Diesel's 1893 patent for his engine design.

September 30, 1955
James Dean and the mystery Porsche

Actor James Dean had just finished filming for the movie *Giant* and was on his way to Salinas, California to make a return to auto racing. During his drive, on this day in 1955, he was pulled over for speeding in his Porsche 550 at about 3:30 in the afternoon. Less than two hours later he was roaring along the highway once again when a 1950 Ford Tudor pulled out in front of him. Dean was unable to stop in time and slammed into the Ford. The collision killed him instantly and seriously injured his passenger, while the driver of the Ford walked away with only minor injuries. The wrecked Porsche soon became a thing of legend. After a tow truck driver handling the wreck was seriously injured, and another driver installed the totaled 550's engine in a different Porsche, then crashed and was killed, many started to believe Dean's car was cursed. Roger Barris took the car on tour in the 1960s, and following a show circuit it was being transported back to LA in the back of a sealed truck. Upon arrival it was discovered the car was gone, and to this day its location remains a mystery.

Also on this day: **1935** – The one millionth Oldsmobile was manufactured. **1937** – Duesenberg ended production of motor cars. **1998** – The Paris Motor Show celebrated its 100th anniversary.

Wax figure of James Dean at Madame Tussauds Hollywood.
(Photo by Loren Javier [342])

1954 Porsche 550 Spyder, similar to the car James Dean died in. (Photo by Jim Bauer [343])

October 1, 1908

The first Model T

The automotive world forever changed on this day in 1908, when the first Ford Model T came off of the assembly line. The Model T, or Tin Lizzy as it came to be known, introduced the middle class to the luxuries of an automobile. As Henry Ford said of the Model T, "I will build a car for the great multitude," and he did. The Model T would remain in production relatively unchanged until 1927, with more than 15 million produced around the world.

Also on this day: 1908 – Ford opened a sales office in Paris, France. **1925** – Dodge Brothers purchased 51 per cent of Graham brothers, and the remaining 49 per cent the following May. **1931** – Ford began production at the Dagenham Plant in east London, the largest factory in Europe at the time.

1908 Ford Model T on display in 1908.
(Photo courtesy Library of Congress collection)

Interior of a 1908 Model T. (Photo by Jack Snell [344])

October 2, 1959

Air-cooled American

The only mass-produced, air-cooled, rear-engine American car was introduced to the public on this day in 1959. The Chevrolet Corvair aimed to be an affordable commuter that would compete with the Volkswagen Beetle and other compacts being introduced by foreign and domestic automakers at the same time, including the Ford Falcon and Plymouth Valiant. The Corvair was a far cry from anything else coming out of Detroit in that era. Aside from its unusual running gear, the Corvair possessed no tailfins or chrome in its grille and rode on low profile tires. The car was championed by Chevrolet General Manager Ed Cole, who made the cover of *Time* magazine, along with the car, just days after it debuted. After winning Car of the Year for 1960 from *Motor Trend*, the Corvair would be surrounded by controversy, in part due to handling concerns brought forth in Ralph Nader's book *Unsafe at any Speed*, before being discontinued in 1969.

Also on this day: 1902 – The Ohio Automobile Company was renamed the Packard Motor Car Company. **1935** – Rolls-Royce debuted the Phantom III. **1949** – Lee Petty drove a Plymouth coupé to his first NASCAR victory at Heidelberg Speedway just outside of Pittsburgh, PA.

Engine of a 1960 Chevrolet Corvair. (Photo by FD Richards [345])

1960 4-Door Corvair Sedan 700 Series.
(Photo by FD Richards [346])

October 3, 1929
The Peugeot 201

The Peugeot 201 was introduced at the Paris Motor Show on this day in 1929, becoming the first Peugeot to feature a zero in the middle of its model number. The small, inexpensive car would carry the automaker through the economic depression that gripped the world, following the collapse of Wall Street in the same month that the 201 debuted. While Peugeot introduced its first gas-powered automobile in the 1890s, the 201 is often referred to as the company's first mass produced model. Originally featuring an efficient 23hp engine, by the time production ended in 1937, the cars were puttering down the street with a 35hp straight four.

Also on this day: **1935** – Peugeot introduced the 402 at the Paris Motor Show. **1967** – Triumph launched the TR5. **1990** – Clarence Avery was inducted into the Automotive Hall of Fame for his design of the first moving automotive assembly line, which was utilized by Ford.

Peugeot 201. (Photos by substantie [347], [348])

October 4, 1983
Setting land speed records

If you were in the Black Rock Desert in Nevada, USA, on this day in 1983, you would not find yourself at the Burning Man festival, but you may have witnessed the land speed record being broken by the British-built Thrust 2. The jet-propelled car was designed by John Ackroyd, and driven by Richard Noble, hitting a top speed of 650.88mph (1047km/h). The record was listed at 633.46mph (1019.45km/h), as that was the average of two runs held within one hour, per regulations of the record. The vehicle was powered by a single Rolls-Royce Avon jet engine from an English Electric Lightning fighter plane from the Cold War era. The land speed record set by Thrust2 was not beaten until 1997, when Royal Air Force pilot Andy Green managed an average speed of 714.144mph (1149.303km/h) driving the ThrustSSC. A second run less than a month later upped the record to 763.035mph (1227.986km/h), where it stands as of 2017.

Thrust SSC, the car used by Richard Noble to break the speed record he set in Thrust2. (Photo by steve p2008 [350])

Also on this day: **1928** – The first Mercedes-Benz with a straight 8 engine, the Nürburg 460, was introduced at the Paris Motor Show. **1946** – American race car driver Barney Oldfield died at age 68. **1973** – Chevrolet unveiled two mid-engined, Corvette prototypes that were equipped with rotary engines.

Thrust 2 at the Coventry Transport Museum. (Photo by David Merrett [349])

October 5, 1919
Ferrari takes the wheel

In his first professional auto race, a young Italian by the name of Enzo Ferrari took fourth place in a hillclimb in Parma, Italy, on this day in 1919. Throughout his racing career, which lasted all of 47 races, Enzo took home 13 first place awards. It is believed he could have won more trophies, but his love for the automobiles prevented him from pushing them too hard. Perhaps that is the reason why he stopped racing cars in the mid 1920s – to pursue his passion for building them. In 1929 Ferrari formed the Scuderia Ferrari racing team in Modena, about the same time he took over as the head of Alfa Romeo's racing department. The first Ferrari badged car wouldn't appear until after WWII. The V12 powered Ferrari 125 Sport debuted May 11, 1947 at the Piacenza racing circuit. Four years later Ferrari would win its first Grand Prix, followed by a World Title the following year.

Enzo Ferrari speaking with reporters during the weekend of the 1967 Italian Grand Prix. (Public domain)

Also on this day: **1935** – The first Donington Grand Prix was held, marking the first Grand Prix race in Britain on a road track. **1955** – The Citroën DS19 launched after nearly 20 years of development. **1964** – The Lincoln Continental in which President John F Kennedy was shot was returned to presidential service after receiving armor plating and a bullet-proof hardtop. It was retired from service in 1978, and now resides at the Henry Ford Museum.

Racecar drivers Enzo Ferrari (far left), Tazio Nuvolari (4th) and Achille Varzi (6th) of Alfa Romeo, with Prospero Gianferrari (3rd) at Colle Maddalena (1930 or 1931). (Public domain)

Alfa Romeo 159 at the Nürburgring. (Photo by Lothar Spurzem [351])

October 6, 1910
Designed to win

The Alfa Romeo 158/159 race cars were entered in 54 Grand Prix races and won 47 of them, making the vehicles some of the most successful racecars to ever hit the track. Orazio Satta Puliga, born on this day in 1910, had just joined Alfa Romeo in 1938, when he was put to work as a designer on this revolutionary race car. Throughout his career he would be responsible for numerous Alfa Romeo designs, including the Alfa Romeo 1900, Giulietta and Giulia. Satta was promoted to Central Director in 1951, and then served as General Vice President between 1969 and 1973 before retiring.

Also on this day: **1940** – Frank Griswold drove an Alfa Romeo to victory at the World's Fair Ground Grand Prix, in Flushing, New York. **1960** – The Pontiac Tempest was introduced.

1955 Alfa Romeo 1900 SS Coupé Touring. (Photo by Andrew Bone [352])

October 7, 1948
Postwar Peugeot

Peugeot can trace its business heritage back to 1810, when the Peugeot company manufactured coffee mills and, later, bicycles. The lion logo would receive trademark status in 1858 thanks to Émile Peugeot. The first Peugeot automobile, a steam tricycle, was assembled in 1889, before a separate automobile company was founded by Armand Peugeot, who named it Société des Automobiles Peugeot. After surviving two world wars, Peugeot debuted its production model 203 on this day in 1948, at the Paris Motor Show, the company's first all new car in the postwar era. Featuring hemispherical cylinder heads, the unique 1290cc four-cylinder offered 41 horsepower. The car was a huge success in France, and by the end of 1950 it would be accountable for nearly 20 per cent of all domestic car sales.

Peugeot 203. (Photo by Ivan Rivera [353])

Also on this day:
1937 – The Renault Juvaquatre was publicly introduced.
1962 – The Ford Mustang I race car made a demonstration debut at the United States Grand Prix at Watkins Glen, New York.

1955 Peugeot 203 C. (Photo by Niels de Wit [354])

Tom Pryce racing at the 1975 US Grand Prix at Watkins Glen.
(Photo by rjb52 [355])

October 8, 1961
The USGP at Watkins Glen

It was a crisp fall day in Watkins Glen, New York, on this day in 1961, when Innes Ireland snagged the checkered flag at the United States Grand Prix. It was the first year the event took place at the picturesque raceway, which lies more than four hours from any major city. Ireland surprised many when he crossed the finish line first driving a Lotus-Climax, as it was his first championship-qualifying Grand Prix win. Ireland would find little success following the 1961 season, but remained an avid F1 competitor through 1966. He would go on to have

a career in journalism, before being elected as president of the British Racing Drivers' Club, a post he held at the time of his death in 1993.

Also on this day: 1960 – The Sheffield Tramway closed, which first went into service in 1873. **1961** – John D Hertz, founder of Hertz Rent-A-Car System, died in Los Angeles. **1978** – Mario Andretti clinched the Formula One World Championship.

Below: Turn 1 and S turn at Watkins Glen.
(Photo by Chris Waits [356])

October 9, 1992
Out of this world Chevrolet

Something out of this world happened on this day in 1992, when a meteorite struck a parked 1980 Chevrolet Malibu in Peekskill, New York. As thousands of people looked on, a meteor later discovered to be 4.4 billion years old lit up the sky over the East Coast of the United States. Upon hearing what 18-year-old Michelle Knapp described as a three car crash, she ran outside to discover a hole in the trunk of her Malibu. Her $300 car was soon worth $10,000 to a meteorite dealer. She was also able to sell the sulphur smelling, 26lb meteorite itself for $69,000 to a group of collectors.

Also on this day: **1953** – The Chrysler Corporation sold the Chrysler Building in New York. **1959** – The first phone call between an airplane and an automobile took place. **1997** – Alfa Romeo launched the 156 in Lisbon. **2007** – Marcos, a British sports car manufacturer announced it was ceasing production.

The Peekskill meteorite in the National Museum of Natural History.
(Photo by Wknight94 [357])

The Chrysler building in 1932. The building was the tallest in the world at the time it was finished. Chrysler Corporation sold it on this day in 1953. (Public domain)

October 10, 1946
Unimog helps rebuild Germany

As Germany began to rebuild after World War II, a need for a versatile agricultural vehicle became apparent. Albert Friedrich answered the call. He designed the Unimog, debuting the prototype on this day in 1946. He would attain a manufacturing agreement with Erhard und Söhne and the first production Unimogs would leave the assembly line the following year. Designed with equal size tires all the way around, a rear loading zone, a hitch and a front-mounted bracket, the vehicle was to be used by farmers in the field and on the highway. In 1951, Daimler-Benz took over the manufacture of Unimogs and began placing the Mercedes symbol on the front of the four wheel drive vehicles.

Also on this day: **1969** – The Mini Clubman was launched. **2006** – The Hummer H3 went into production.

The Mini Clubman, like this 1970 model, launched on this day in 1969.
(Photo by davocano [358])

1977 Mercedes Unimog. (Photo by Andrew Bone [359])

October 11, 1928
Long name, fast driver

Alfonso Antonio Vicente Eduardo Angel Blas Francisco de Borja Cabeza de Vaca y Leighton, Marquis of Portago, better known as Alfonso de Portago, was a Ferrari race car driver, Olympic bobsledder and stunt pilot from Spain, who was born on this day in 1928. One of his first transportation feats wasn't by land but by air, when the millionaire heir flew his plane beneath the London Bridge at age 17, winning a $500 bet. After meeting a US Ferrari importer in 1953, Alfonso began a successful racing career. He took first at many prestigious events, including the Tour de France automobile race, the Grand Prix of Oporto and the Nassau Governor's Cup. Alfonso and his co-driver were killed in a crash on May 12, 1957 during the Mille Miglia, after a tire blowout caused him to lose control and career into the crowd, resulting in the deaths of nine spectators.

Also on this day: **1932** – Mack Trucks patented its bulldog mascot, as designed by A F Masury. **1996** – Ford Motor Company purchased the naming rights to Detroit, Michigan's indoor American football stadium, dubbing it Ford Field.

Memorial to victims of Mille Miglia at the site of Portago's fatal crash.
(Public domain)

The Mack Trucks bulldog mascot was patented on this day in 1932.
(Photo by Sheila Sund [360])

October 12, 1868
Audi founder is born

An early Audi logo. *(Photo by Axel Schwenke [362])*

Audi founder August Horch was born on this day in 1868 in the village of Winningen, Rhenish Prussia. After receiving a degree in engineering, Horch worked for Karl Benz from 1896 until he founded A Horch & Co in 1899, in Cologne, Germany, desiring to build his own cars. Following a dispute with investors, Horch left his own company and set up a competing automaker, this time called Horch Automobil-Werke GmbH. Legal action brought by his former partners denied him use of the Horch name on his new vehicles, as it was still a registered trademark of the former company. Horch and his new financiers gathered at his home to discuss new names. Horch's son was studying Latin at the time, when

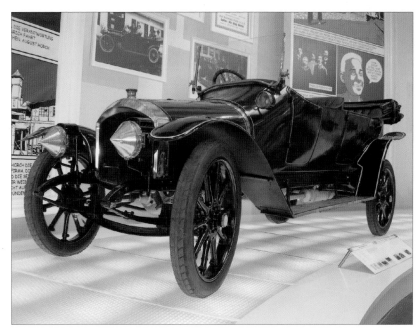

An Audi Type A, the first Audi vehicle, manufactured between 1910-1912.
(Photo by Bildergalerie [361])

he piped up with the suggestion Audi, the Latinization of Horch, both of which mean 'to listen.'

Also on this day: **1933** – Rover launched the model 10. **1948** – Morris Minor cars went on sale in Britain. **1993** – The one millionth Toyota Camry was manufactured.

October 13, 1916
GM incorporates

General Motors Company incorporated on this day in 1916, officially becoming General Motors Corporation and acquiring all stock from the former business. Founded by William Durant in 1908, GM quickly began to acquire numerous automobile companies, starting with Buick Motor Company the day after GM was founded. Oldsmobile, Cadillac, Cartercar, Elmore, Ewing and Oakland would all soon

The General Motors Renaissance Center in Detroit, GM's world headquarters. (Public domain)

fall under the GM umbrella. General Motors would become one of the largest automotive holding companies in the world, and has since remained a top automobile manufacturer.

Also on this day: **1933** – The last Invicta was manufactured. **1957** – Bing Crosby, Louis Armstrong, Frank Sinatra and Rosemary Clooney hosted *The Edsel Show*, an hour long TV special to promote the new Edsel automobiles. **1966** – The Jaguar 420 was introduced at the London Motor Show.

A man sits in his 1916 Buick. Buick was the first company owned by General Motors. (Photo sourced by simpleinsomnia [363])

October 14, 1857
No horse for Haynes

When the Duryea brothers built the first motorized vehicle in the United States, it was designed so that it could still be pulled by a horse as a secondary means of power. Less than a year after the Duryeas debuted their automobile in 1893, Elwood Haynes, born on this day in 1857, test drove a wagon he had started building in his own kitchen. Haynes' car, however, was built with zero intention of ever being hooked up to a horse, except on one particular day. As a crowd gathered to watch the test

Elwood Haynes, circa 1910. (Public domain)

drive in Kokomo, Indiana, Haynes worried that his automobile may cause injuries to onlookers. To prevent the possibility of harm he had a horse pull the vehicle away from the people. Once at a safe distance he fired up the engine and enjoyed a successful test drive.

Also on this day: **1965** – Oldsmobile introduced the 1966 Toronado, the first high volume front-wheel drive car produced in the United States since Cord ended production in 1937. **1997** – Toyota launched the hybrid Prius. **2013** – Driving a Land Rover Discovery, Britons Stephen Cooper and Robert Belcher established a new record for driving from London to Cape Town, South Africa, a distance of nearly 10,000 miles, in 10 days, 3 hours and 16 minutes.

Elwood Haynes in his first car, the 1894 Pioneer, in a photo taken circa 1910. (Public domain)

October 15, 1924
Mr Lee Iacocca

Lee Iacocca during an introductory meeting after being named president of Ford Motor Company. (Photo by Thomas O'Halloran [364])

Some have careers; some have magic. Lido Anthony 'Lee' Iacocca, born on this day in 1924, fit the latter. As one of the most influential men in modern American automotive history, Iacocca was responsible for incredible feats between the 1950s and 1990s with Ford and Chrysler. After joining Ford as an engineer in 1946, he quickly found his calling in marketing. He launched Ford's successful 56 for $56 campaign, which allowed people to make $56 monthly payments on a new 1956 Ford. A promotion to VP would have him participating in the development and launch of the Ford Mustang and Lincoln Mark III, among many other models. After becoming Ford's President in 1970, he oversaw the introduction of the Ford Pinto. Despite incredible profits, he was dismissed from Ford in 1978, likely due to clashes with Henry Ford II. He was quickly picked up by Chrysler, and as president of the floundering company he worked to turn the nearly bankrupt business around. He negotiated government bailouts and launched multiple cars that would ensure cash flow to Chrysler, including the Chrysler Town & Country and Dodge Caravan.

Also on this day: 1930 – The Bentley 8 Litre was introduced at the Olympia Motor Show. **1998** – Richard Brown set the two-wheeled British Land Speed record of 216.55mph driving a rocket powered motorcycle. **2004** – The US National Highway Traffic Safety Administration lifted a ruling that hearse manufacturers had to install anchors for child-safety seats in their vehicles, a law that went into effect in 1999 for all personal automobiles sold in the country.

The Ford Mustang, introduced in 1964, was one of Iacocca's most successful projects as an executive at Ford. (Photo by RL GNZLZ [365])

October 16, 1947
Land Rover is a go

Executives at former British automaker Rover officially approved the 'Landrover' marque on this day in 1947. The original prototype, designed to be a 'go anywhere' vehicle, was built on a Jeep chassis by Rover Company designer Maurice Wilks and his brother Spencer on Maurice's farm. By the Amsterdam Motor Show the following April, when the vehicle debuted, the name had been changed to Land Rover, and an off-road champion was born.

Also on this day: 1951 – The Austin A30 was introduced at Earls Court Motor Show in London. The car was a direct response to the Morris Minor. **1951** – The Hudson Hornet was announced. **1995** – The Skye Bridge that spans Loch Alsh to connect the Isle of Skye with mainland Scotland was opened.

1951 Series 1 Land Rover. (Photo by Graham Robertson [366])

The interior of a Series 1 Land Rover. (Photo by blastpaintrestore [367])

October 17, 1935
A dozen for Rolls-Royce

Rolls-Royce introduced its first V12 automobile on this day in 1935. The Phantom III consisted of only the chassis and mechanical parts, with bodywork completed by the coachbuilder of the buyer or dealer's choice. The 447cu in aluminum V12 engine powered the 4050lb chassis, which could reach a weight of more than 7000lb, once fitted with a body. The massive size of the car limited its performance; one test showed a maximum speed of just 87mph. Production of the Phantom III ceased in 1939, with the last chassis being fitted with a body and delivered to its owner in 1947. Rolls-Royce wouldn't produce another V12 until the introduction of the 1998 Silver Seraph.

Also on this day: 1931 – Henry Birkin drove a Maserati 26M to win the Mountain Championship at Brooklands. **1962** – The Triumph Spitfire debuted at the London Motor Show. **1968** – *Bullitt*, starring Steve McQueen hit movie theaters, featuring a high octane seven-minute car chase through San Francisco, California. **2000** – Alice Huyler Ramsey, the first woman to drive across the United States, was inducted into the US Automotive Hall of Fame.

1937 Rolls-Royce Phantom III. (Photo by Brian Sims [368])

Interior of 1937 Rolls-Royce Phantom III Vesters & Neirinck Coupé 4.
(Photo by Jack Snell [369])

October 18, 1939
The Hall of Fame

To preserve the memories of the men and women who contributed great efforts to the automotive industry around the world, a group known as Automobile Old Timers founded The Automotive Hall of Fame in New York City on this day in 1939. After three different names throughout its first 30 years in existence, and multiple location changes, the name was finally settled as The Automotive Hall of Fame, and a permanent home was established in Dearborn, Michigan. The museum honors more than 800 people who have had an impact on automotive history, including, but in no way limited to, founders, financiers, inventors, marketers, racers, engineers, designers, dealers, mechanics, and union officials.

Also on this day: 1919 – Rolls-Royce America Inc, was established. **1956** – Elvis Presley was slapped by a Memphis, Tennessee gas station manager when he refused to stop signing autographs, which the manager said was disrupting business. Elvis punched the manager, Ed Hopper. Hopper was later charged with assault.

1919 Rolls-Royce Silver Ghost Type J141 Coupé. Rolls-Royce America Inc, was established on this day in 1919. (Photo by David Merrett [370])

Rock'n'roller and Cadillac aficionado Elvis Presley got into a small fight with a Memphis gas station attendant while signing autographs for fans on this day in 1956. He's seen here in 1957 in a promotional photo for Jailhouse Rock.

October 19, 1897
Crossing Great Britain

During the time he acted as a director and deputy chairman at Daimler, Henry Sturmey was also an inventor, passionate cyclist and an early editor for multiple cycling and automotive publications, including *Autocar*. He would use the magazine to promote Daimler automobiles in Britain, but perhaps his best feat of marketing genius ended on this day in 1897, when he completed a heavily publicized journey from John O'Groats to Land's End, driving a Coventry-built Daimler. The journey earned Sturmey a spot in the record books as the first to drive the length of Great Britain by automobile.

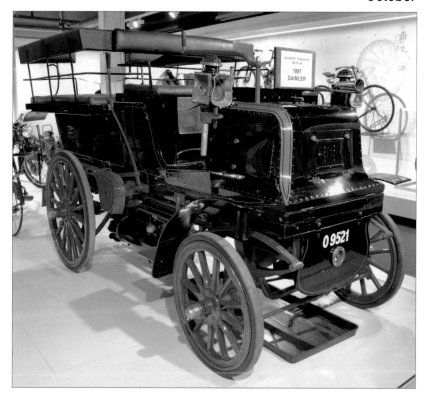

1897 Daimler Grafton Phaeton at the British Motor Museum. Said to be the oldest Coventry built Daimler. (Photo by Karen Roe [372])

1897 Daimler at the Coventry Transport Museum. (Photo by Thomas's Pics [371])

Also on this day: **1965** – The MGB GT went on sale. **1971** – Alberto Pirelli, founder of Pirelli Tires, died at age 89. **1997** – Cory McClenathan became the first driver in the history of National Hot Rod Association drag racing to top 320mph in a quarter mile run, when he hit 321.77mph in Ennis, Texas.

October 20, 1902
Big day for Cadillac

Born out of the failed Henry Ford Company, Cadillac manufactured its first vehicle on this day in 1902. Following a dispute between Henry Ford and his investors, Ford left his own company. When the financial backers called upon engineer Henry Leland to appraise the assets from the now defunct business, Leland convinced William Murphy and Lemuel Bowen to start a new company using single cylinder engines that he produced. Utilizing the former Ford factory at Cass Street and Amsterdam Avenue in Detroit, Cadillac would begin production two months after its August founding. Cadillac models debuted at the 1903 New York Auto Show where the company received approximately 2000 orders for its finely crafted vehicles.

1903 Cadillac Model A Runabout. (Photo by brewbooks [373])

Also on this day: **1965** – The last Volvo 544 was manufactured. Approximately 440,000 of the cars had been manufactured over eight years. **1995** – Vauxhall introduced the Vectra to replace the Cavalier.

October 21, 1897

Oldie, but a goodie

The oldest existing automotive manufacturer in the Western Hemisphere came to be on this day in 1897, when Louis Clark recruited his brothers John and James, his father Charles, and friend William Morgan to start the Pittsburg Motor Vehicle Company. Two years later, the company moved from Pittsburgh, Pennsylvania to Ardmore, changing its name to Autocar Company. After building the first motorized truck in the United States in 1899, followed by several small passenger cars, the company turned its focus to commercial vehicles. By 1911, Autocar was manufacturing only trucks. After selling out to White Motor Company, following a short lived post-WWII boom, Autocar would exchange hands multiple times throughout the next 50 years until once again becoming independently operated as a subsidiary of an Illinois based holding company. Autocar is headquartered in Indiana, where it manufactures severe duty trucks.

A retired Autocar truck. (Photo by Mike [374])

1915 Autocar. (Photo by Greg Gjerdingen [375])

Also on this day:
1929 – Henry Ford and Thomas Edison dedicated the Edison Institute in Dearborn, Michigan, celebrating the 50th anniversary of electric light. **1978** – Elite Heritage Motors reintroduced the Duesenberg name with the Duesenberg II.

1936 Volkswagen Beetle Prototype.
(Photo by Bruno Kussler Marques [376], [377])

October 22, 1936

VW hits the streets

More than 21.5 million production models stemmed from the prototype that was taken for a test drive for the first time on this day in 1936. Under contract from Adolf Hitler and the Nazi party, Ferdinand Porsche was tasked with building Germany a People's Car. The VW Type 1 prototype was designed with a top speed of 62mph, perfect for Germany's new autobahn, and priced for the working class German. A small run of the cars were manufactured before World War II, but mass production of the Beetle, as it would come to be known, wouldn't begin until after the war when British authority handed the Wolfsburg plant back to the Germany government. The cars rolled off the assembly line between 1938 and 2003, earning the title of most-manufactured car built on a single platform.

Also on this day: **1952** – The three-wheeled Reliant Regal Mark I was shown to the public at the London Motor Show. **1954** – The Ford Thunderbird went on sale. **1969** – The Datsun 240Z debuted.

October 23, 1911
English T

The Ford Motor Company began its intercontinental expansion on this day in 1911, when the first Model Ts left a factory in Trafford Park, Manchester, England, the first Ford assembly plant outside of North America. Three years after production started Britain's first moving assembly line was installed at the plant, allowing the factory to pump out more than 20 vehicles per hour. Following an expansion of the plant after World War I, production increased significantly, and, by the beginning of the 1920s, 41 per cent of all registered cars in Britain were Fords. For better access to a deep-water port Henry Ford ordered a new plant to be built along the River Thames in Dagenham, which was completed in 1923.

A Model T Depot Hack in England.
(Photo by pyntofmyld [378])

Also on this day: 1938 – The new Mercury marque from Ford was unveiled to the press. **1955** – In his Formula One debut, Briton Tony Brooks drove a British Connaught B-Type to victory at the Syracuse Grand Prix in Sicily, becoming the first British driver piloting a British car to win a Grand Prix since 1924. **2007** – Nissan announced the GT-R.

Nissan introduced the GT-R, such as this 2008 model, at the Tokyo Motor Show on this day in 2007. (Photo by Debarshi Ray [379])

This DeLorean was built for exhibition purposes following the release of Back to the Future 2.
(Photos by Brian Corey)

October 24, 1975
A time machine in the making

There was only one that didn't need roads – John Z DeLorean, an American automotive executive with a storied career, founded DeLorean Motor Company on this day in 1975. The company built a sole model, the DMC-12, which first appeared as a prototype in October 1976. The vehicle, which has gained a cult following and is widely known for its role as a time machine in the *Back to the Future* movies, only saw production between 1981-1983 before the company went bankrupt following drug trafficking charges against the founder. DeLorean would later be found not guilty. A majority of the approximate 9200 cars produced were assembled in Dunmurry, Northern Ireland. Each featured a rear mounted Peugeot-Renault-Volvo fuel injected V6 engine with either a 5-speed manual transmission or 3-speed automatic. Most of the DeLoreans were left unpainted, giving the car its iconic bare metal look.

Also on this day: 1931 – The George Washington Bridge, spanning the Hudson River to connect New Jersey and New York City, was dedicated by President Franklin Delano Roosevelt. **2007** – Subaru unveiled the Impreza WRX STI at the Tokyo Motor Show.

October 25, 1975
An incredible jump

During a broadcast of *Wide World of Sports* on US television channel ABC on this day in 1975, motorcycle stuntman Robert Craig 'Evel' Knievel jumped 14 Greyhound buses at Kings Island, near Cincinnati, Ohio, making it his longest successful jump. Throughout Evel Knievel's career he attempted more than 75 jumps riding Harley Davidsons, some of which resulted in horrific crashes. He is said to have suffered at least 433 bone fractures, earning him a Guinness World Record for the most broken bones in a lifetime. Following the Kings Island jump, Evel announced a short lived retirement. Just more than a year later he would jump seven buses in the Kingdome in Seattle, Washington. He felt the jump was less thrilling than others he completed, and apologized to the crowd.

Also on this day: 1972 – The three millionth Mini rolled off the assembly line. **1977** – Michael Edwardes was named chairman of British Leyland.

Evel Knievel wax figure at Madame Tussauds, Las Vegas.
(Photo by Dutch Boyd [380])

An Evel Knievel Harley-Davidson XR-750 suspended in the air as if jumping at the Harley-Davidson Museum. (Photo by Danemroberts [381])

October 26, 1926
Cord buys Duesenberg

August and Fred Duesenberg were self-taught master mechanics who used their skills to build fantastic racecars and engines, opening their first shop in 1913 in St. Paul, Minnesota. Their cars managed astonishing feats of speed, claiming multiple victories at Indy races, and, in 1923, Jimmy Murphy became the first American to win the French Grand Prix, driving a Duesy. When the brothers started production of the Model A, the first car to be mass produced with a straight 8 engine, they quickly discovered they were much better

1922 Duesenberg Model A Dual Cowl Phaeton by Fleetwood. (Photo by Rex Gray [382])

1931 Duesenberg Model J. (Photo by Rain0975 [383])

Interior of a Duesenberg Model J, featuring a bar. (Photo by Brian Corey)

1957 Chevrolet 150 two door sedan. Buck Baker, 1957 NASCAR Champion, drove a '57 Chevrolet with race number 87, dubbed Black Widow, with a similar paint scheme. (Photo by Greg Gjerdingen [384])

engineers than salesmen, leading E L Cord to acquire Duesenberg as part of Auburn Automobile Company, on this day in 1926. By the end of the next decade, the Great Depression would kill the brand that sold cars for as much as $25,000 to the rich and famous, at a time when a Ford Model A could be had for under $500.

Also on this day: 1909 – General Motors purchased Cartercar **1966** – The Toyota Corolla was introduced in Tokyo.

October 27, 1957
The first consecutive champion

A dramatic 250 lap NASCAR race unfolded on the ⅓ mile dirt track in Greensboro, North Carolina on this day, capping off the 1957 racing season. An accident on lap 35 knocked multiple racers out of the event, and sent Marvin Panch end over end in his Ford. However, after landing on his wheels, Panch completed 16 more laps before the car called it quits. Numerous crashes led to a long afternoon for the 2500 fans shivering in the grandstands. Elzie Wylie 'Buck' Baker Sr, in his Black Widow 1957 Chevrolet, and Lee Petty in his Oldsmobile swapped the lead four times throughout the race. Finally, on lap 191 Baker pulled ahead and led the rest of the race. Baker took home the $1000 grand prize and secured his second consecutive Grand National Series

Buck Baker's 1949 Oldsmobile from his early NASCAR career.
(Photo by Brian Snelson [385])

Championship trophy, making him the first driver to ever win it two years in a row.

Also on this day: 1924 – The Charlotte Speedway hosted more than 50,000 spectators on its opening day. Tommy Milton drove a Miller to victory. **1945** – Ferdinand Porsche was arrested for war crimes. **2006** – Automotive designer Albrecht Graf Goertz, responsible for the BMW 503 and 507, died at age 92.

October 28, 1942
Slow down for war

During WWII, Americans, along with people in many nations, were subject to rations of all sorts, including gasoline and rubber, making it nearly impossible to get new tires. In an effort to reduce consumption related to all things automobile, the State of Utah imposed a 'Patriotic Speed Limit' of 35mph (56km/h) on this day in 1942. This came after a call by the federal government for

35 miles per hour speed limit sign.
(Photo by KOMUnews [386])

a nationwide 'Victory Speed Limit' of the same speed the previous May. Studies had shown that tires were subject to 50 per cent less wear when traveling at 35mph opposed to 60mph (100km/h). Not only did the lower speed limit save tires, it saved lives. Total accidents decreased 35 per cent between 1941 and 1943 in the state of Utah, with fatal accidents being cut in half in the same time frame.

Also on this day: **1942** – The Alaska Highway was completed. The route spanned 1700 miles from the continental United States, through Canada, and into Alaska. **1971** – Ferrari unveiled the 365GT4.

October 29, 1954
The last true Hudson

After Detroit area department store founder Joseph L Hudson offered financial support to eight local businessmen interested in starting a car company, the group decided to name it after its investor. Once production started in 1909, Hudson would set the record for the

Ferrari unveiled the 365 GT4 on this day in 1971 for the 1972 model year. (Photo by nakhon100 [387])

1954 Hudson Hornet convertible.
(Photo by John Lloyd [388])

1954 Hudson Super Jet.
(Photo by Greg Gjerdingen, [389])

highest amount of vehicles sold in the first year of existence, at 4508 automobiles, 17th overall in the industry. After decades of growth, the company suffered following the end of WWII, resulting in a merger with Nash to create American Motors. About six months after the companies combined forces, the last true Hudson rolled off the assembly line on this day in 1954. The Hudson name would live on as rebadged Nashes for three more years.

Also on this day: **1971** – Allman Brothers Band guitarist Duane Allman died at age 24 in a motorcycle accident in Macon, Georgia, USA. **1986** – Prime Minister Margaret Thatcher opened the final section of the M25, London's 117 mile orbital motorway.

October 30, 1963
The original Lamborghini

When Enzo Ferrari refused to see a wealthy customer who had some concerns about his recently purchased Ferrari, that customer pledged to build his own sports car out of spite. The Lamborghini 350GTV prototype debuted on this day in 1963 at the Turin Motor Show – the same day Automobili Ferruccio Lamborghini SpA was officially founded. Bricks were placed under the bonnet of the Lamborghini at the show, as Ferruccio Lamborghini was displeased with the engine created by the ex-Ferrari engineers he'd hired, saying it was too similar to those in Ferraris. Between 1964 and 1966 assembly workers hand-built approximately 135 350GT when manufacturing began on the production version of the prototype.

Also on this day: **1909** – The fifth Vanderbilt Cup race was held on Long Island, New York. **1988** – Ayrton Senna clinched the Formula One World Championship with a win in Suzuka. **1998** – Saturn unveiled the first three door coupé at the New England International Auto Show.

October 31, 1957
Toyota USA

Toyota began chasing its American dream on this day in 1957 when Toyota USA headquarters was established in Hollywood, California in a defunct Rambler dealership. When sales of the Toyopet commenced the following year, it was soon discovered it would not be the first choice for a second car for American families, as Toyota hoped. The year saw the sale of only 286 of the small, underpowered vehicles, and one Land Cruiser, causing Toyota to re-evaluate its entry into the US car market. The Toyopet would be discontinued and the large Land Cruiser would be the only offering from the Japanese automaker until it introduced the Corona in 1965. Within a decade Toyota would be the number one selling import brand in the United States, thanks to the success of the Corona and the Corolla.

Also on this day: **1957** – Chevrolet announced the Impala as a 1958 model. **1967** – The first Baja 1000 off-road race began. The 849 mile (1366km) race was won by Vic Wilson and Ted Mangels in a Meyers Manx buggy, with a time of 27 hours and 38 minutes. **2010** – A 1964 Aston Martin DB5, formerly owned by Sir Paul McCartney, was sold at auction for £344,400.

Interior of 1958 Toyopet.
(Photo by James Case [393])

Lamborghini 350GT (1964-1966). The first production Lamborghini.
(Photo by NAParish [390])

1966 Lamborghini 350 GT.
(Photo by Clemens Vasters [391])

1958 Toyota Toyopet. (Photo by InSapphoWeTrust [392])

November 1, 1946
License to drive

The 1903 Motor Car Act made it a punishable offense to operate an automobile without a license in the United Kingdom, but no test was required to obtain one. A volunteer test would be introduced more than three decades later, as part of the Road Traffic Act of 1934, with a Mr J Beene becoming the first person to pass it. Only three months later the evaluation became mandatory, and initially saw a pass rate of 63 per cent. When World War II broke out in Europe, all driving tests were suspended in the UK as examiners were being retasked with other duties that included fuel rationing and overseeing traffic. New drivers' licenses wouldn't be issued again until this day in 1946, more than a year after victory in Europe.

Also on this day: **1895** – *The Horseless Age*, America's first automobile magazine, was published. **1955** – Studebaker unveiled the Hawk. **1972** – The Standard Oil Company was reorganized as the Exxon Corporation. **1979** – The struggling Chrysler Corporation received a $1.5 billion bailout from the US Government.

People learning to drive in the UK are required to place an L plate on their vehicle.
(Photo by Lee Haywood [394])

Below: 1956 Studebaker Golden Hawk. The Hawk was introduced on this day in 1955. (Photo by Ali Mannan [395])

November 2, 1983
Minivan mayhem

A few short years before automotive executives Lee Iacocca and Hal Sperlich found themselves kicked to the curb outside of Ford headquarters, the two spearheaded a new concept car codenamed Mini-Max. Henry Ford II, who was known to regularly butt heads with Iacocca, was unimpressed and shut down the project. Iacocca and Sperlich would be let go, but were soon welcomed with open arms to a struggling Chrysler Corporation. With Iacocca as President, the two brought their concept back to life. Renamed the Magic-wagon during development, the project would result in production vehicles that the *New York Times* would describe as "the hot cars coming out of Detroit." Chrysler gave birth to the minivan on this day in 1983, when the Plymouth Voyager and Dodge Caravan began to roll off the assembly line. Combining the drivability of a passenger car with the storage and seating capacity of a cumbersome station wagon, the minivans were an immediate hit, which helped pull Chrysler out of its financial hardship.

Also on this day: **1935** – Cord debuted the 810 at the National Automobile Show in New York City. **1999** – Ford of Canada delivered 16 battery-powered, zero emission Ranger pickup trucks to customers in Quebec, Canada, marking the first sale of fully electric cars by a major automaker in Canada.

Rear seating area of the first Plymouth Voyager.
(Photo by Greg Gjerdingen [396])

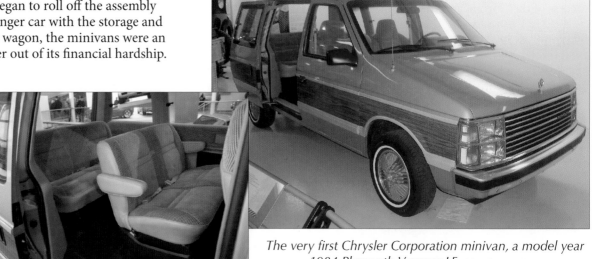

The very first Chrysler Corporation minivan, a model year 1984 Plymouth Voyager LE. (Photo by Brian Corey)

November 3, 1900
Let the showboating begin

What is considered the first modern auto show took place at Madison Square Garden in New York City, on this day in 1900. It was not the first auto show, nor was it even the first show at Madison Square Garden, but it was the first really big show. It cost a whopping 50 cents to get in, equivalent to about $13 in 2017. Guests were treated to displays from more than 66 exhibitors, yet only about 31 actual vehicles. The event, sponsored by the Automobile Club of America, saw more than 10,000 people come for a peek throughout the week. It was at this show that Ransom E Olds debuted a prototype for his Runabout. None of the automakers that partook in the show are still in business.

Also on this day: **1965** – The Lamborghini Miura chassis was unveiled at the Turin Motor Show, where it received multiple orders, despite not having a body. **2007** – Construction of Ferrari World theme park in Abu Dhabi began.

Madison Square Garden building, circa 1900-1910, location of the first modern auto show. (Public domain)

The chassis for the new Lamborghini Miura was unveiled at the Turin Motor Show on this day in 1965. The chassis was enough to secure multiple orders. When customers received their Miura chassis it would have this beautiful coachwork attached. (Photo by Bruno Kussler Marques [397])

A very small portion of the LeMay collection at the former Marymount Military Academy near Tacoma, Washington. The crowd watches as cars go over the auction block.

(Photo by Brian Corey)

November 4, 2000
A record collection

At the time of his death, on this day in 2000, Harold E LeMay had amassed one of the largest personal collection of automobiles ever. It contained upwards of 3000 cars, trucks, motorcycles, military vehicles, buses and other modes of transport, and included thousands more pieces of automotive memorabilia. Harold started a trash collection company in Spanaway, Washington following high school, which led to the founding of Harold LeMay Enterprises just after WWII. His company primarily remained a refuse business, which continues to operate throughout Washington State, but grew to include towing companies and an auction house. He used his self-built wealth to always buy and never sell, as it has been said he never sold a car in his lifetime. Among the many vehicles are countless rare and one of a kind autos, and in 1997 he was awarded a Guinness Book of World Records title for the largest private auto collection.

Also on this day: **1910** – At the Olympia Motor Show in London the

America's Car Museum in Tacoma, Washington, was built in honor of Harold LeMay and houses parts of his collection. (Photo by Brian Corey)

Morgan Company introduced its original three wheeled vehicle. **1990** – The 500th ever Formula One Grand Prix, the Australian Grand Prix, was won by Nelson Piquet in a Benetton.

November 5, 1895
The Selden patent

When George B Selden received US Patent No 549,160 on this day in 1895, for his gasoline powered automobile, it essentially granted him a monopoly over the blossoming auto industry in America. After organizing a payment method and automakers organization, he was able to accept royalties from all gas-powered vehicles manufactured in the country. That is, until he was challenged by Henry Ford in a years-long court battle. But that's a story for a different day (September 15).

Also on this day:
1908 – Henry Ford lost an election for a US Senate seat. **1959** – Paul Vincent Galvin, co-inventor of the first automobile stereo, and co-founder of Motorola, died at the age of 64. **1999** – Ford announced the 6.0 Power Stroke diesel engine.

George B Selden (right) driving an automobile in 1905.
(Illustration based on public domain photo)

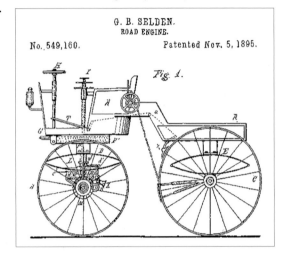

George B Selden drawing for the Selden Road-Engine, US Patent 549,160. (Public domain)

November 6, 1988
Polish victory lap

Alan Kulwicki had just won his first NASCAR Winston Cup race. With his adrenaline pumping he turned his car around and drove it the wrong way around Phoenix International Raceway following the Checker 500, which took place on this day in 1988, thus giving birth to the Polish victory lap. Now a tradition in many genres of auto racing, the Polish victory lap involves the winner of a race driving the wrong way around the track, often waving the checkered flag out of the window. Kulwicki, who was of Polish descent, was nicknamed the Polish Prince, and following his death in a light aircraft accident in 1993, the Polish victory lap name was solidified. Kulwicki was a successful NASCAR driver, winning Rookie of the Year in 1986, and the 1992 Winston Cup Championship, a title he never got to defend.

Also on this day: 1947 – The first post-WWII Rolls-Royce and Bentley automobiles landed in the United States. **2000** – A petrol tanker truck crashed in Lagos, Nigeria, killing as many as 200 people.

Alan Kulwicki's 1988 car, which he used for his Polish victory lap.
(Photo by transplanted mountaineer [398])

The 2014 RWDNS race winner performs a Polish victory lap at the Tilleda Thunder On Ice racing series.
(Photo by Royal Broil [399])

November 7, 1980
The King of Cool

The 'King of Cool' Steve McQueen passed away on this day in 1980 due to pleural mesothelioma, a cancer associated with asbestos exposure. Born Terence Steven McQueen on March 24, 1930, he would go on to make a name for himself in Hollywood and on the racetrack. Starring in such films as *The Cincinnati Kid*, *The Thomas Crown Affair*, *The Getaway*, *The Sand Pebbles*, and *Papillon*, McQueen was well known on the screen. His other passion, which was reflected in many of his movies, including *Bullitt*, was auto racing. *Bullitt* features a nearly 11-minute car chase scene, in which McQueen's character drives a 1968 390 V8 Ford Mustang GT Fastback through the streets of San Francisco in pursuit of a 1968 375hp 440 Magnum V8-powered Dodge Charger.

Wax figure of Steve McQueen at Madame Tussauds. (Photo by Loren Javier [400])

Jaguar XKSS formerly owned by Steve McQueen. (Photo by Bryce Womeldurf [401])

Also on this day: **1885** – Canada's first transcontinental railway was completed. **1940** – High winds caused the Tacoma Narrows Bridge in Washington State, USA to collapse. The suspension bridge, the third longest in the world at the time, had opened just four months earlier. **1969** – The 250,000th Chevrolet Corvette was manufactured.

1911 Hupmobile roadster. (Photo by Daderot [402])

November 8, 1908
What's Hup-ening

Bobby Hupp's successful test drive of a Hupmobile through the streets of Detroit, Michigan had his investors sipping champagne. The Hupp Motor Car Corporation was incorporated on this day in 1908, and publicly debuted its Model 20 at the 1909 Detroit Auto Show. Henry Ford later remarked, "I recall looking at Bobby Hupp's roadster at the first show where it was exhibited, and wondering whether we could ever build as good a small car for as little money." Once Hupp received sufficient orders for the new automobile, production began. More than 500 cars were built by fall of 1909, and the next year production increased to more than 5000.

Also on this day: **1918** – General Motors absorbed the Canadian McLaughlin Motor Company. **1935** – British racing driver Peter Arundell was born. He would score 12 championship points with team Lotus in 13 World Championship Grand Prix starts. **1982** – Finnish motorcycle racer Mika Kallio was born. He would be named the 2002 Rookie of the Year.

1910 Hupmobile 20 interior. (Photo by F D Richards [403])

November 9, 1960

Rising through the ranks

Following WWII, Colonel Charles Thornton founded a firm made up of military men, to help large manufacturing businesses adjust to civilian production profitability. After being hired by Ford Motor Company, the young group of military engineers, financiers and others became known as the Quiz Kids by the suits and ties at Ford. They rebranded themselves as the Whiz Kids, and quickly earned respect from executives, as they dug Ford out of a financial mess. One of the former soldiers recruited by Thornton was Robert McNamara. After playing a pivotal role in the introduction of the highly successful Ford Falcon in 1959, McNamara was appointed president of Ford on this day in 1960, the first person to hold the title outside of the Ford family since John S Gray, Ford's first president from 1903 to 1906. Just five weeks after accepting the position, he was offered the position of Secretary of Defense for the President John Kennedy administration, which he accepted.

Official portrait Department of Defense portrait of Robert McNamara. (Public domain)

McNamara pushed for smaller cars, such as the 1961 Lincoln Continental. Between 1958-1960 Lincoln lost $60 million as it sold much larger versions of its vehicles. (Photo by Greg Gjerdingen [404])

Also on this day: **1927** – American racing driver Sherwood Johnston was born. He would win the 1952 SCCA National Sports Car Championship. **1941** – Starting at 3am, Budapest switched to driving on the right, nearly four months after the rest of Hungary. **1962** – The Ford Rotunda was destroyed by fire.

November 10, 1914

The first Dodge

In 1900 Horace and John Dodge started a machine shop named Dodge Brothers Company, which provided parts to the booming new auto industry. They were soon producing chassis, engines and other components for companies including Olds Motor Vehicle Company and Ford Motor Company. After nearly 15 years in the parts business the first complete Dodge Brothers automobile rolled off the assembly line on this day in 1914, at the Dodge main factory in Hamtramck, Michigan. The Dodge Model 30 was designed to compete with the Model T, but offered some interesting features that were unique for the era. The all-steel-bodied Dodge, as opposed to common wood-framing under steel sheeting, sported a 12-volt electrical system, a 35hp four cylinder engine and a sliding gear transmission. The advancements on early Dodge cars and

The Dodge Brothers, Horace on the left, John on the right, riding in their first car, near the Dodge Brothers Motor Car Company Plant in Hamtramck, Michigan. (US Library of Congress, call number HAER MICH,82-HAMT,1—313)

trucks helped push the automaker to second in sales in the United States as early as 1916. Following the unrelated deaths of the brothers in 1920, the business was sold by their wives, and in 1928 Dodge became a part of Chrysler Corporation.

Also on this day: **1934** – Lucien Bianchi, an Italian-Belgian race car driver, was born. He would die in 1969 during preparation for the 24 Hours of Le Mans. **2007** – The Mini Clubman was made available for purchase in the UK.

November 11, 1926
First woman in Formula One

On May 18, 1958, Maria Teresa de Filippis made her Formula One debut at the Monaco Grand Prix, driving a Maserati 250F. While she failed to qualify for the race by 5.8 seconds, she became the first woman to participate in Formula One racing. Born on this day in 1926, de Filippis began her racing career at age 22, when she won her first race in a Fiat 500. She would go on to finish second in the 1954 Italian sports car championship season. She caught the eye of Maserati and the team brought her in as the works driver. A pioneer in women's auto racing, de Filippis would participate in five World Championship Grand Prix races before stepping out of the driver's seat at the end of the 1950s.

A Maserati 250F, like that in which de Filippis made her F1 debut.
(Photo by ian mcwilliams [405])

Also on this day:
1926 – The US numbered Highway System was established. **1960** – Robert Byron, winner of the first sanctioned NASCAR race, died of a heart attack at age 45. **1978** – *The Dukes of Hazzard* crew filmed the iconic jump of the General Lee that takes place in the opening credits, on this day in 1978, on the campus of Oxford College in Georgia.

Red Byron's race car. Byron, who died on this day in 1960, was the winner of the first sanctioned NASCAR race. (Photo by David Berkowitz [406])

An Oldsmobile advertisement from 1907.

CUMULATIVE EVIDENCE PROVES THE

OLDSMOBILE

the car that does things—the car for any exploit—for touring, for hill climbing, for general utility.

The Oldsmobile, Model "A," Touring Car for 1907—a thoroughly tested car, built along the successful lines of Model "S" for 1906, but with greater horse power, greater capacity and more finished qualities.

The conclusive evidence of the capacity of these cars continues to accumulate. Can you get away from the following convincing facts?

The Hill Climbing Ability, again demonstrated by the recent record climb up Twin Peaks, San Francisco. Here Model "A" not only sets a new mark of 2 minutes 29 seconds, cutting 1 minute 1 second from the old record, but was the first and only car to ever make the run to the highest apex.

Motor Endurance, again demonstrated on November as at Cleveland, when Model "A" completed a 200-hour non-stop run. A copy of sworn statements giving details of this run will be sent to those interested on request.

Touring Quality, demonstrated on the 300-mile non-stop run made by Model "A" from Detroit, Mich., to Cincinnati O., in 14 hours and 12 minutes, actual running time. This run was made on the high gear. When Cincinnati was reached the car was driven to the top of Vine

Street Hill, still on the high gear. The car which made this remarkable demonstration of touring and hill climbing ability was taken fresh from the factory and represented the average run of stock cars.

Roadability, demonstrated by the 75 mile run from New York to Poughkeepsie over difficult hills and trying road conditions with the high speed lever sealed in. Also in the Santa Barbara, California, run, and the St. Catharines to Toronto, Canada, high-speed-lever-sealed-in run.

If you are an Oldsmobile owner, send us your name, address, number of model and date of purchase and we will send you regularly the Oldsmobile News Letter, a weekly publication devoted to the interest of Oldsmobile enthusiasts.

For further reasons address Dept. S. A.
OLDS MOTOR WORKS, Lansing, Mich., U. S. A.
Member of Association Licensed Automobile Manufacturers

November 12, 1908
Developing Oldsmobile

On this day in 1908, the newly formed General Motors (GM) purchased Oldsmobile. At the time, Oldsmobile was losing money after its latest product, a six-cylinder model, failed to sell in the volume of the popular Curved Dash. Following the purchase from Ransom E Olds, GM introduced the Oldsmobile Model 20 for 1909, which was more or less the 1908 Buick Model 10 with a longer wheelbase and some changes to the exterior. The rear-wheel drive, four-door model had a 22bhp four-cylinder engine, giving it sufficient power and fuel economy. A total of 6575 Oldsmobile vehicles were manufactured in 1909, with 5325 of them being the Model 20.

Also on this day: **1914** – English auto racer Peter Whitehead was born. **1979** – US President Jimmy Carter orders a stop to all petroleum imports from Iran, in response to a hostage situation in Tehran. **1998** – Daimler-Benz completed a merger with Chrysler.

Below: Exterior and interior of a 1908 Oldsmobile Touring. (Photos by Joe Ross [407], [408])

November 13, 1940

The Jeep prototype

About two months before this day in 1940, American Bantam Car Company delivered a prototype of what would come to be known as the Jeep to the US Army. Officials were impressed, but not completely sold, the Army claimed ownership of the design and passed the blueprints on to Willys-Overland, with a few requests for changes. Willys delivered the upgraded prototype on this day in 1940; in turn it would receive the first government contract to produce the highly capable vehicles. Ford would later be recruited to produce nearly identical Jeeps as WWII manufacturing ramped up, and, between the two companies, approximately 640,000 Jeeps were built for WWII. Bantam, a much smaller firm, was tasked with manufacturing Jeep trailers.

World War II era Jeep. (Photo by Falcon® Photography [409])

Also on this day: 1927 – The Holland Tunnel linking New Jersey and New York City under the Hudson River opened to traffic. **1934** – The ten millionth Chevrolet was manufactured. **1971** – *Duel*, the first full length film from director Steven Spielberg, was released on television network ABC, featuring a demonic tanker truck driver chasing another driver down a lonesome desert highway.

US President Theodore Roosevelt rides in a Jeep in Casablanca, Morocco in 1943 while greeting US troops. (Photo courtesy Library of Congress, reproduction number LC-USW33-027834-ZC)

November 14, 1965/1971

Two wins today

Richard Petty won not one, but two, NASCAR series races on this day, one each in 1965 and 1971. The 1965 race, the first event of the 1966 season, took place in Augusta, Georgia, where Petty had

1966 Plymouth Belvedere raced by Richard Petty. (Photo by Jason Goulding [410])

claimed the pole position. Petty battled Bobby Isaac and Tony Lund for the lead throughout the race, but was able to take the checkers in his Petty Enterprises Plymouth, winning a $1700 purse. The 1971 Capital City 500 in Richmond, Virginia, fell on the same date after rain delayed it from its scheduled September 10 start. Petty beat out Bobby Allison for first place, giving him the overall points lead for the season and earning him his third championship title.

Also on this day: 1940 – The Alvis car plant in Coventry, England was destroyed during a Nazi air raid. **1945** – Tony Hulman purchased the Indianapolis Motor Speedway from Eddie Rickenbacher for $750,000. **1996** – General Motors first production electric car, the EV1, was manufactured in Lansing, Michigan.

An advertisement for the November 14, 1966 race at Augusta International Speedway.

November 15, 1965
Breaking barriers

The jet-powered Spirit of America, driven by Craig Breedlove, established a new land speed record on this day in 1965, when a speed of 600.601mph (966.574km/h) was achieved while racing across the Bonneville Salt Flats in Utah. Breedlove was the first person to break the 400mph (644km/h), 500mph (805km/h), and now the 600mph barriers. Gary Gabelich would outdo Breedlove five years later when he drove the rocket-powered Blue Flame to 622.407mph (1001.1km/h) at the same location.

Also on this day: 1930 – The Moon Motor Company went into receivership. 2004 – The Citroën C4 became available for purchase in the United Kingdom.

A Moon Motor Car. The company went into receivership on this day in 1930.
(Photo by Jason Taellious [412])

The Spirit of America on exhibit at the Museum of Science and Industry in Chicago, Illinois. (Photo by 'self' [411])

November 16, 1901
Electric speed

Coney Island, New Jersey is well known for its classic and contemporary amusement park rides, but on this day in 1901 it was home to a different kind of wild ride. A soup of automobiles, including eight gas-powered, six steam-powered and one electric vehicle, known as the Torpedo Racer, bolted down a one mile course in a show of speed and ability. Andrew Riker and his lean and low battery powered Torpedo Racer crossed the finish line in third place out of the entire field, but in doing so he set a new US land speed record for electric motor carriages at a harrowing 57mph (92km/h).

"Finish of 1st Am[erican] auto race at Springfield, IL - A L Riker in electric, winner." 1900, Long Island, New York.
(Library of Congress, reproduction number LC-DIG-ppmsca-19358, public domain)

Also on this day: 1904 – The first reported automobile theft in Los Angeles took place. The White steam car was later recovered. 1956 – Terry Labonte, American stock car driver and two-time NASCAR champion, was born. 1981 – Production of the Vauxhall Astra began in Britain.

Illustration of Andrew Riker with mechanic on the Torpedo Racer.
(Original image public domain)

November 17, 1927

Double-decked

On this day in 1927, Leyland introduced the Titan double-decker bus. The bus would be built primarily for markets in the United Kingdom between 1927 and 1942, and again between 1945 and 1969, but it also found success in export markets, including Australia and South Africa.

1940 Roe bodied Leyland Titan.
(Photo by Jon's pics [413])

The original buses, model TD1, featured a six-cylinder, 6.8-liter front-mounted engine that produced 90-98bhp, and could carry 48 seated passengers. At 25ft long and 13.1ft tall, with a weight of 5⅝ tons, the bus rode on pneumatic tires, giving it a legal top speed of 20mph. By the time the TD2 was introduced in 1931, more than 2350 TD1s had been manufactured.

1929 Leyland Titan TD1. (Photo by Jon's pics [414])

Also on this day: **1957** – Carroll Shelby drove a Maserati 450S to victory in an SCCA National event in Riverside, California. **1986** – Renault executive Georges Besse was assassinated outside his Paris home. Anarchist group Action Directe was assumed to have conducted the hit in retaliation for major layoffs issued to save the company. Two women were sentenced to life in prison for the murder. **1998** – Newly formed DaimlerChrysler began trading on the New York Stock Exchange.

November 18, 1960

So long, DeSoto

Chrysler introduced DeSoto in 1928 to offer mid level luxury. By the end of the year Chrysler would also acquire Dodge, giving them two makes aimed at the same crowd. Chrysler executives placed DeSoto as a mid-luxury vehicle, between Chrysler and Dodge, but the new make started to suffer from identity problems, and sales struggled as an array of strange designs were introduced. After finding stability, following the near fatal disaster that was the Airflow, the brand achieved relative success through the 1950s. A recession at the end of the decade led to Chrysler's decision to cut DeSoto, an announcement made on this day in 1960. The final DeSotos would roll off the assembly line on November 30 and a flash sale would be put into effect to sell off the remaining models.

1934 DeSoto Airflow coupe. (Photo by Greg Gjerdingen [415])

Also on this day: **1916** – The last major automobile race in the US before the country's entry into World War I, the American Grand Prize, was held. Co-drivers Gil Anderson and Howard Wilcox were victorious, scoring $7500. **2012** – The first United Grand Prix was held in Austin, Texas.

1961 DeSoto, the final model year for the brand. (Photo by John Lloyd [416])

November 19, 1959
The end of Edsel

Too much money, too much hype, too much of the same old thing. The Edsel was a brand new car line from Ford, filling the gap between Ford and its luxurious Lincoln line, but when the new brand debuted on September 4, 1957, amid high expectations, the press and the public were quick to shrug. Sharing numerous cosmetic and mechanical components with other Ford models, the car did little to stand out, aside from a large vertical grille that was gawked at by many consumers. The financial fiasco that followed quickly sunk the brand, leading Ford to announce its discontinuation on this day in 1959. When production ceased at the end of November, only 2846 units were produced for the 1960 model year, leading to a final production total of 118,297 Edsels built between 1957 and 1960.

Also on this day: **1912** – Thomas Neal was named as the first chairman of General Motors. **1993** – An agreement was made between General Motors and Toyota to sell the Chevrolet Cavalier as the Toyota Cavalier in Japan.

1958 Edsel Citation. (Photo by Rain0975 [412])

1960 Edsel Villager. (Photo by Greg Gjerdingen [418])

The front end of a 1953 Kaiser Henry J. The final one left the assembly line on November 20 1953 as a 1954 model. (Photo by A Davey [420])

November 20, 1923
Yellow means ...

Stop. Go. Those were the only commands offered by traffic lights since the first one was installed in London in 1868. That all changed when the US Patent Office issued patent number 1,475,074 on this

A yellow caution light shines on a three position traffic light. (Photo by TheDigitel Beaufort [419])

day in 1923. Before the introduction of the caution light, the fast and often unforeseen change of the light signals, from stop to go, was regularly blamed for accidents. When inventor Garrett Morgan received the patent for his three-position traffic light, which provided a warning light that signaled the change from go to stop, the safety of intersections would be forever improved. Morgan later sold the rights to his patent to General Electric for $40,000.

Also on this day: **1953** – The final Henry J rolled off the assembly line as a 1954 model that was indistinguishable from 1953 models, aside from the serial number. **2011** – Ferrari designer Sergio Scaglietti died at age 91.

November 21, 1970

Meeting the Boss

Ford introduced the Boss 351 Mustang on this day in 1970 for the 1971 model year at the Detroit Auto Show. The vehicles featured an eight-cylinder, 16-valve V8 pushing 330bhp. The engine had an aluminum intake manifold, solid lifters, dual-point distributor, a six-quart oil pan, cast-aluminum valve covers and 4-barrel carb system, allowing the Mustang to scream from 0-60mph in 5.8 seconds. Only 1806 Boss 351 Mustangs were built in 1971.

Also on this day: **1919** – The Fox Motor Company was founded. **1967** – Ken Block, American race car driver and co-founder of DC Shoes, was born.

1971 Ford Mustang Boss 351. (Photo by crudmucosa [421])

November 22, 1893

Harley Earl's birthday

As a Stanford dropout Harley J Earl joined his father's coachbuilding business, Harley Automobile Works, which was churning out custom car bodies for some of Hollywood's biggest stars. Following a Cadillac dealer's acquisition of the family business, Earl, born on this day in 1893, was observed by Cadillac General Manager Lawrence Fisher while touring dealerships around the country. Fisher watched as Earl used innovative methods to design bodies, leading him to invite Earl to develop a body for Cadillac's new companion brand LaSalle in 1927. The success of the LaSalle led to Earl being named director of General Motor's new Art and Color Section. Earl's career manifested into one of legend in the auto industry. After becoming the first styling person to be named as a VP of a large corporation, Earl would play a role in the introduction of many cars of great importance, including the Buick Y-Job in 1939, considered the first concept car. He also approved

Ford Cleveland engine block, the bare bones of the engine that powered the Mustang Boss 351. (Photo by Nick Johns [422])

1953 Chevrolet Corvette. Harley Earl was instrumental in the introduction of the Corvette. (Photo by Joe deSousa [423])

1927 LaSalle, the design that led to Earl being hired by General Motors. Note the right hand drive, as this is an Australian car. (Photo by Sicnag [424])

Frank Hershey's 1948 Cadillac design, which ushered in the era of fins. Perhaps his greatest contribution was Project Opel, better known by its production name, Corvette.

Also on this day: **1957** – The Ferrari 250 Testa Rossa was introduced. **1963** – President John F Kennedy was shot while riding in a Lincoln Continental convertible in Dallas, Texas. He would later die from his wounds. **1995** – Briton Colin McRae won the World Rally Championship.

November 23, 1951
The first Poles

Fabryka Samochodów Osobowych was established by the communist government of Poland to produce automobiles in a country facing years of rebuilding, following WWII. A factory was built along the Vistula River in Warsaw, and produced the first Polish manufactured automobiles, which began to roll off of the assembly line on this day in 1951. The FSO Warszawa was assembled under license from Soviet automaker GAZ, whose similar vehicle was named Pobeda, 'victory' in English.

Also on this day: **1945** – English race car driver Tony Pond was born. **1954** – A gold plated 1955 Chevrolet Bel-Air rolled off the assembly line, marking the production of the 50 millionth General Motors vehicle.

FSO Warszawa hatchback. (Photo by photobeppus, [425])

November 24, 1951
A mighty merger

When Austin and Morris agreed to merge, on this day in 1951, to form British Motor Corporation (BMC), it became the largest automaker in Britain, and the fourth largest in the world, falling behind General Motors, Chrysler and Ford. The new company would continue to operate both brands as unique, claiming they would not produce the same models. However, the introduction of the Mini at the end of the decade saw both brands offering a version.

Also on this day: **1965** – A 70mph speed limit was set on the M1 in the United Kingdom. **1973** – Germany imposed a speed limit on its Autobahn due to the 1973 oil crisis. It was lifted after four months.

A later generation Warszawa 223.
(Photo by Felix O [426])

1951 Austin A40 Sports. (Photo by Sicnag [427])

1951 Morris Oxford. (Photo by Niels de Wit [428])

November 25, 1973

No gas on Sundays

President Nixon issued a ban on purchasing gasoline on Sundays on this day in 1973. (Public domain)

The Organization of Arab Petroleum Exporting Countries declared an oil embargo in October 1973 against Canada, Japan, the Netherlands, the United Kingdom, and the United States, in response to American involvement in the Yom Kippur War. The circumstances led to US President Richard Nixon issuing an indefinite ban on Sunday gasoline sales, on this day in 1973. The ban would last until the embargo ended the following March, but other fuel saving legislation from the era remained in place, including a national speed limit of 55 miles per hour, and the ability to turn right when faced with a red traffic light. Each of these measures was designed to improve fuel efficiency.

Also on this day: **1844** – Karl Benz was born. **1925** – Ford Motor Company completed its first airplane. **1949** – Cadillac manufactured its one millionth car. **1990** – A windstorm sent the Lacey V Murrow floating bridge – which connected Seattle, Washington to Bellevue and other eastern suburbs across Lake Washington – to the bottom of the lake.

November 26, 1948

The first Australian

J A Holden & Co became a leading saddlery in South Australia soon after it was founded in 1856. When the founder's grandson joined the company almost 50 years later, he added automotive upholstery repair to the company's services. Following WWI, a subsidiary was formed, Holden Motor Body Builders, which produced car bodies in Adelaide, South Australia. The next decade would have HMBB building car bodies for Austin, Chrysler, DeSoto, Ford, Morris, Hillman, Humber, Hupmobile and Willys-Overland, before the company was bought by General Motors. When the Australian government began to encourage growth of the Australian auto industry, Holden executives made a compromise with GM to build a Chevrolet-based, Australian car. The Holden 48-215 – the first mass-produced Australian badged automobile – began rolling off the assembly line on this day in 1948, generating a waiting list of buyers that took more than a year to fill.

Also on this day: **1963** – Porsche introduced the Carrera GTS Type 904, a vehicle designed to bring Porsche back to its racing heritage. **1898** – Pete DePaolo, winner of the 1925 Indy 500, was born.

Warning to gas stealers during the 1973 oil crisis. (Photo by David Falconer/National Archives, Records of the Environmental Protection Agency, public domain)

1950 Holden FX sedan. (Photo by Sicnag [429])

151 Holden 45-215 Ute, referred to as the FX. (Photo by Alden Jewell [430])

November 27, 1949
Bringing the trophy to Japan

Race car driver Masanori Sekiya achieved his greatest fame behind the wheel as the first Japanese-born winner of 24 Hours of Le Mans. Born on this day in 1949, Sekiya first participated in the all day race in 1985. He quickly came to love the event, even marrying in the town before the 1987 competition, but he did not limit his career to Le Mans, as he raced in Formula 3000, Formula Nippon, and won first place in the Japanese Touring Car Championship in 1994. After a fourth place finish in 1993, Sekiya returned to Le Mans in 1995, driving a McLaren F1 GTR for Kokusai Kaihatsu Racing, with co-drivers J J Lehto of Finland and Yannick Dalmas of France. Just two laps shy of 300, the team took home the first place trophy in the GT1 class, and in the overall rankings.

Also on this day: **1945** – British race car driver and television presenter Alain de Cadenet was born. **1996** – The final Cadillac Fleetwood left the assembly line. **2007** – Three time Indy 500 winner Helio Castroneves won the televised contest *Dancing with the Stars* with partner Julianne Hough.

A McLaren F1 GTR, similar to the car Masanori Sekiya drove in the 1995 24 Hours of Le Mans to become the first Japanese winner.
(Photo by DoomWarrior [431])

The Lark McLaren F1 GTR.
(Photo by Matthew Lamb [432])

November 28, 1895
The first race in America

The first organized automobile race in the United States took place on this day in 1895, following a July 10 announcement from the *Chicago Times-Herald* that it would host the race, with a winning prize of $5000 (equivalant to roughly $143,000 in 2017). While 83 vehicles signed up for the race, only six arrived for the start, as many automobiles were incomplete or damaged en route to the event. Of the vehicles, two were electric and four were gas-powered, including three Benz and one Duryea Motor Wagon. The Duryea, driven by Charles Duryea, finished the 54 mile course ahead of the pack in seven hours and fifty-three minutes, traveling an average of 7mph (11km/h). Second place went to a Benz, imported by H Mueller & Co.

Also on this day: **1993** – The first Irish F1 driver, Joseph Kelly, passed away. **2000** – Bill France Jr stepped down as president of NASCAR. His father was the founder of the racing organization.

Charles Duryea in the vehicle he built and raced to victory at the Chicago-Times Herald race.
(Photo from US National Museum. Library of Congress reproduction number: LC-USZ62-16250)

November 29, 1906
Lancia is founded

A group of Fiat racing drivers, including Vincenzo Lancia, and his friend Claudio Fogolin, founded Lancia & C Fabbrica Automobili, on this day in 1906, in Turin, Italy. The company found commercial success with its first vehicle, the Tipo 51, a 12hp that remained in production from 1907 through 1912. Lancia was known for innovation, and became the first manufacturer to offer production V4 and V6 engines, as well as independent suspension. By the end of the 1960s, Lancia was losing great sums of money, and a bid by Fiat to take over the company was accepted. The company was reorganized, and found great success in the marketplace after many dominating rally racing performances throughout the 1970s and 1980s.

Also on this day: **1975** – Two time Formula One Champion Norman Graham Hill died when the plane he was piloting crashed near London. Riding with him was fellow racer Tony Brise, team designer Andy Smallman, and three team mechanics, all of whom perished. **1987** – The Calder Thunderdome in Australia hosted its first race.

November 30, 1960
Scouting the competition

A merger of five harvesting and manufacturing firms in 1902 resulted in the founding of International Harvester Company (IH). The business originally focused on producing heavy machinery, including tractors and other agricultural equipment, but began truck production in 1907 at the company's McCormick Works factory in Chicago. Nearly 50 years later, IH expanded its operation by offering a competitor to the civilian Jeep, the International Scout, which first left a Fort Wayne, Indiana assembly line on this day in 1960. The vehicle featured a variety of two-door body styles, including a full-length roof, half cab pickup, or a soft top, each available with a 4x4 drivetrain.

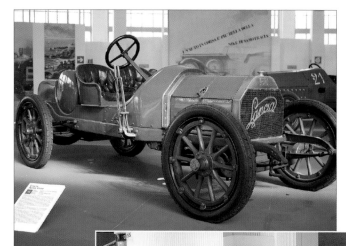

1908 Lancia Alfa Sport, originally called the Tipo 51. (Photo by tomislav medak [433])

1909 Lancia Beta Torpedo. (Photo by Semnoz [434])

A 1907 International Harvester light truck, the first year International produced trucks. (Photo by Brian Corey)

A 1963 International Scout 80. (Photo by dave_7 [435])

Also on this day: **1901** – The Henry Ford Company was organized, which would later fail, giving way to Henry Ford founding the Ford Motor Company two years later. **1950** – The Paris Motor Show saw the launch of the upscale Renault Fregate.

December 1, 1913
The moving assembly line

The first moving assembly line in the automotive industry began to churn out complete Model T's on this day in 1913 at the Ford Highland Park Assembly Plant. Henry Ford yearned for maximum efficiency in the production of his vehicles, as this would allow him to offer an inexpensive, reliable automobile to the masses. By combining aspects of previous, still, assembly lines, with methods borrowed in part from slaughterhouses and breweries, Ford was able to reduce the time it took to build a Model T from more than 12 hours to about 1 hour and 30 minutes. The assembly line reduced the man hours necessary to build vehicles while increasing output, resulting in less expensive cars that didn't sacrifice quality.

Also on this day: **1914** – Maserati was founded. **1989** – Ford Motor Company acquired Jaguar. **1990** – The two Channel Tunnel sections that were started from the UK and France meet 40 meters under the seabed.

Workers busy on Ford's Highland Park moving assembly line
(Courtesy Ford Motor Company)

Mass production took Ford around the world. This Buenos Aires assembly plant opened in 1921.
(Public domain)

December 2, 2002
Toyota's first hydrogen vehicles

In a staggering show of advanced technology Toyota delivered the first market-ready fuel cell vehicles on this day in 2002. After ten years of research and development, six Toyota Fuel Cell Hybrid Vehicles (FCHVs) were produced, of which four were leased to the Japanese government, and two were delivered to researchers at the University of California, Irvine and Davis. The FCHVs emit only water vapor as an emission, because it is able to power its motors and recharge its batteries with electricity that is generated by combining hydrogen and oxygen. This led to Toyota launching the Mirai in 2015, the first hydrogen fuel cell vehicle to be sold on a large scale.

Toyota Highlander FCHV in 2011 in the UK.
(Photo by Dominic Alves [436])

Also on this day: **1899** – British racer John Cobb was born. **1916** – The Uniontown Board Speedway in Pennsylvania held its first event, which was won by Louis Chevrolet behind the wheel of a Frontenac.

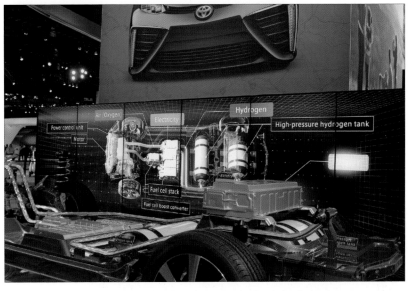

2015 Toyota Mirai chassis alongside digital display.
(Photo by California Air Resources Board [437])

December 3, 1979

Stepping out of Pace

At a time when Detroit was still pushing gas guzzling land yachts, the AMC Pacer was a novel idea. Introduced in February 1975 more than 145,000 Pacers sold in their first year of production, but sales soon slumped, and only 280,000 total vehicles left the plant during its five year run. Advertised as 'the first wide small car,' the Pacer featured a surface area that was nearly 37 per cent glass, giving rise to the name, Flying Fishbowl. A general lack of power, minimal storage, and fuel economy that was lower than that of competing Asian and German imports, all contributed to the end of production of the Pacer on this day in 1979.

Also on this day: **1948** – The Kaiser-Frazer Corporation bought the Willow Run factory, originally built by Ford to manufacture airplanes for WWII. **1990** – Wendell Scott, the first African American NASCAR race car driver, died at age 69.

1975 AMC Pacer D/L.
(Photos by Greg Gjerdingen [438], [439], [440])

December 4, 1915

The Peace Ship sets sail

Henry Ford had a history of supporting unusual causes, often in more unusual ways. But perhaps no feat was more widely mocked than his World War I peace ship, an amateur attempt at ending the fighting. Henry Ford chartered the ocean liner Oscar II and invited famous peace activists to accompany him on a journey to Europe. The idea was to gain enough publicity to bring peace to the nations at the root of the war. The ship launched from New York Harbor on this day in 1915 and immediately faced hardship. Aside from being dubbed the 'Ship of Fools' by many members of the press, fighting among the activists and an outbreak of influenza aboard the ship that left Henry physically ill, prompted him to abandon his mission, and return to the US just four days after landing in Norway.

Also on this day: **1916** – American racing driver Iggy Katona was born. **1974** – Leo Goossen, an American race car designer, died at age 82.

Left: Oscar II Peace Ship with Capt G W Hempel and Henry Ford.
(Public domain)

Right: Press photo of the 'Peace Ship' leaving New York on December 4, 1915. (Public domain)

December 5, 1977
A new car on the horizon

The first mass-produced front-wheel drive cars from the Chrysler Corporation, the Dodge Omni and Plymouth Horizon, were introduced on this day in 1977. Not only were they the first front-wheel drive vehicles produced in large quantities from Chrysler, they are among the first from any American automaker. Along with the introduction of the K-car platform, these compact cars are heralded as a savior to Chrysler during a time when it was losing millions of dollars per year, prior to hiring Lee Iacocca as President. Previous front-wheel drive cars from American manufacturers include the Cord 810 and Cadillac Eldorado.

Also on this day: **1946** – South African racing champion Sarel Daniel van der Merwe was born. **1973** – The United Kingdom issued a 50mph speed limit in order to conserve petrol during the 1973 oil crisis. **1985** – Frankie Muniz, American actor, race car driver and star of *Malcolm in the Middle*, was born.

December 6, 1976
One fast woman

Alvord Desert in the state of Oregon hosted Kitty O'Neil and her team as she chased the women's land speed record on this day in 1976. Kitty was working as a stuntwoman when she met Bill Fredrick, a stunt technology maker, who built the SMI Motivator, the car which she would eventually pilot in her quest to conquer the existing women's land speed record of 308.506mph (496.492km/h). She landed a $20,000 contract to pilot the vehicle, under the stipulation that she could not pursue the broader land speed record of 630.478mph (1014.656km/h), as it was to be broken by stuntman Hal Needham in the same car. When the dust settled during her record setting attempt, she found she had smashed the women's record with an official speed of 512.710mph (825.127km/h).

1986 Plymouth Horizon. (Photo by Greg Gjerdingen [441])

1986 Dodge Omni GLH-S Shelby. (Photo by Greg Gjerdingen [442])

Also on this day: **1948** – Formula One World Champion Keijo 'Keke' Rosberg was born in Solna, Sweden. **1954** – Volkswagenwerk GMBH registered Volkswagen as a trademark, although the name had been in use for many years. **1961** – Two time 24 Hours of Le Mans winner Manuel Reuter was born in Mainz, Western Germany.

The SMI Motivator, the vehicle in which Kitty O'Neil broke the women's land speed record. (Illustration by Brian Corey)

F1 World Champion Keke Rosberg, seen here in 1979, was born on this day in 1948. (Photo by Gilberto Benni [443])

December 7, 1931
End of the A

Henry Ford saw no need for a new model in the mid 1920s. His Model T filled the market as an affordable option to consumers. Henry's son Edsel worked tirelessly to convince his father that a new car was indeed necessary, and falling sales eventually persuaded Henry to agree. Edsel led the design team for the car that was to replace the world's best-selling automobile, although Henry would take most of the credit for the Model A, after close to 2 million units sold in the 18 months following its launch on December 2, 1927. Despite the success, Ford began discontinuation of the Model A on this day in 1931. When factories were back up to full speed in March of 1932 they were retooled to manufacture the four-cylinder Model B and the Model 18, Ford's first car to feature the company's famous flathead V8 engine.

Also on this day: **1979** – The final MG Midget was manufactured. **2009** – Silverstone was awarded a 17-year contract to host the British Grand Prix, starting in 2010.

Interior of a Ford Model A DeLuxe Roadster. (Photo by Jack Snell [444])

1931 Ford Model A DeLuxe Coupe. (Photo by Jim Hammer [445])

December 8, 1981
Mitsubishi lands in America

In 1971 Chrysler Corporation purchased 15 per cent of Mitsubishi, allowing the Japanese company to sell the Mitsubishi Galant as a rebadged Dodge Colt, in order to compete in the growing small car market in the US. Less than a decade later Chrysler was bleeding financially and Mitsubishi was not pleased with sales performance. In 1980 Chrysler sold its Australian manufacturing division to Mitsubishi, in order to avoid bankruptcy, and in 1981 Mitsubishi founded Mitsubishi Motors North America, Inc to sell cars with its own name on them in the US. The first Mitsubishi badged vehicles arrived on US shores on this day in 1981. For the 1982 model year, 30,000 vehicles were sent to the US, including the Tredia, Cordia and Starion models, followed by the Mighty Max pickup truck.

Also on this day: **1861** – Early automotive executive William Crapo Durant was born in New York. **1945** – Toyota received permission to begin production of buses and trucks from occupying forces, following the end of WWII.

1982 Mitsubishi Tredia. (Photo by Riley [446])

A well used 1983 Mitsubishi Cordia Turbo. (Photo by Riley [447])

December 9, 2005
Recall the Routemaster

London's iconic double decker public transport buses went into service in February of 1956, following seven years of design and development. The Routemaster, as it is officially known, was built by the Associated Equipment Company, and Royal Park Vehicles saw production through 1968, but the end of the assembly line did not mean the end of service. A total of 2786 Routemasters were produced for service, and as many as 1280 remain. The original design featured independent front suspension, power steering and a fully automatic transmission, all firsts for a bus. The aging

1966 Routemaster JJD 408D. (Photo by Paul Robertson [449])

Routemasters were recalled from routine service on this day in 2005, replaced by more modern buses, although one heritage route through central London is still operated by the vintage buses as of 2017.

Interior of a classic Routemaster.
(Photo by James Petts [448])

Also on this day:
1920 – Italian motorcycle racing champion Bruno Ruffo was born. **2007** – Brazilian race car driver Rafael Sperafico was killed in a crash at the Autódromo José Carlos Pace motorsport circuit in São Paulo.

December 10, 1915
One million Fords

The Ford Model T was manufactured from 1908 until 1927. With more than 15,000,000 produced overall, it was the best selling car in the world until the Volkswagen Beetle surpassed it in production numbers in 1972. It was the car that launched the moving assembly line for the auto industry, which allowed Ford to crank out T after T in two hours or less. It was this mass production that gave way to the 1,000,000th Ford, which rolled out of the River Rouge factory in Detroit on this day in 1915. That year Ford produced a total of 308,162 vehicles, with the base model selling for $390. The next year production went up by nearly 200,000 units, and the price fell by $45. The Model T would be named the most influential car of the 20th century in 1999's Car of the Century competition.

1915 Ford Model T, similar to the one millionth that left the assembly line. (Photo by Don O'Brien [450])

Also on this day: 1912 – Charles Nash was elected President of General Motors. **1920** – Co-founder of Dodge Brothers, Horace Dodge, died on this day at age 52. **1970** – Lee Iacocca became President of Ford Motor Company.

Hood ornament of a 1915 Ford Model T.
(Photo by Walter [451])

December 11, 1894
The first auto show

When four automakers gathered to display their vehicles in Paris, France, on this day in 1894, at the Internationale de Velocipidie et de Locomotion Automobile, the world's first auto show began. The event would give way to the 1898 Salon de l'Automobile, organized by French automotive pioneer Albert de Dion. The event is known today as Mondial de l'Automobile, or Paris Motor Show. The biennial show has since become one of the most important industry auto shows, often playing host to more than one million visitors checking out the latest lineups, new models and concept cars from automakers all over the world.

First International Automobile Exhibition at the Tuileries in 1898, organized by the ACF. (Public domain)

Also on this day: 1920 – English motorcycle racer and journalist Denis Jenkinson was born. **1961** – Philco Corporation became a subsidiary of Ford. **2010** – Nissan sold its first all electric Leaf in North America.

Nissan sold its first Leaf in the United States on this day in 2010, similar to this 2011 model. (Photo by Masahiko OHKUBO [452])

December 12, 2010
Tom Walkinshaw Racing

Tom Walkinshaw, British racecar driving and founder of Tom Walkinshaw Racing, passed away on this day in 2010 at the age of 64. His racing career began in 1968 behind the wheel of an MG Midget. He soon began racing Formula Three and Two, and, in 1974, he was hired by Ford to drive the British Touring Car Circuit, of which he won his class. Walkinshaw founded the racing team and engineering firm that bears his name two years later. Starting in 1982 TWR developed a close relationship with Jaguar, and for nearly the next dozen years they were the prime choice of cars for the team to build upon, starting with the Jaguar XJ-S. TWR achieved wins at Le Mans in Jaguar vehicles in 1988 and 1990. The team won twice more, in 1996 and 1997, with a Porsche WSC-95. Tom Walkinshaw Racing closed shop in 2002, with its assets and facility purchased by Menard Competition Technologies.

Also on this day: 1923 – Dodge celebrated the production of its one millionth vehicle.

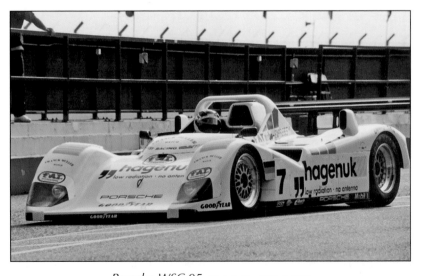

Porsche WSC-95. (Photo by Tony Harrison [453])

1984 TWS Jaguar XJ-S. (Photo by Sicnag [454])

December 13, 2003
Boots take a walk

A craze took over American highways and byways in the 1950s as gas stations became more than a place to refuel your car. Roadside attractions were lit with neon, and often included outstanding feats of architecture, or featured novelties such as huge rockets, smiling dinosaurs or, in one case, the world's largest hat and cowboy boots. Seattle, Washington's Hat'n'Boots gas station opened in 1954 on Highway 99 in Georgetown, and two years later a patent would be issued for its unique building design. The iconic gas station struggled following the opening of Interstate 5, which bypassed the area, leading to its closure in 1988. After playing a role in multiple movies, the City of Seattle moved the dilapidating Hat'n'Boots to a permanent location in Oxbow Park on this day in 2003, preserving a piece of Americana for generations to come.

Hat n' Boots in 1977. (Picture courtesy of Library of Congress, photograph by John Margolies, reproduction number, e.g., LC-MA05-1)

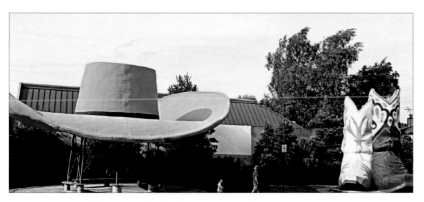

Hat and boots in Oxbow Park, Seattle, WA. (Photo by Joe Wolf [455])

Also on this day: **1957** – The final first generation Ford Thunderbird left the assembly line, giving way for the two-seater to become a four-seater.

December 14, 1909
The last brick is laid

The original track surface at Indianapolis Motor Speedway was a cruel mixture of limestone, gravel, tar and oil. This resulted in a course so rough it popped nearly all of the tires of the motorcycles that took to it opening day. Before competition resumed, the track needed to be sanded down, but driver's then battled a never settling dust. As one man said, "Driving at Indy was like flying through a meteor shower." Multiple deaths during early racing events at the Speedway were attributed to the poor track conditions. This led to course founder Carl Fisher resurfacing the track with bricks. It was on this day in 1909 the last brick at Indy was laid, leading to the nickname 'The Brickyard.' The bricks remained in place for more than 50 years, before the installation of asphalt. A row of original brick remains on the track today, marking the start/finish line.

The last remaining bricks at Indianapolis Motor Speedway make up the start/finish line. (Photo by Josh Hallett [456])

A 1987 AMC Eagle, similar to the last one that rolled off the assembly line on this day in 1987. (Photo by Greg Gjerdingen [457])

Also on this day: **1931** – Rolls-Royce acquired Bentley. **1987** – The final American Motors Eagle station wagon rolled off the assembly line. **2004** – The Millau Viaduct cable bridge spanning the River Tarn in southern France was dedicated, becoming the tallest vehicle bridge in the world.

December 15, 1930
The Highway Code

Part of the United Kingdom's Road Traffic Act of 1930 included the development of a Highway Code, a draft of which was first issued on this day in 1930. *The Highway Code* would be officially published by the Ministry of Transportation the following April, and could be purchased for one penny. The code featured 18 pages of information and advice to drivers, including the use of hand signals they should give, and how to understand hand signals issued by traffic officers. The second edition was published three years later, and featured illustrations of road signs for the first time. The booklet is continuously revised and features guidelines and rules for automobiles, motorcycles, pedestrians, cyclists and animals.

Also on this day: **1915** – Hercules Motor Manufacturing Company was founded. **1941** – A no-strike policy was formed for war industries by the American Federation of Labor Council. **1967** – The Silver Bridge, spanning the Ohio River to connect Point Pleasant, West Virginia and Gallipolis, Ohio, collapsed, killing 46 people.

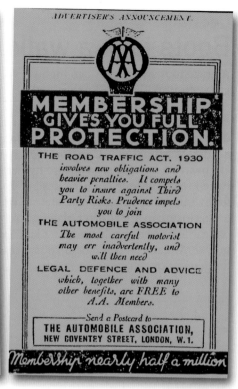

Front cover of the first Highway Code, and advert on inside front cover.

December 16, 1949
Saab goes into production

Saab's initial production passenger car, the 92, left the Trollhättan Assembly factory for the first time on this day in 1949. Originally an airplane manufacturer, Saab began its automotive branch in 1945, when engineers and designers started work on their first prototype, known as the Ursaab, or original Saab. As could be expected from an airplane company, the 92 was extremely aerodynamic, featuring a body stamped from a single piece of sheet metal. The reduced drag was beneficial to the small 25hp engine, allowing for the coupé to travel approximately 105km/h (65mph). Saab's surplus of green paint from WWII aircraft production led to the color being used as the original color on the first 92s, nearly 20,000 of which were produced before Saab introduced its next model, the 93, in 1955.

1950 Saab 92. (Photo by Greg Abbott [458])

Saab 92 B. (Photo by Andrew Bone [459])

Also on this day: **1925** – Construction of the Queensway Tunnel between Liverpool and Birkenhead began. **1992** – Toyota began manufacturing vehicles in Europe, when production started at its plant in Burnaston, Derbyshire.

December 17, 1963
Breathe cleanly

The Clean Air Act of 1963 was passed into law in the United States on this day in 1963, providing a range of guidelines to help reduce and prevent pollution. The act aimed to address current environmental problems caused by pollution, as well as provide resources to begin research into techniques that would minimize future pollution and lay the groundwork for emission regulations. However, it was not until the 1970 Clean Air Act that the auto industry felt major pressure to begin seeking solutions. Under this piece of legislation the automobile makers were required to cut their product's emissions by approximately 90 per cent. Upon signing the Clean Air Act of 1963 President Lyndon B Johnson stated, "Now, under this legislation, we can halt the trend toward greater contamination of our atmosphere. We can seek to control industrial wastes discharged into the air. We can find the ways to eliminate dangerous haze and smog."

President Lyndon B. Johnson. (Public domain)

Also on this day: 1954 – British Petroleum Company, known as BP, was formed. **1968** – Paul Tracy, Canadian race car driver and sports broadcaster, was born. **1998** – Construction of a new General Motors plant in Shanghai, China was completed.

Paul Tracy, born on this day in 1968, is seen here at the 2008 Toyota Grand Prix of Long Beach. (Photo by Regular Daddy at English Wikipedia [460])

December 18, 1898
The first land speed record

On this day in 1898, Count Gaston de Chasseloup-Laubat set the first official land speed record during a competition hosted in northern France by French automobile magazine *La France Automobile*. Soaring into the record spot in his electric Jeantaud, Chasseloup-Laubat completed a 1km pass (0.62 miles) in 57 seconds, with an average speed of 63.13km/h (39mph). After a series of speed duels throughout January and March 1899, resulting in back and forth victories and records between him and Camille Jenatzy, Chasseloup-Laubat remained victorious.

Count Gaston de Chasseloup-Laubat in his electric Jeantaud. (Public domain)

Georges Bouton and Count Gaston de Chasseloup-Laubat on a steam powered Trépardoux & Cie Dog Cart de route in 1885. (Public domain)

Finally, on April 29, 1899, less than five months after the original record was set, Jenatzy made the first run that surpassed 100km/h (62mph), and ended up with an average speed of 105km/h (65mph). This record would stand for three years and begin the passion to accelerate automotive speed technology.

Also on this day: 1907 – American race car driver Bill Holland was born. **1949** – Alberto Ascari drove a Ferrari 166 to victory at the Buenos Aires Grand Prix. **1954** – English racer John Booth was born.

December 19, 1924

Ghost of a Ghost

The final Rolls-Royce Silver Ghost manufactured in London was sold on this day in 1924. It was for this car that the term 'The best car in the world' was coined, thus making the Silver Ghost an exquisite choice of the elite, including US President Woodrow Wilson. The luxury line was introduced in 1906 as the 40/50, and one chassis was named Silver Ghost. While other chassis received titles of their own, the press regularly referred to the cars as Silver Ghost, leading to Rolls-Royce officially recognizing the name in 1925. After manufacturing stopped in England, the cars saw continued production at the American Springfield factory for two more years. A total of 7874 Silver Ghosts were built between 1906 and 1926, before its successor, the Phantom I made its debut.

Also on this day: **1938** – Henry Ford II, grandson of Henry Ford, was elected to the Ford Motor Company Board of Directors. **1986** – The final Ford Capri was built, rolling out of the Halewood assembly plant. **1999** – Ferdinand Porsche was named 'Car Engineer of the Century.'

Above: 1924 Rolls-Royce Silver Ghost Roadster with coachwork by Merrimac; right: the dashboard.
(Photos by David Merett [461], [462])

December 20, 1989

Roger & Me

In the midst of record profits, a series of decisions approved by General Motors CEO Roger Smith led to the closing of several auto plants in Flint, Michigan, in favor of cheaper labor in Mexico. The shuttering of manufacturing facilities, starting in 1986, was documented by Michael Moore in his film *Roger & Me*, which debuted on this day in 1989. The closing of the plants reduced the number of GM autoworkers in Flint from 80,000 in 1978 to 50,000 in 1992. As of August 2015, conservative estimates put the number of GM employees in the Flint area at just 7200. The documentary follows the downfall of jobs and the uprising of crime; all while Moore tries to score an interview with Smith. Despite mixed reviews, *Roger & Me* is recognized as being an important commentary on the life and history of the people living and working in the auto industry, which led to the US Library of Congress selecting it for preservation.

Also on this day: **1922** – New York City retired its horse-drawn fire service. **1957** – The first second-generation, and first four-seat production Ford Thunderbird was manufactured, for the 1958 model year. **1977** – British automobile executive Sir Reginald Rootes passed away in London at age 81.

Michael Moore at the 66th Venice International Film Festival in September 2009. (Photo by nicolas genin [463])

1958 Ford Thunderbird.
(Photo by Greg Gjerdingen [464])

December 21, 1945
A general accident

On December 8, 1945, chief of staff, Major General Hobart Gay, invited General George S Patton to go pheasant hunting off base from the German post he was overseeing. During the journey he stated, "How awful war is. Think of the waste." Just moments later the Cadillac he was riding in the back seat of collided with an American army truck at a relatively low speed. Other occupants suffered minor injuries but Patton hit his head on the divider glass, which resulted in paralysis. On this day in 1945 he died from those injuries. The infamous car crash was widely speculated as an assassination of the general in order to silence his criticism of allied war leaders.

Also on this day: **1926** – The first Rolls-Royce Phantom I built in the United States was delivered to Harry Orndorff in Rhode Island. **1931** – The Kissel Motor Car Company was liquidated. **2000** – Citroën sold more than 100,000 vehicles in the UK in a single year for the first time.

December 22, 1937
The Lincoln Tunnel opens

The Lincoln Tunnel, passing underneath the Hudson River between Manhattan in New York City and Weehawken, New Jersey, opened on this day in 1937. The cost of the tunnel was a staggering $85 million (approximately equivalent to $1.44 billion in 2017), and was funded by the depression era Public Works Administration. When the tunnel opened, access cost 50 cents per automobile (approximately $8.50 in 2017) . The single original tunnel is 8216ft long (2504m), but since its opening two more tubes have been added to handle increased traffic flow.

Also on this day: **1910** – The Fisher Closed Body Company was organized to manufacture enclosed automobile cabs. **1960** – The one millionth Morris Minor was manufactured.

George S Patton in France in 1918 with a Renault FT light tank during WWI. (Public domain)

Below: General George S Patton in a command vehicle during a visit to Los Angeles in June 1945 following Victory in Europe. (Public domain)

Inside the Lincoln Tunnel (Photo by James Loesch [465])

Entrance to Lincoln Tunnel heading toward New Jersey. (Photo by Paul Sableman [466])

December 23, 1942
The Renault 4CV

It would be five years before the prototype that Renault unveiled on this day in 1942 would become the market-ready 4CV. When the production model launched in 1947, the rear-wheel drive, rear-engine, four-door supermini lagged in sales, but things began to turn around within the year. By the middle of 1949, nearly 40,000 of the

A 1:43 scale model of the 1942 Renault 4CV prototype. Model by Eligor. (Photo by Andrew Bone [467])

cars had been purchased. Production of the 4CV lasted through 1961, and by the time the last one rolled off the assembly line it had become the first French car to sell more than one million units.

Also on this day: 1915 – The White Motor Company was incorporated. **1956** – Italian race car driver Michele Alboreto was born. **1987** – French motorcycle racer Thomas Bourgin was born.

Renault 4CV. (Photo by Andrew Bone [468])

December 24, 1801
The Puffing Devil

British inventor and mining engineer Richard Trevithick introduced a steam-powered contraption he named the Puffing Devil, on this day in 1801. Trevithick, who would go on to patent the first high-pressure steam engine, demonstrated his new transportation device by carrying six passengers along Fore Street, and then up Camborne Hill in Camborne, UK. Just three days later the machine broke down, and operators left it unattended with the fire still burning. The water in the steam engine evaporated and the vehicle was destroyed, as the flames didn't die away. He went on to build a series of steam locomotives, furthering development of the modern railroad and steam transportation.

Also on this day: 1961 – General Motors accepted William Mitchell's design of the 1963 Buick Riviera and the 1963 Chevrolet Corvette. **2000** – John Cooper, co-founder of Cooper Car Company, died at age 77.

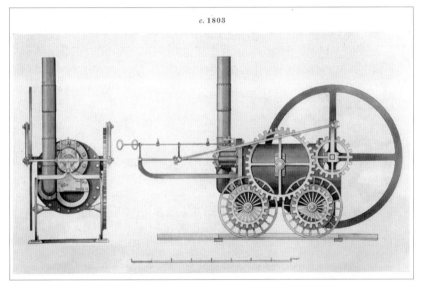

Trevithick followed up the Puffing Devil with the Coalbrookdale locomotive shown here. (Public domain)

William Mitchell's design for the 1963 Corvette was accepted by General Motors on this day in 1961. (Photo by Greg Gjerdingen [469])

December 25, 1985
Going the distance

David Turner and Tim Pickhard's 847 mile trip from Lands End, England to John O'Groats, Scotland, was no ordinary Christmas drive. By the time their four-day journey concluded on this day in 1985, they had set a new distance record for an electric vehicle on a single charge. To set the record, a Rover Leland Sherpa was outfitted with a Lucas electric motor. To set a new record of this type, Swedes Nic Megert and Anton Julmy took a 22,339.7km (13881.2 mile) trip around Europe that lasted from July 29 to August 28, 2016.

A 1981 Sherpa, similar to the one converted to battery power for the record drive on 25 December 1985. (Photo by Riley [470])

A 1947 Ford Sportsman. Ford introduced its first 'Woodie' convertible on 25 December in 1946. (Photo by Greg Gjerdingen [471])

Also on this day: 1878 – Louis Chevrolet was born in Switzerland. **1946** – Ford delivers the first wood-bodied convertible, dubbed the Sportsman.

December 26, 1933
Nissan signs up for business

Nissan can trace its roots back to the first Japanese automaker, Kwaishinsha Motor Car Works, of which the three investors named the first car DAT, an acronym of their surnames. After introducing its first car in 1914, the company was later renamed to DAT Jidosha & Co, and, in 1931, a smaller car was introduced, the DAT Type 11, which was known as the Son of DAT, and later Datsun. In 1931, the maker of Datsun became affiliated with Tobata Casting, which was part of the Nihon Sangyo holding company, or Nissan for short. On this day in 1933 Jidosha-Seizo Kabushiki-Kaisha (Automobile Manufacturing Co, Ltd) was founded by the holding company to take over all automobile production for Tobata. In June of 1934, the business name was changed to Nissan Motor Company.

Son of DAT, the Datsun Type 11, 1932 model. (Photo by HKT3012 [472])

Also on this day: 1956 – Preston Tucker, automotive executive and entrepreneur, died at the age of 53. **1985** – Ford introduced the Taurus.

A set of Nissan and Datsun Z cars from different generations. (Photo by thinktk [473])

December 27, 1941
The start of US tire rationing

The United States Federal Office of Price Administration (OPA) began its first rationing program to support WWII efforts on this day in 1941, limiting the number of tires any automobile driver could own to five. The OPA was originally designed as a consumer protection agency to stabilize

Williams County, North Dakota. H R Lampan, chairman of the tire rationing board. (Photo courtesy of Library of Congress, reproduction number: LC-USF34-065059-D)

prices and rents to prevent unwarranted increases. When the war began in December 1941, it shifted to limiting purchases of certain goods, including tires, cars, metal, typewriters, bicycles and food, among others. The OPA did issue a number of certificates to obtain new tires, but those were limited to vehicles deemed as essential, such as transport trucks for foods or fuels, public transportation, and safety and sanitary vehicles. After the war ended on both fronts, rationing in the US continued through 1945, with tire rationing not ending until December 31 of that year.

Also on this day: 1900 – German race car driver Hans Stuck was born. **1933** – The first Buicks to feature independent front suspension were introduced. **1993** – Belgian race car driver André Pilette died at age 75.

May 1942, Washington DC: congested parking downtown after both tire and gas rationing had been put into force. (Photo courtesy of Library of Congress, reproduction number: LC-USF34-082477-C)

December 28, 1923
A very presidential present

Having a birthday during the holiday season can be difficult for some people who think their special day will be forgotten. That wasn't the case on this day in 1923 when US President Woodrow Wilson received a Rolls-Royce Silver Ghost for his 67th birthday. Left by anonymous friends, the Rolls had even been modified with a higher windshield and roof, so Wilson could wear his top hat. Wilson was the

President Woodrow Wilson received this specially made Rolls-Royce for his 67th birthday from an anonymous friend, later found to be Bernard Baruch. (Photo by Hugh Miller, courtesy Woodrow Wilson's Presidential Library Archive [474])

first president to really understand the appeal of the motorcar, and was a champion of national road-building, paving the way for America's highway system.

Also on this day: **1938** – Florence Lawrence, AKA the Biograph Girl, died after purposefully consuming poison. Florence was considered the first movie star, and she was also the inventor of the mechanical brake light, mechanical turn signals and electric windshield wipers, none of which she patented or ever received compensation for. **1953** – Production of the Chevrolet Corvette moved from Flint, Michigan to St Louis, Missouri.

Florence Lawrence sits behind the wheel of a Lozier open touring car with 1912 Pennsylvania license plates. The famous actress and inventor killed herself on this day in 1938.
(Photo courtesy of Wisconsin Center for Film and Theater Research)

December 29, 1800
It's going to be a Goodyear

Charles Goodyear did not start Goodyear Tire & Rubber Company, but it is named for him. Goodyear is often credited with inventing vulcanized rubber, which allowed for the manufacture and long-term use of rubber products, including tires. Goodyear, born on this day in 1800, was a self-taught chemist who became obsessed with natural rubber in the early 1830s. He wanted to make it a viable material for production of numerous products, as untreated rubber would perish after a few months. Goodyear achieved this when he discovered how to lengthen the life of rubber by curing it with sulphur and heat. He

Charles Goodyear.
(Illustration from Scientific America., public domain)

Stripping tube on mandrel before sending to cure, Goodyear Tire Factory, Akron, OH.
(Photo courtesy Library of Congress, reproduction number LC-USZ62-113947, public domain)

received a US patent for the process, now called vulcanization, in June of 1844, eight weeks after Englishman Thomas Hancock filed for a similar patent. It is believed Hancock experimented on samples of rubber from Goodyear to learn about vulcanization. It was not until 38 years after Goodyear died that Frank Seiberling founded Goodyear Tire & Rubber Company.

Also on this day: **1929** – Wilhelm Maybach, German automobile designer and engineer, died at age 83. **1962** – British racing driver Graham Hill won his first World Drivers' Championship. **1967** – Hyundai Motor Company was founded in South Korea.

December 30, 1983

Miles and miles and miles

British auto racer Violette Cordery had stamina. In 1926 she co-drove a 19.6 hp Invicta around Autodromo Nazionale Monza for 10,000 miles, (16,000km), setting a new long distance record for the track. Her racing career started about five years earlier when she participated in her first hillclimb at the age of 20. She would tackle multiple genres of racing, including motorcycles and sprints. While achieving success on all tracks, she was best known for her distance drives. Following Autodromo, she conducted a world tour through Europe, Africa, Australia, India, Canada and the United States, and, in 1929, she, along with her sister Evelyn, covered 30,000 miles (48,000km) at Brooklands over about 30,000 minutes – nearly 21 days – averaging 61.57mph (99km/h). She lived a quiet life after retiring in 1938, living peacefully until her death on this day in 1983.

Also on this day: **1918** – Henry Ford resigned as president of Ford Motor Company. **1936** – The United Auto Workers union began its first sit-down strike. **1942** – English race car driver Guy Edwards was born.

December 31, 2002

Legends go their own ways

The Great Depression was incredibly hard on Bentley, pushing it into receivership. Its financial downfall led to Rolls-Royce acquiring the company under the name British Central Equitable Trust in 1931. The automakers would continue their own production lines, with Rolls-Royce focusing on utmost luxury, and Bentley pursuing power and performance for a top of the line driving experience. In 1998 Rolls-Royce and Bentley were put up for auction by their current owner, Vickers plc. Volkswagen outbid BMW to acquire Bentley and the rights to Rolls-Royce model names, its mascot and grille shape. However, the Rolls-Royce name and logo were owned by a separate entity, to which BMW paid for licensing rights. Under a temporary deal BMW would supply engines to VW for Rolls-Royce cars, so Volkswagen could use the name. It was on this day in 2002 that Rolls-Royce became a sole product of BMW, splitting it from Bentley after 71 years.

Violette Cordery at the wheel of the 'Eric-Campbell' 10hp in 1919.
(Public domain)

Former English race car driver Guy Edwards, born on this day in 1942, drove this 1976 Penthouse Rizla car for Hesketh Racing.
(Photo by Ben Sutherland [475])

Also on this day: **1878** – Karl Benz filed for a patent for his two-stroke gas engine. **1948** – Malcolm Campbell, English journalist, race car driver, and land speed record holder, died at age 63 of natural causes. **1955** – General Motors became the first US corporation to make more than $1 billion in a single year.

A 2002 Bentley Continental T. (Photo by Vetatur Fumare [476])

A 2002 Rolls Royce Phantom. (Photo by David Merrett [477])

Appendix: picture sources

Pictures that have been reproduced under Creative Commons licenses are detailed here, with author name and web address.

January

[1] Ernesto Andrade, https://www.flickr.com/photos/dongkwan/2624109828/in/photolist-4ZTfqU-4ZTj9h
[2] emperornie, https://flic.kr/p/cgdiPj
[3] Flominator, https://commons.wikimedia.org/w/index.php?curid=2787271
[4] Greg Gjerdingen, https://flic.kr/p/H193LE
[5] Vetatur Fumare, https://flic.kr/p/nRe8kq
[6] Iwao, https://flic.kr/p/p6GZo7)
[7] Joe Ross, https://flic.kr/p/24VxVf
[8] Joe Ross, https://flic.kr/p/QVMcf9)
[9] Greg Gjerdingen, https://flic.kr/p/fMxNfX
[10] Greg Gjerdingen, https://flic.kr/p/eCdihS
[11] Yahya S, https://flic.kr/p/w3Z4hv
[12] ilikewaffles11, https://flic.kr/p/w4Pbfx
[13] Jeff Wilcox, https://flic.kr/p/2txGmQ
[14] Lothar Spurzem, https://commons.wikimedia.org/w/index.php?curid=1468350)
[15] Tim Green, https://commons.wikimedia.org/w/index.php?curid=20674501
[16] James, https://flic.kr/p/eiXqwV
[17] Jack Snell, https://flic.kr/p/pZgGdu
[18] Greg Gjerdingen, https://flic.kr/p/UUBErr
[19] Karrmann, https://commons.wikimedia.org/w/index.php?curid=2256584
[20] Tucker Automobile Club of America, Inc, https://commons.wikimedia.org/w/index.php?curid=501861
[21] Riley, https://flic.kr/p/St2Uxy
[22] Daryl Mitchell, https://flic.kr/p/qaqUud
[23] Yahya S, front view: https://flic.kr/p/pVsMgR; side view: https://flic.kr/p/qzEDYs
[24] big-ashb, https://flic.kr/p/hjfHFf
[25] LSDSL, https://commons.wikimedia.org/w/index
[26] N A Parish, https://flic.kr/p/TLZ9rZ
[27] Mic, https://flic.kr/p/8GYRuj
[28] Contri, https://flic.kr/p/8HK1GH

February

[29] Buch-t, GFDL, https://commons.wikimedia.org/w/index.php?curid=20635679
[30] Claus Ableiter, GFDL, https://commons.wikimedia.org/w/index.php?curid=3575541
[31] Oli R, https://commons.wikimedia.org/w/index.php?curid=2437393
[32] Alden Jewell, https://flic.kr/p/P9u1ct
[33] Michel Curi, https://flic.kr/p/pKqzQh
[34] Jack Snell, https://flic.kr/p/yHbHwe
[35] Jorbasa Fotografie, https://flic.kr/p/foYhRT
[36] 孝杰 林, https://flic.kr/p/hVGLkn)
[37] KOMUnews, https://flic.kr/p/zvwkXD
[38] RL GNZLZ, https://flic.kr/p/vSF2rE)
[39] Don O'Brien, https://flic.kr/p/tojxrK
[40] Sicnag, https://flic.kr/p/o6vWJ9
[41] zombieite, https://flic.kr/p/of8bD7
[42] zombieite, https://flic.kr/p/nZEHR8
[43] zombieite, https://flic.kr/p/ogSA72
[44] John Lloyd, https://flic.kr/p/6MYSQH
[45] Jack Snell, https://flic.kr/p/dzYxnZ
[46] Iwao https://flic.kr/p/bnUs2D
[47] Greg Gjerdingen, purple Prowler: https://flic.kr/p/nAzgQq
[48] Greg Gjerdingen, yellow Prowler: https://flic.kr/p/phoaBC
[49] Ben Garrett, https://flic.kr/p/o7VWQn
[50] F D Richards, https://flic.kr/p/fN4FWq
[51] Darryl Moran, https://commons.wikimedia.org/w/index.php?curid=10235308
[52] Freewheeling Daredevil, https://flic.kr/p/4s7uk5)
[53] Thomas's Pics, https://flic.kr/p/ocqNeQ)
[54] Supermac1961, https://flic.kr/p/6DSvny
[55] Nascarking, https://commons.wikimedia.org/w/index.php?curid=38582044
[56] GabboT, https://flic.kr//p/qPmQKn
[57] Lothar Spurzem, https://commons.wikimedia.org/w/index.php?curid=886151
[58] Stuart Seeger, https://commons.wikimedia.org/w/index.php?curid=4012263
[59] Jake Archibald, https://flic.kr/p/ctcCb9
[60] Przemysław JahrAutorem, https://commons.wikimedia.org/w/index.php?curid=4317921
[61] Andrew Duthie, https://flic.kr/p/dwhNbn
[62] BiTurbo228, https://flic.kr/p/cq5VfU
[63] TuRbO_J, https://flic.kr/p/DbqfLz
[64] NAParish, https://flic.kr/p/6HvxFx
[65] Stuart Seeger, http://www.flickr.com/photos/stuseeger/202557320/
[66] Stuart Seeger, https://commons.wikimedia.org/w/index.php?curid=3528998
[67] Lothar Spurzem, https://commons.wikimedia.org/w/index.php?curid=903911

March

[68] Christian Sinclair, https://flic.kr/p/aGocbe
[69] Nathan Bittinger, https://flic.kr/p/4mp4qY
[70] Peter Turvey, https://commons.wikimedia.org/w/index.php?curid=36244619
[71] Ben, https://flic.kr/p/aBeZNgj
[72] Ben, https://flic.kr/p/aBf1dn
[73] Jay Clark, https://flic.kr/p/7vPF17
[74] Sicnag, https://flic.kr/p/y51VwU)
[75] Sicnag, https://flic.kr/p/y52973
[76] Sicnag, https://flic.kr/p/yJrrxq
[77] F D Richards, https://flic.kr/p/Ldx5Xc
[78] F D Richards, https://flic.kr/p/LJ2Hr1
[79] big-ashb, https://flic.kr/p/hjdfQW
[80] Tim O'Brien, https://commons.wikimedia.org/wiki/File%3AJanetGuthrie.jpg
[81] Dan Wildhirt, https://commons.wikimedia.org/w/index.php?curid=11048406
[82] Karen Roe, https://flic.kr/p/Jw9hyL
[83] Mac H (media601), https://flic.kr/p/y1N55C
[84] Marion Doss, https://flic.kr/p/5eDDP5
[85] Derivative work: Altair78, photo by Luftfahrrad, https://commons.wikimedia.org/w/index.php?curid=4900463
[86] Freewheeling Daredevil, https://commons.wikimedia.org/w/index.php?curid=3611507
[87] Seattleretro, https://commons.wikimedia.org/w/index.php?curid=10051918
[88] Patrick Pelster (selbst fotografiert), https://commons.wikimedia.org/w/index.php?curid=7890186
[89] Greg Gjerdingen, https://flic.kr/p/HUHA4j
[90] Tee Cee, https://flic.kr/p/zLwSQv
[91] Mario Mancuso, https://flic.kr/p/e7ZLEz
[92] Jack Snell, https://flic.kr/p/dczoFp
[93] mark6mauno, https://flic.kr/p/zY4tS
[94] Freewheeling Daredevil, https://commons.wikimedia.org/w/index.php?curid=3612726
[95] Kristoferb, https://commons.wikimedia.org/w/index.php?curid=16244509)
[96] James Stewart, https://flic.kr/p/6S2wiK
[97] Zach Catanzareti, https://flic.kr/p/J46mqw
[98] dodge challenger1, https://flic.kr/p/5fCD2x
[99] Michael Kumm, https://flic.kr/p/4mSJDo
[100] Michael Kumm, https://flic.kr/p/4mNFyR
[101] Michel Curi, https://flic.kr/p/qenaMR
[102] Lutz H, https://commons.wikimedia.org/w/index.php?curid=14498295
[103] Stuart Seeger, https://commons.wikimedia.org/w/index.php?curid=5495665
[104] Dan Smith, https://commons.wikimedia.org/w/index.php?curid=300566
[105] Joe Ross, https://flic.kr/p/PKz43r
[106] Riley, https://flic.kr/p/DRauPA

April

[107] Greg Gjerdingen, https://flic.kr/p/tijj5y
[108] Greg Gjerdingen, https://flic.kr/p/ti9sNy
[109] Morio, https://commons.wikimedia.org/w/index.php?curid=27655258
[110] Rudolf Stricker, https://commons.wikimedia.org/w/index.php?curid=3705638
[111] S 400 HYBRID, https://commons.wikimedia.org/w/index.php?curid=10911755
[112] Skblzz1, https://commons.wikimedia.org/w/index.php?curid=1956703
[113] Raynardo, https://en.wikipedia.org/wiki/Golden_Submarine#/media/File:The_Golden_Submarine.jpg
[114] Joseph Brent, https://flic.kr/p/7R4RRj
[115] Joseph Brent, https://flic.kr/p/7R4SNW
[116] Karen Roe, https://flic.kr/p/MAHi71
[117] rhino not for sale, https://commons.wikimedia.org/w/index.php?curid=30009567
[118] Joost Evers/Anefo, Nationaal Archief, https://commons.wikimedia.org/w/index.php?curid=45258333
[119] Dave Hogg, 2.0 https://flic.kr/p/93sqPX
[120] Yasser Alghofily, https://flic.kr/p/6i5a2W
[121] FD Richards, https://flic.kr/p/gdy7rh
[122] Michel Curi, https://flic.kr/p/oVmijM
[123] Nic Redhead, https://flic.kr/p/crFTUQ)
[124] Simon Davison, https://flic.kr/p/2NeLWU
[125] Sicnag, https://flic.kr/p/jpA23h
[126] dodge challenger1, https://flic.kr/p/5fCD2x
[127] Bryce Womeldurf, https://flic.kr/p/9wEHEf
[128] John Lloyd, https://flic.kr/p/aD6zU7
[129] Devin Noh, https://flic.kr/p/RAsaih
[130] Ben, https://flic.kr/p/dXqQWb
[131] Martin Lee, https://flic.kr/p/Rzz34P
[132] lecates, https://flic.kr/p/Jy14F
[133] Sicnag, https://flic.kr/p/T55ZP8
[134] Jason Goulding, https://flic.kr/p/dW1JKT
[135] David Berry, https://flic.kr/p/b9T8ni
[136] iowagto, https://flic.kr/p/AEP1T
[137] Illustration sources: (Top) By Rex Gray, https://flic.kr/p/85oC4U; (Center) Ferruccio Lamborghini, courtesy Automobili Lamborghini SpA, PRESS DATABASE – Attribution, https://commons.wikimedia.org/w/index.php?curid=1213551; 1963 GTV – By Craig Howell from San Carlos, CA, USA, cropped and adjusted by uploader Mr.choppers; (Bottom) Lamborghini 350 GTV, https://commons.wikimedia.org/w/index.php?curid=17959273
[138] Joe Ross, https://flic.kr/p/4r89U8
[139] FD Richards, https://flic.kr/p/fMLJzt

May

[140] Stuart Seeger, https://flic.kr/p/jY7gu
[141] Martin Lee, https://www.flickr.com/photos/kartingnord/14028517703/
[142] dun_deagh, https://flic.kr/p/cNZAZJ
[143] John Pease, https://flic.kr/p/ikF5rb
[144] Michel Curi, https://flic.kr/p/qenaMR
[145] Karen Roe, https://flic.kr/p/e4Xee6
[146] Illustration based on original photo by Valder137, https://commons.wikimedia.org/w/index.php?curid=35672126
[147] Jack Snell/Erick, https://flic.kr/p/eNgJrw
[148] Mark van Seeters, https://flic.kr/p/72Sujq
[149] ideogibs, http://www.flickr.com/photos/ideogibs/2113890097/
[150] Sherry Lambert Stapleton, https://commons.wikimedia.org/w/index.php?curid=2894377
[151] M Peinado, https://flic.kr/p/8H9tRV
[152] Geoff Jones, https://commons.wikimedia.org/w/index.php?curid=12245293
[153] Sicnag, https://flic.kr/p/ydyYKM
[154] Paul Williams, https://flic.kr/p/8hSKug
[155] lix, https://flic.kr/p/9XSo9v
[156] Josh Hallett, https://flic.kr/p/3rDBCC
[157] Josh Hallett, https://flic.kr/p/3rDj9Q
[158] TTTNIS, https://commons.wikimedia.org/w/index.php?curid=29182784
[159] Iwao, https://flic.kr/p/bTVG2p
[160] marek.boeckmann, https://flic.kr/p/o3jTcV
[161] Will Pittenger, https://commons.wikimedia.org/w/index.php?curid=4788200
[162] Spikerogan, https://commons.wikimedia.org/w/index.php?curid=22938827
[163] Royal Broil, https://flic.kr/p/ekmG9K
[164] SarahStierch, https://commons.wikimedia.org/w/index.php?curid=40594000
[165] Doctorindy, https://commons.wikimedia.org/w/index.php?curid=18636390
[166] GTHO, https://commons.wikimedia.org/w/index.php?curid=31169813
[167] GTHO, https://commons.wikimedia.org/w/index.php?curid=10649136
[168] Greg Gjerdingen, https://flic.kr/p/L3HJcw
[169] Jack Snell, https://flic.kr/p/yL2wnH
[170] Zombieite, https://flic.kr/p/o4NGA5
[171] Bibliothèque Nationale de France, http://gallica.bnf.fr/ark:/12148/btv1b6913057v.r=1908%22grand%20prix%22itala?rk=85837;2
[172] CreepShot, https://flic.kr/p/dU1eLp
[173] RL GNZLZ, https://flic.kr/p/ne3W9Q
[174] R-E-AL, https://commons.wikimedia.org/w/index.php?curid=7445888
[175] H Michael Miley, https://flic.kr/p/Via5GM
[176] H Michael Miley, https://flic.kr/p/Via5VH
[177] How I See Life, https://flic.kr/p/6imdhM
[178] FD Richards, https://flic.kr/p/zf7UQK
[179] Luc106, https://commons.wikimedia.org/w/index.php?curid=45809765
[180] Shelby Bell, https://flic.kr/p/HU1F7N
[181] John Lloyd, https://flic.kr/p/c6GKew
[182] John Lloyd, https://flic.kr/p/c6GLYj
[183] The359, https://flic.kr/p/4RXRzQ
[184] Artem Svetlov, https://flic.kr/p/tpLGuw.
[185] Vitaly Kuzmin, http://vitalykuzmin.net/?q=node/493, https://commons.wikimedia.org/w/index.php?curid=25628916

June

[186] Cullen328, https://commons.wikimedia.org/w/index.php?curid=51385430
[187] Lothar Spurzem, https://commons.wikimedia.org/w/index.php?curid=886185
[188] Morio, https://commons.wikimedia.org/w/index.php?curid=25308136
[189] Sicnag, https://flic.kr/p/xGVM9X
[190] Mikaël Restoux, https://commons.wikimedia.org/w/index.php?curid=1506914
[191] Tony Hisgett, https://flic.kr/p/QhGdeS
[192] califlier001, https://flic.kr/p/kfeBaH
[193] Ben Garrett, https://flic.kr/p/hSX7Cr
[194] Mike Roberts, https://flic.kr/p/N2ZG6
[195] Paul Hudson, https://flic.kr/p/or2pqT
[196] Michel Curi, https://flic.kr/p/pNqFZu
[197] AmateurArtGuy, https://flic.kr/p/Gko547.
[198] nakhon100, https://flic.kr/p/a6dv9i
[199] EditorASC at en.wikipedia, https://commons.wikimedia.org/w/index.php?curid=6642471
[200] Carterhawk, https://commons.wikimedia.org/w/index.php?curid=9474767
[201] Greg Gjerdingen, https://flic.kr/p/ac3ndR
[202] Arvin Govindaraj, https://flic.kr/p/dN2xBb
[203] Artem Svetlov, https://flic.kr/p/yzXa2d
[204] Robert Couse-Baker, https://flic.kr/p/bqE5TG
[205] David Merrett, https://flic.kr/p/eZvuta
[206] Sicnag, https://flic.kr/p/E4RGTq
[207] René, https://flic.kr/p/9CeUrH
[208] Andrew Basterfield, https://flic.kr/p/8gXEMm
[209] Hurstad, https://commons.wikimedia.org/w/index.php?curid=9732428
[210] Stahlkocher, https://commons.wikimedia.org/w/index.php?curid=2062136
[211] Adam Singer, https://flic.kr/p/22bHGS
[212] Alexandre Prévot, https://commons.wikimedia.org/w/index.php?curid=48768681
[213] Lothar Spurzem, https://commons.wikimedia.org/w/index.php?curid=1167285
[214] Original photo by James Temple, derivative work by Ligabo, https://commons.wikimedia.org/w/index.php?curid=10042145
[215] Doug Letterman, https://flic.kr/p/fPzbqP
[216] RL GNZLZ, https://flic.kr/p/pwwCix
[217] Morten Brunbjerg Bech, https://flic.kr/p/tKkJG
[218] Fekist, https://commons.wikimedia.org/w/index.php?curid=2160525
[219] Dietmar Rabich, https://commons.wikimedia.org/w/index
[220] Dietmar Rabich, https://commons.wikimedia.org/w/index
[221] Rex Gray, https://flic.kr/p/kF857b

July

[222] Greg Gjerdingen, https://flic.kr/p/fZXxuT
[223] Greg Gjerdingen, https://flic.kr/p/ySe4od
[224] Nick Ares, https://flic.kr/p/6ZwdCk)
[225] Joe Ross, https://flic.kr/p/bkqVbu
[226] Riley, https://flic.kr/p/U6jmji
[227] Mark Spearman, https://flic.kr/p/r7vnjF
[228] Bundesarchiv, https://commons.wikimedia.org/w/index.php?curid=5418816
[229] fremantleboy, own work on base of image: Landkreise.svg by DieBuche, https://commons.wikimedia.org/w/index.php?curid=2146821
[230] Pedro Ribeiro Simões, https://flic.kr/p/8W7c3g
[231] ilikewaffles11, https://flic.kr/p/h2znxo

[232] ocean yamaha, https://flic.kr/p/hmQEu
[233] Lothar Spurzem, https://commons.wikimedia.org/w/index.php?curid=1181064
[234] Manoj Prasad (front view) https://flic.kr/p/pBEdvr
[235] Manoj Prasad, (rear view) https://flic.kr/p/pBo35V
[236] Bob Adams, https://flic.kr/p/E6npdT
[237] H Michael Miley, https://flic.kr/p/fooRzh
[238] brewbooks, https://flic.kr/p/3akRDe
[239] Supermac1961, https://flic.kr/p/9YvkrX)
[240] Karen Roe, https://flic.kr/p/JH13TQ
[241] Scott Daniels, https://flic.kr/p/kEuugg
[242] Sicnag, https://flic.kr/p/prr2s9
[243] Rick Dikeman, https://commons.wikimedia.org/w/index.php?curid=24471
[244] Marco Pagni, https://flic.kr/p/c2kvEo
[245] Robin Corps, https://flic.kr/p/6BL1Av
[246] Joanna Poe, https://flic.kr/p/r72tUS
[247] rg-fotos, https://flic.kr/p/9ieE2w
[248] Jack Snell, https://flic.kr/p/nD82jE
[249] theregeneration, https://flic.kr/p/5pfsf8
[250] Geni, https://commons.wikimedia.org/w/index.php?curid=51673872
[251] Andrew Bone, https://www.flickr.com/photos/andreboeni/27461734514/in/photolist-hc3UvB-6XteLi-brMRRt-JLVddr-HQGyVh-DtfYq9-JE6d1v-qM2i6H
[252] Paul Williams, https://flic.kr/p/e6YURX
[253] Rob, https://flic.kr/p/btiFag
[254] RL GNZLZ, https://flic.kr/p/T9FgYj
[255] RL GNZLZ, https://flic.kr/p/JqwnB1)
[256] Anackire, https://flic.kr/p/uAq4c9
[257] Christian Madden, https://commons.wikimedia.org/w/index.php?curid=4976910
[258] N8huckins, https://commons.wikimedia.org/w/index.php?curid=34711540
[259] Jim Summaria, https://commons.wikimedia.org/w/index.php?curid=5626785
[260] Tony Hisgett, https://flic.kr/p/QcfYnT
[261] FD Richards, https://flic.kr/p/fn3UMt
[262] Jack Snell, https://flic.kr/p/ghWp3V
[263] Jason Goulding, https://flic.kr/p/dwXSzG

August

[264] Stuart Seeger, https://flic.kr/p/4rmS5C
[265] Martin Lee, https://flic.kr/p/nkAdEG
[266] Willy Pragher, https://commons.wikimedia.org/w/index php?curid=46534377
[267] David Berry, https://flic.kr/p/csZiv7
[268] David Berry, https://flic.kr/p/csZip3
[269] RL GNZLZ, https://flic.kr/p/mut47c
[270] Riley, https://flic.kr/p/VLUttb
[271] John Pease, https://flic.kr/p/iixMed
[272] Bernard Spragg, https://flic.kr/p/dn4A2w
[273] Surreal Name Given, https://flic.kr/p/9DbDWT
[274] Lothar Spurzem, https://commons.wikimedia.org/w/index.php?curid=3170595
[275] Adam Singer, https://flic.kr/p/8LkWgC
[276] Ylitvinenko, https://commons.wikimedia.org/w/index.php?curid=53215366
[277] Jack Snell, https://flic.kr/p/eKQa4G
[278] Greg Gjerdingen, https://flic.kr/p/nGHc7Y
[279] Jasen Miller, https://flic.kr/p/9XcUKf
[280] jodelli, https://flic.kr/p/4RKr4t
[281] jodelli, https://flic.kr/p/btsKNH
[282] Jerry Lewis-Evans, https://flic.kr/p/ffuZXu
[283] Greg Gjerdingen, https://flic.kr/p/umL9Yk
[284] the 216, https://flic.kr/p/5b62a8
[285] SAS Scandinavian Airlines, http://images.flysas.com, public domain, https://commons.wikimedia.org/w/index.php?curid=35129841
[286] Supermac1961, https://flic.kr/p/8hqAi9
[287] Greg Gjerdingen, https://flic.kr/p/HQXi7A
[288] Greg Gjerdingen, https://flic.kr/p/eCfTNS
[289] Sludge G, https://flic.kr/p/9iuQkh
[290] Simon Davison, https://flic.kr/p/N97D5
[291] Rain0975, https://flic.kr/p/p9RktJ
[292] Joe Ross, https://flic.kr/p/QVMc7J
[293] Nick Ares, https://flic.kr/p/54o9vA
[294] Martin Pettitt, https://flic.kr/p/8CbtUQ
[295] Paul Williams, https://flic.kr/p/ahsqHW
[296] DeFacto, https://commons.wikimedia.org/w/index.php?curid=3609044
[297] DeFacto, https://commons.wikimedia.org/w/index.php?curid=2273227
[298] Niagara, https://commons.wikimedia.org/w/index.php?curid=21009058
[299] C5813, https://commons.wikimedia.org/w/index.php?curid=48497695
[300] Lothar Spurzem, https://commons.wikimedia.org/w/index.php?curid=903972
[301] Bob Tilden, https://flic.kr/p/6QACsA
[302] Alberto from Spain, https://flic.kr/p/P2N7zj)

September

[303] Jerry 'Woody,' https://flic.kr/p/5TBhzG
[304] Greg Gjerdingen, https://flic.kr/p/HoWU2G
[305] Autoviva, https://flic.kr/p/9nir4Y
[306] David Merrett, https://flic.kr/p/djS5gn
[307] Martin Lee, https://flic.kr/p/FcBGEE
[308] cole24_, http://www.flickr.com/photos/22831849@N00/276233455/
[309] Roger Wollstadt, https://commons.wikimedia.org/w/index.php?curid=16991211
[310] mroach, https://flic.kr/p/5du3nA
[311] Staffan Vilcans, https://flic.kr/p/6sAQ4S)
[312] Oxyman, https://commons.wikimedia.org/w/index.php?curid=4303815
[313] Firing up the quattro, https://flic.kr/p/9JbUud
[314] Kat, https://flic.kr/p/aeweDM
[315] Greg Gjerdingen, https://flic.kr/p/UUCqcT
[316] Mike, https://flic.kr/p/4JvJXQ
[317] FAHansson, https://commons.wikimedia.org/w/index.php?curid=58174036
[318] DanielPenfield, https://commons.wikimedia.org/w/index.php?curid=28044470
[319] Karen Roe, https://flic.kr/p/Kpd42i
[320] Jack Snell, https://flic.kr/p/evrW3y
[321] John Lloyd, https://flic.kr/p/aD2JbZ
[322] RL GNZLZ, https://flic.kr/p/EH8ZRv
[323] Dan, https://flic.kr/p/8Rocrb
[324] Susan Dussaman, https://flic.kr/p/9CaAAu
[325] Ron Cogswell, https://flic.kr/p/CXP7LJ
[326] David Merrett, https://flic.kr/p/djiyVs
[327] RL GNZLZ, front: https://flic.kr/p/fJbh8T,
[328] RL GNZLZ, rear: https://flic.kr/p/p2P5uX
[329] Christopher Hilton, https://commons.wikimedia.org/w/index.php?curid=60811503
[330] Andrew Bone, https://flic.kr/p/PT6Tiq
[331] Kzaral, https://flic.kr/p/6EHb6p
[332] Rikita, https://commons.wikimedia.org/w/index.php?curid=23017396
[333] emperornie, https://flic.kr/p/oYDWC6
[334] Nic Redhead, https://flic.kr/p/cgBRjd
[335] Phil Kalina, https://flic.kr/p/pkcdu1
[336] hell0094, https://flic.kr/p/6WVbEj
[337] Marco Verch, https://flic.kr/p/adKaXS
[338] Stephan Wershoven, https://flic.kr/p/L6JYsz
[339] Andrew Bone, https://flic.kr/p/USiRiJ
[340] RL GNZLZ, https://flic.kr/p/qv84XA
[341] I, Luc Viatour, https://commons.wikimedia.org/w/index.php?curid=1433279
[342] Loren Javier, https://flic.kr/p/9Etghd
[343] Jim Bauer, https://flic.kr/p/e67JhF

October

[344] Jack Snell, https://flic.kr/p/ocJhKK
[345] FD Richards, https://flic.kr/p/fvag5m
[346] FD Richards, https://flic.kr/p/fuueTa
[347] substantie, (front) https://flic.kr/p/WqrFzg,
[348] substantie, (interior) https://flic.kr/p/WyvWpL
[349] David Merrett, https://flic.kr/p/9tGdpf
[350] steve p2008, https://flic.kr/p/j7WExM
[351] Lothar Spurzem, https://commons.wikimedia.org/w/index.php?curid=1025457
[352] Andrew Bone, https://flic.kr/p/SUnEjV
[353] Ivan Rivera, https://flic.kr/p/56Ru8t
[354] Niels de Wit, https://flic.kr/p/euwTaU
[355] rjb52, https://commons.wikimedia.org/w/index.php?curid=4112806
[356] Chris Waits, https://flic.kr/p/8duT7o
[357] Wknight94, https://commons.wikimedia.org/w/index.php?curid=16925714
[358] davocano, https://flic.kr/p/mmpiBG
[359] Andrew Bone, https://flic.kr/p/JA1v6h
[360] Sheila Sund, https://flic.kr/p/fjdWnD
[361] Bildergalerie, https://commons.wikimedia.org/w/index.php?curid=6705112
[362] Axel Schwenke, https://flic.kr/p/ekGREY
[363] simpleinsomnia, https://flic.kr/p/nDj5Ns
[364] Thomas O'Halloran, US Library of Congress, ds 07053, http://hdl.loc.gov/loc.pnp/ds.07053
[365] RL GNZLZ, https://flic.kr/p/znRSVR
[366] Graham Robertson, https://flic.kr/p/caEgTo
[367] blastpaintrestore, https://flic.kr/p/npd2yR
[368] Brian Sims, https://flic.kr/p/fuHybo
[369] Jack Snell, https://flic.kr/p/rNVjHU
[370] David Merrett, https://flic.kr/p/HAJMks
[371] Thomas's Pics, https://flic.kr/p/S2k1tG
[372] Karen Roe, https://flic.kr/p/MDmbDe
[373] brewbooks, https://flic.kr/p/3akjSe
[374] Mike, https://flic.kr/p/5gPCkV
[375] Greg Gjerdingen, https://flic.kr/p/acr7aa
[376] Bruno Kussler Marques, front: https://flic.kr/p/cBcEP3
[377] Bruno Kussler Marques, rear: https://flic.kr/p/cBcFk7
[378] pyntofmyld, https://flic.kr/p/ngb9kR
[379] Debarshi Ray, https://flic.kr/p/f59jMX
[380] Dutch Boyd, https://flic.kr/p/bBqJmP
[381] Danemroberts, https://commons.wikimedia.org/w/index.php?curid=7469538
[382] Rex Gray, https://flic.kr/p/kuAd8H
[383] Rain0975, https://flic.kr/p/pPdoxK
[384] Greg Gjerdingen, https://flic.kr/p/JdYVLE
[385] Brian Snelson, https://commons.wikimedia.org/w/index.php?curid=7281445
[386] KOMUnews, https://flic.kr/p/zskTL
[387] nakhon100, https://commons.wikimedia.org/w/index.php?curid=37769861
[388] John Lloyd, https://flic.kr/p/9xgpUF
[389] Greg Gjerdingen, https://flic.kr/p/umzPA6
[390] NA Parish, https://flic.kr/p/6HvmHv
[391] Clemens Vasters, https://flic.kr/p/q6Rq9w
[392] InSapphoWeTrust, https://flic.kr/p/afbour
[393] James Case, https://flic.kr/p/pXNCvW

November

[394] Lee Haywood https://flic.kr/p/7psiwT
[395] Ali Mannan, https://flic.kr/p/JjMMYa
[396] Greg Gjerdingen, https://flic.kr/p/Pbmixx
[397] Bruno Kussler Marques, https://flic.kr/p/cBcCD9
[398] transplanted mountaineer, https://commons.wikimedia.org/w/index.php?curid=2786757
[399] Royal Broil, https://flic.kr/p/kPB8yr
[400] Loren Javier, https://flic.kr/p/9Ettt3
[401] Bryce Womeldurf, https://flic.kr/p/Vjkeif
[402] Daderot, https://commons.wikimedia.org/w/index.php?curid=51460982
[403] F D Richards, https://flic.kr/p/LGP7bm
[404] Greg Gjerdingen, https://flic.kr/p/KdzKrJ
[404a] Douglas Wilkinson, https://commons.wikimedia.org/wiki/File:1915-dodge-archives.jpg
[405] ian mcwilliams, https://commons.wikimedia.org/w/index.php?curid=11780856
[406] David Berkowitz, https://flic.kr/p/9ZFj7w
[407] Joe Ross, exterior: https://flic.kr/p/4kaes8
[408] Joe Ross, interior: https://flic.kr/p/4keieh
[409] Falcon® Photography, https://flic.kr/p/We7mrS
[410] Jason Goulding, https://flic.kr/p/etjtoQ
[411] 'self', https://commons.wikimedia.org/w/index.php?curid=1443714
[412] Jason Taellious, https://flic.kr/p/a7PGQi
[413] Jon's pics, https://flic.kr/p/cCay1
[414] Jon's pics, https://flic.kr/p/gDPDm
[415] Greg Gjerdingen, https://flic.kr/p/UH1LSp
[416] John Lloyd, https://flic.kr/p/9xgqfp
[417] Rain0975, https://flic.kr/p/p9UdsT
[418] Greg Gjerdingen, https://flic.kr/p/HWBuSC
[419] TheDigitel Beaufort, https://flic.kr/p/8Y9M5a
[420] A Davey, https://flic.kr/p/5hRTGo
[421] crudmucosa, https://flic.kr/p/xoonYY
[422] Nick Johns, https://commons.wikimedia.org/w/index.php?curid=12059078
[423] Joe deSousa, https://flic.kr/p/oB1jkZ
[424] Sicnag, https://flic.kr/p/SQbtWP
[425] photobeppus, https://flic.kr/p/fjMvBz
[426] Felix O, https://commons.wikimedia.org/w/index.php?curid=7947281
[427] Sicnag, https://flic.kr/p/mTPRBv
[428] Niels de Wit, https://flic.kr/p/eD7ZDJ
[429] Sicnag, https://flic.kr/p/pB7N66
[430] Alden Jewell, https://flic.kr/p/UEwcAM
[431] DoomWarrior, https://commons.wikimedia.org/w/index.php?curid=3957170
[432] Matthew Lamb, https://commons.wikimedia.org/w/index.php?curid=49763828
[433] tomislav medak, https://commons.wikimedia.org/w/index.php?curid=7635722
[434] Semnoz, https://commons.wikimedia.org/w/index.php?curid=625173
[435] dave_7, https://flic.kr/p/frTN3d

December

[436] Dominic Alves, https://flic.kr/p/aCAYsP
[437] California Air Resources Board, https://flic.kr/p/qbkEUL
[438] Greg Gjerdingen, Front ¾ view: https://flic.kr/p/LSuj9G
[439] Greg Gjerdingen, interior view: https://flic.kr/p/MGBm3B
[440] Greg Gjerdingen, rear ¾ view: https://flic.kr/p/MDUPfY
[441] Greg Gjerdingen, https://flic.kr/p/G8jBy2
[442] Greg Gjerdingen, https://flic.kr/p/caXwfU
[443] Gilberto Benni, https://commons.wikimedia.org/w/index.php?curid=5295240
[444] Jack Snell, https://flic.kr/p/epKdPm
[445] Jim Hammer,, https://flic.kr/p/8i8Jem
[446] Riley, https://flic.kr/p/cWwmdS
[447] Riley, https://flic.kr/p/tJpPUY
[448] James Petts, https://flic.kr/p/T6uQ27
[449] Paul Robertson, https://flic.kr/p/atDZQG
[450] Don O'Brien, https://flic.kr/p/7R4VpK
[451] Walter, https://flic.kr/p/aEpf2v
[452] Masahiko OHKUBO, https://flic.kr/p/a9CUAM
[453] Tony Harrison, https://commons.wikimedia.org/w/index.php?curid=3883888
[454] Sicnag, https://commons.wikimedia.org/w/index.php?curid=17234624
[455] Joe Wolf, https://flic.kr/p/nEwuQi
[456] Josh Hallett, https://flic.kr/p/3rDj9Q
[457] Greg Gjerdingen, https://flic.kr/p/KsYcSi
[458] Greg Abbott, https://flic.kr/p/PoaoVP
[459] Andrew Bone, https://flic.kr/p/dveaxC
[460] Regular Daddy at English Wikipedia, https://commons.wikimedia.org/w/index.php?curid=18340222
[461] David Merrett, https://flic.kr/p/Tckom3
[462] David Merrett, https://flic.kr/p/SciXLc
[463] nicolas genin, https://commons.wikimedia.org/w/index.php?curid=7920625
[464] Greg Gjerdingen, https://flic.kr/p/JeSf7L
[465] James Loesch, https://flic.kr/p/93a6YF
[466] Paul Sableman, https://flic.kr/p/7YtYj1
[467] Andrew Bone, https://flic.kr/p/RMLwET
[468] Andrew Bone, https://flic.kr/p/dve1EA
[469] Greg Gjerdingen, https://flic.kr/p/cn3jwL
[470] Riley, https://flic.kr/p/d8v8HY
[471] Greg Gjerdingen, https://flic.kr/p/yxzutG
[472] HKT3012, https://commons.wikimedia.org/w/index.php?curid=43539628
[473] thinktk, https://flic.kr/p/5mqtUx
[474] Hugh Miller, Woodrow Wilson's Presidential Library Archive, https://flic.kr/p/7zZrJS
[475] Ben Sutherland, https://flic.kr/p/o4ruV9
[476] Vetatur Fumare, https://flic.kr/p/gJbVBU
[477] David Merrett, https://flic.kr/p/6fWzTs

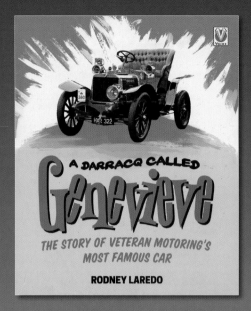
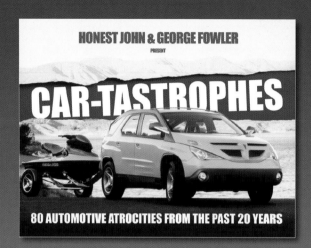
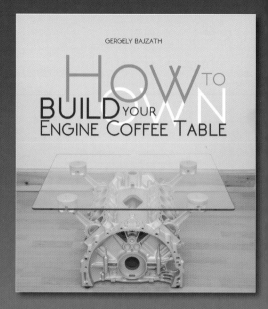

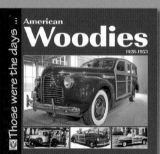
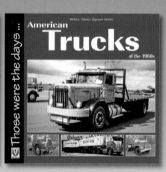
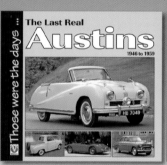
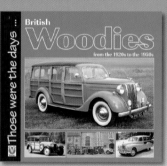

Index

24 Hours of Le Mans 14, 15, 25, 37, 66, 68, 73, 81, 82, 90, 92-97, 107, 113, 129, 141, 144, 166, 175, 179, 182

24 Hours of Daytona 23, 94, 107

Alfa Romeo 18, 36, 71, 89, 95, 96, 123, 148, 150

AMC – *See* American Motors Corporation

American Motors Corporation 13, 30, 37, 54, 126, 178, 183

Andretti, Mario 31, 37, 55, 66, 116, 149

Argetsinger, Cameron 38

Auburn Automobile Company 119, 159

Audi 36, 39, 61, 64, 66, 74, 84, 90, 96, 99, 137, 151, 176

Austin Motor Company Limited 63, 65, 128, 132, 139, 144, 153, 173, 174

Autocar 156

Autodromo Nazionale Monza 76, 115, 124, 133, 134, 141, 191

Baker, Erwin 71, 73, 122, 136

Barnato, Woolf 15, 38, 113

Beetle – *See* Volkswagen Type 1

Bentley Boys 95, 113

Bentley Motors Limited 9, 15, 38, 64, 95, 113, 122, 153, 164, 183, 191

Benz, Karl 21, 40, 55, 109, 151, 174, 191

Birkin, Tim 95

Bohlin, Nils 104, 143

British Motor Corporation 75, 128, 139, 173

Brooklands 63, 67, 71, 73, 76, 91, 95, 113, 116, 119, 126, 154, 191

Bugatti 14, 48, 63, 64, 125, 127

Buick Motor Company 8, 16, 32, 40, 54, 56, 61, 67, 75, 78, 87, 110, 113, 138, 152, 167, 172, 188, 189

Buick, David 40

Burman, Bob 57, 83

Cadillac 7, 16, 19, 24, 26, 31, 40,

50, 60, 110, 114, 123, 127, 138, 139, 152, 154, 155, 172, 174, 177, 179, 187

Camaro 13, 34, 74, 121

Checker Motors Corporation 93

Chevrolet 6, 9, 11, 13, 15, 16, 26-28, 32, 34, 47, 53, 54, 56, 61, 63, 64, 67-69, 74, 85, 86, 99, 100, 106, 118, 121, 131, 138, 139, 141, 146, 147, 150, 149, 161, 165, 168, 171-174, 177, 188-190

Chrysler 6, 8, 14, 20, 22, 30, 39, 42, 45, 47, 48, 54, 64, 68, 72, 76, 78, 82, 86, 87, 98, 115, 117, 124, 131, 133, 140, 150, 153, 162, 166, 167, 170, 173, 175, 179, 180

Chrysler, Walter 8, 54, 87, 117

Citroën 7, 14, 25, 62, 65, 80, 113, 148, 169, 187

Citroën, André 25

Cord 6, 20, 71, 93, 109, 119, 141, 152, 158, 159, 162, 179

Cordery, Violette 191

Corvette 15, 16, 28, 29, 32, 62, 64, 85, 99, 100, 106, 115, 121, 131, 147, 165, 172, 188, 190

Cugnot, Nicolas-Joseph 36

Cummins Engine Company 8, 24, 124, 135

Curved Dash 42, 68, 86, 111, 167

Daimler, Gottlieb 27, 40, 55, 71, 98, 129

Datsun 10, 141, 156, 189

Davenport, Thomas 102

Daytona 500 30, 31, 32, 34, 37, 41, 44, 50

de Filippis, Maria Teresa 77, 167

de Portago, Alfonso 151

de Silva, Walter 36

Dean, James 145

DeLorean Motor Company 47, 101, 157

DeLorean, John Z 47, 123, 157

Desoto 20, 98, 117, 131, 170, 174

Diesel, Rudolf 36, 145

Drive-in movie theater 75

Duesenberg Motors Company 66, 89, 112, 122, 123, 145, 156, 158, 159

Durant, William C 11, 26, 40, 54, 69, 78, 89, 113, 114, 135, 138, 152, 180

Duray, Arthur 88

Duryea Motor Wagon Company 132, 134, 141, 152, 175

Earl, Harley 15, 24, 172

Earnhardt, Dale, Sr 32, 51

Edsel 135, 152, 171

Fabryka Samochodów Osobowych (FSO) 79, 89

Fangio, Juan Manuel 34, 35, 108, 117

Ferrari 14, 18, 23, 25, 35, 37, 40, 62, 64, 66, 67, 74, 77, 90, 93, 96, 99, 108, 110, 117, 129 133, 148, 151, 160, 161, 163, 171, 172, 185

Ferrari, Enzo 14, 62, 67, 93, 110, 148, 161

Firestone Tire & Rubber Company 26, 56, 117

Fisher Body 11, 110, 187

Ford GT40 23, 38, 60, 62, 73, 92, 94

Ford, Henry, II 17, 62, 72, 91, 101, 106, 135, 141, 145, 153, 162, 186

Ford Motor Company 6, 7, 10, 11, 13, 14, 16, 17, 19, 20, 22-24, 29, 31, 32, 34, 37, 38, 39, 42-48, 50, 51, 53, 54, 56, 57, 59-62, 66, 71-73, 75, 76, 80-82, 84-86, 90-95, 99, 100, 101, 103, 105, 106, 109-114, 116-121, 124-126, 130-132, 134-136, 138, 140, 141, 143-149, 151, 153, 155-157, 159, 162, 164-168, 171-174, 176-178, 180-183, 186, 189, 191

Ford Quadricycle 57, 59, 86

Ford, Edsel 6, 7, 59, 72, 81, 135, 180

Ford, Henry 11, 14, 17, 24, 31, 38, 53, 56, 57, 59, 62, 72, 80, 81, 84–86, 91, 92, 94, 101, 106, 112,

114, 117, 135, 136, 138, 141, 143, 145, 146, 148, 153, 155-157, 162, 164, 165, 176-178, 180, 186, 191

Formula One (F1) 7, 14, 18, 19, 25, 27, 28, 34, 35, 37, 38, 50, 52, 53, 60, 66, 67, 69, 70, 72, 76, 77, 85, 89, 101, 103, 105, 107, 108, 117, 121, 124, 127, 129, 133, 143, 144, 149, 157, 161, 163, 167, 175, 176, 179, 182

FSO – *See* Fabryka Samochodów Osobowych

General Motors 7, 9, 11-13, 15-17, 19, 21, 22, 24, 26, 27-29, 31, 40-42, 47, 48, 51, 54, 64, 67-69, 73, 78, 80, 89, 99, 108, 110, 114, 119, 123, 124, 130, 131, 134, 135, 138-140, 152, 159, 165, 167, 168, 171-174, 181, 185, 186, 188, 191

Grand Prix 7, 10, 15, 22, 34, 35, 37, 38, 40, 42, 47, 48, 52, 53, 58, 59, 60, 64, 66, 67, 69, 72, 74, 76, 77, 79, 83, 85, 86, 88, 89, 91, 95, 96, 97, 100, 101, 103, 105, 107, 108, 113, 114, 117, 119, 122-129, 133, 134, 138, 141-144, 148, 149, 151, 157, 158, 163, 165, 167, 170, 180, 185

Gurney, Daniel 18, 37, 60, 101, 103

Guthrie, Janet 41

Haynes, Elwood 152

Hells Angels 46

Hertz, John, Sr 58, 149

Highway Code, The 184

Hispano-Suiza 15, 88,

Holden 138, 174

Honda 38, 58, 66, 86, 111, 142

Horch, August 151

Hudson Motor Car Company 13, 28, 33, 37, 66, 90, 100, 110, 130, 153, 160

Hummer 48, 67, 80, 150

Hupmobile 33, 165, 174

Hybrid vehicle 43, 132, 152, 177

Hydrogen fuel cell vehicle 58, 177

Index

Hyundai Motor Company 33, 111, 190

Iacocca, Lee 62, 90, 91, 133, 140, 153, 162, 179, 181
Indianapolis 500 8, 37, 41, 57, 61, 74, 77, 78, 83, 84, 116, 174, 175
Indianapolis Motor Speedway 41, 57, 71, 74, 76, 83, 87, 100, 122, 140, 168, 183
Internal combustion engine 18, 21, 40, 42, 108, 129
International Harvester Company 176

Jaguar 7, 25, 28, 37, 39, 41, 45, 47, 50, 52, 55, 61, 67, 96, 107, 115, 132, 139, 140, 141, 144, 152, 165, 177, 182
Jeantaud 185
Jeep 10, 19, 22, 24, 26, 38, 47, 153, 168, 176
Jellinek, Emil 17, 56, 143
Johnson, Dick 66
Jowett 144

Kaiser-Frazer Corporation 8, 16, 24, 51, 83, 97 127, 171, 178
Karmann Ghia 106, 110
KIA Motors Corporation 111
Kimber, Cecil 59
Knievel, Evel 158

Lamborghini 33, 36, 46, 64, 65, 67, 72, 74, 161, 162
Lamborghini, Ferruccio 33, 67, 161
Lancia 67, 176
Land Rover 7, 21, 50, 68, 99, 134, 136, 152, 153
Land speed record 9, 11, 19, 23, 35, 49, 52, 88, 135, 138, 147, 153, 169, 179, 185, 191
Le Mans – See 24 Hours of Le Mans
Leland, Henry 24, 31, 50, 92, 114, 155, 188
LeMay, Harold 163
Levitt, Dorothy 101
Lincoln Motor Company 7, 24, 31, 47, 49, 50, 83, 90, 148, 153, 166, 171, 172

Lotus 6, 67, 77, 83, 86, 91, 96, 149, 165

Mack Trucks, Inc 29, 151
Maserati 18, 39, 43, 44, 60, 67, 73, 77, 89, 129, 135, 154, 167, 170, 177
Maybach, Wilhelm 27, 39, 40, 55, 89, 126, 129, 142, 190
Mazda 22, 27, 68, 75, 83, 106, 111
McLaren, Bruce 19, 35, 85, 93, 94, 108, 175
McNamara, Robert 131, 166
McQueen, Steve 154, 165,
Mercedes-Benz 9, 17, 20, 21, 25, 27, 34, 35, 39, 43, 56, 63, 67, 72, 89, 91, 92, 96, 101, 108, 124, 126, 132, 143, 144, 147, 150, 167, 175
Mercury 7, 32, 37, 119, 157
MG 38, 59, 69, 76, 140, 180, 182
Michelin Tire Company 14
Mille Miglia 95, 151
Mini 35, 45, 88, 94, 108, 128, 144, 150, 158, 166, 173
Minivan 98, 162
Mitsubishi 48, 64, 104, 180
Model A 24, 92 159, 180
Model T 31, 56, 62, 81, 85, 86, 117, 119, 131, 140, 146, 162, 168, 179
Monorail 91
Monza – See Autodromo Nazionale Monza
Moore, Michael 186
Morris Motors Limited 59, 67, 128, 151, 153, 173, 174, 187
Mustang 20, 38, 61, 62, 73, 120, 121, 135, 140, 141, 149, 153, 165, 172

Nader, Ralph 27, 47
NASCAR (National Association for Stock Car Auto Racing) 18, 28, 30, 32-34, 37, 40, 41, 44, 48, 50, 60, 68, 75, 76, 88, 92, 98, 119, 132, 146, 159, 164, 167-169, 175, 178
Nash Motors 13, 54, 87, 114, 160, 181
Neon 6, 98
Nissan Motor Company 10, 15, 18, 21, 23, 32, 75, 85, 157, 182, 189

Nürburgring 15, 34, 62, 93, 96, 120, 144, 148

O'Neil, Kitty 179
Oldfield, Barney 11, 18, 57, 94, 112, 147
Oldsmobile 9, 16, 33, 42, 67, 68, 86, 111, 113, 114, 128, 130, 138, 145, 152, 159, 163, 166, 167
Opel Automobile GmbH 9, 17, 21, 41, 57, 59, 77, 134, 138, 142, 172
Organization of the Petroleum Exporting Countries (OPEC) 137

Pacer 13, 37, 178
Packard Motor Car Company 8, 47, 64, 101, 122, 124, 125, 141, 146
Patrick, Danica 50, 63, 83
Petty, Lee 34, 44, 117, 146, 159
Petty, Richard 32, 40, 44, 92, 101, 168
Peugeot 6, 57, 110, 111, 118, 121, 133, 147, 149, 157
Pikes Peak International Hill Climb 91, 121
Plymouth 6, 18, 19, 22, 30, 34, 88, 98, 117, 119, 131, 140, 146, 162, 168, 179
Pontiac 7, 9, 13, 34, 47, 60, 67, 119, 138, 141, 148
Porsche 15, 31, 45, 51, 52, 68, 76, 82, 88, 94, 101, 103, 121, 129, 132, 145, 156, 159, 174, 182, 186
Porsche, Ferdinand 22, 31, 82, 88, 116, 132, 156, 159, 186
Prost, Alain 35, 66, 69, 74
Prototype 8, 110, 16, 28, 32, 42, 44, 48, 67, 75, 76, 82, 86, 88, 105, 107, 109, 113, 134, 147, 150, 153, 156, 157, 161, 163, 168, 184, 188

Renault 15, 35, 60, 82, 97, 102, 104, 121, 149, 157, 170, 176, 187, 188
Riker, Andrew 134, 169
Rolls-Royce 12, 24, 37, 51, 60, 70, 90, 97, 99, 104, 105, 116, 130, 138, 146, 147, 154, 164, 183, 186, 187, 190, 191
Rolls, Charles 1, 70

Roth, Ed 39
Route 66 98
Royce, Henry 51, 70, 97

Saab 116, 124, 132, 184
Saturn Corporation 9, 50, 67, 84, 161
Schumacher, Michael 7, 35, 52, 96, 100, 107, 125, 127, 129
SEAT 17, 36, 56, 73
Segrave, Henry 43, 52, 119
Selden, George 15, 72, 138, 164
Self-starter 92
Senna, Ayrton 50, 59, 69, 161
Shelby American Inc 20, 64, 73, 82, 170, 179
Shelby, Carroll 20, 64, 73, 170
Silver Ghost 60, 70, 154, 186, 190
Studebaker 22, 28, 30, 39, 43, 46, 47, 76, 100, 110, 112, 124, 162
Subaru 75, 103, 157

Thunderbird 29, 32, 45, 90, 100, 106, 135, 156, 183, 186
Todt, Fritz 102
Toyoda, Sakichi 30
Toyota Motor Company 10, 24, 30, 43, 51, 54, 75, 131, 141, 142, 151, 152, 159, 161, 171, 177, 180, 184, 185
Trevithick, Richard 188
Trickle, Dick 76
Tucker, Preston 17, 121, 141, 189

Unimog 150
Unser, Al, Sr 77, 116

Vanderbilt Cup 9, 61, 161
Volkswagen (VW) 5, 10, 27, 31, 36, 41, 44, 58, 76, 80, 82, 88, 97, 104, 106, 118, 131-133, 138, 146, 156, 179, 181, 191
Volkswagen Type 1 10, 27, 31, 36, 41, 44, 54, 76, 82, 97, 104, 106, 118, 132, 138, 146, 156, 181
Volvo Cars 60, 82, 85, 95, 104, 131, 155, 157

Watkins Glen International 38, 113, 140, 149
Weinermobile 108
Willow Run 22, 51, 79